TALES FROM THE T

CU00536187

'The busiest and best pub in our m.   ... . Puddings.
The Johnson brothers were clever businessmen who knew that if
trouble started it could ruin their takings. That's why they had the best
security, the elite of the underworld. Their motto was to stop the
trouble before it started. Most of the time they did.'
Terry Murphy - Licensee of the Bridge House, Canning Town

'There were some great pubs in the East End in the sixties but the
Puddings topped them all. Only one pub came near it and that
belonged to me!'
Sammy McCarthy - Former British featherweight boxing champion

'One of my most vivid memories from the Two Puddings is having a
fantastic 18th birthday celebration there with my mates. This came as
a huge shock to Eddie though as I'd already been working behind the
bar for him for a year!'
Sam Shepherd - Star of the film _Bronco Bullfrog_

'Playing at the Two Puddings was like playing in an East End Mecca
of music and you knew as a band that if you played there you were
certainly making inroads locally. A venue that demanded respect.'
David Essex - Singer and actor

'I loved the Two Puddings. Apart from the best live music, it had the
best birds in London too!'
**Billy Murray - Actor: _McVicar, East Enders, Call Of Duty: Modern
Warfare_**

'The Puddings, was one of those rare, special places that always had
a great atmosphere. I used to go with my mates, who were all about
6' 2" to 6' 4", where as I'm 5' 8". They would provide me with a beer
crate to stand on so I could have a decent conversation with them!
To this day they still remind me of it. Great times.
John Claridge - Photographer

ABOUT THE AUTHOR

Eddie Johnson was born in Limehouse, East London in 1932 and grew up within a tightly-knit family in a tiny, terraced house on a lively street in Old Ford, Bow.

He remembers seeing George Lansbury, the leader of the Labour Party, MP for Bow and eminent pacifist, when he visited Smeed Road Infant School to speak to the young pupils. This made a lifelong impression.

He was evacuated three times during the war but was in the East End during the worst of the blitz.

In 1950-52 he did his National Service, spending one year in the Royal Military Police and one year in the Highland Light Infantry and serving overseas in Tobruk, Tripoli and Malta.

After coming out of the army he fell into a series of dead-end jobs and, at a loose end, regretfully became a bit of a hooligan, regularly getting drunk and fighting in dance halls. One night in London's West End, he received a near fatal stab wound in the stomach. This incident changed his life as, whilst recovering, he fell in love with his wife to be Shirley. She was a great influence in steering him away from the rougher influences in his life.

After marriage they moved to Walthamstow, where they had two children, Andrew and Matthew, and Eddie worked quite happily in the docks as a tally clerk.

With his brother Kenny he also started running dances in various parts of London and helped run the Jive Dive, a famous club in Forest Gate.

In 1962, when the opportunity arose to take over the Two Puddings public house in Stratford, he reluctantly took it as his wife was so keen. He thought he would be there for a couple of years at most yet he remained licensee until 2000.

Eugene, their third son, was born in the hospital next door to the Two Puddings during the mid-1960s and their fourth son Gerard was born 1st January 1973, seconds after midnight, and consequently featured on national television and newspapers as the first British person born a European.

Eddie now lives in a quiet part of Suffolk but is an inveterate writer of letters to the *Independent* newspaper, and others, about the unfairness he perceives in the world.

George Lansbury would be proud to know that he still attends anti-war marches whenever the occasion demands.

TALES FROM THE TWO PUDDINGS

STRATFORD, EAST LONDON'S OLYMPIC CITY, IN THE 1960'S

EDDIE JOHNSON

FIFTY FIRST **51** STATE PRESS

LONDON

TALES FROM THE TWO PUDDINGS

Published by Fifty First State Press

www.51statepress.com

First published in Great Britain in 2012

ISBN 978-0-9572090-0-8

Edited by Matt Johnson

Artwork by Martin Lewis Design

Front Cover photograph by Alf Shead:
Shirley Johnson (centre) in the Two Puddings with
Peter Ferdinando, Johnny Bruce, Charlie Johnson,
Mickey King, Rocky Bob and friends

DEDICATED TO MY WONDERFUL SONS
ANDREW, MATTHEW, EUGENE AND GERARD,
MY BEAUTIFUL GRANDSONS
JACK AND GEORGE
AND THEIR LOVELY
MUM AND NAN, SHIRLEY

Tales From The Two Puddings

Contents

Foreword

The Past Is Another Country

Early Days, Early Doors

The Cooks, The Cleaners, The Burglar and Her Lover

The Flying Angels

A Carnival Of Lost Souls

The Magic Door

The Good Times Roll

The Devil's Kitchen

THE WORLD'S GREATEST PUB

THE BOYS IN BLUE

THE GETAWAY

TALES FROM THE TWO PUDDINGS

Foreword

It's a Strange Life for a Kid, Living Above a Pub

In many families, certain tales are told and re-told so many times that, over the years, they become part of the collective identity of the clan. With Stratford now being steamrollered by the Olympic juggernaut, it seemed an appropriate time for our dad to finally commit to paper some of the tales from our family's time there.

He's always been a wonderful raconteur and storyteller. When my brothers and I were little, he'd sit us on his lap and entertain us with stories of growing up a 'blitz kid' and roaming the streets of '40s East London with his gang, rummaging amongst the rubble the doodlebugs had left the night before, and engaging in street battles with neighbouring gangs.

These tales from Stratford in the '60s are from a similarly lost world; a world that's been more thoroughly flattened - by rapacious property developers and inept council officials - than the Luftwaffe could ever have dreamed of doing. It's a world now largely replaced by vast, soul-sapping shopping centres, and privately funded but shoddy, monolithic housing estates.

In the '60s, an East London pub was a very male-dominated environment. Our dad, uncles and their friends all seemed to be large men adorned in dark suits and ties, with huge hands and broken noses. There were plenty of strong female characters around, though, including our mum who, though a deeply empathetic, kind person, was also strong-willed and glamorous, and played her full part in helping turn the Two Puddings into one of the social epicenters of the East End during that era.

Earliest memories, by definition, are often our most intense. As a child, I was well aware of the energy radiating through that building; its continual bustle and commotion, telephones constantly ringing, people always dropping by, and, especially at night-times on weekends, the entire structure seeming to vibrate. Upstairs, my brothers and I would listen to the sound of hundreds of people having a raucous time as laughter and music drifted up through the floorboards. From the little flat above, we'd look out over Stratford Broadway, with its neon signs and roar of traffic, honestly believing we were living on the Broadway of the Drifters song popular at the time.

It's a strange life for a kid, living above a pub. There was a sense of 'otherness' when I compared experiences with school friends. Most of them, in my childhood, at least, seemed to live in rows of small residential houses with parents who'd head off to nine-to-five jobs every morning. It was a happy childhood, though. Often the last sound we'd hear before drifting off to sleep - and the first when we'd awake - would be our mum and dad laughing and chatting about characters and incidents from the previous session in the pub. The customers were nice to us, and the staff were kind, too, child-minding us on many occasions. Although unsavoury or violent incidents did occur downstairs, our parents tried to shield us from it as best they could whilst, in our own naïve way, we would try piecing it together from overheard snippets of hushed conversation. Children have very big ears.

As we weren't allowed to play in the streets outside, the Broadway being a very busy road, we embarked upon adventures closer to hand. My brothers and I knew every inch of the Puddings, from its basement boiler room to its rooftop balcony. During daytime closing hours, the place became our own secret kingdom; there was always something slightly eerie but exciting about venturing into the darkened pub and dance hall. Reverberating with ghosts from the night before, the smell of tobacco smoke and perfume still clinging to its walls, its floors slightly sticky underfoot from spilt drinks and discarded chewing gum, we'd mess around on the instruments left on stage by the bands currently in residence or (I feel ashamed to admit) occasionally burgle the 'blind box' in order to buy sweets and American comics from the shop next door. Sneakily, we'd help ourselves to too many bottles of coke and packets of crisps from behind the bar, gleefully ruining our appetite for the dinner our mum was cooking upstairs.

Even after we were no longer physically living above the pub, my brothers and I loved going back. During school holidays, we'd take turns to accompany our dad on his customary Monday meetings with his brothers in their infamous 'office'. With its dusty old velvet curtains tightly drawn against the daylight, its huge, cartoon-sized safes crouching in the corners, there they would sit, around their old wooden desk, counting money, exchanging gossip, and hatching plans - proceedings illuminated by a bare light bulb dangling from the high ceiling.

As we grew into adulthood, my brothers and I would still sometimes go back to the pub to have a pint, chat with the staff, and wander around the place, reminiscing. I've always believed that buildings soak up human moods and emotions, magnifying or reflecting them. I always found the Puddings to have a benign atmosphere. For almost four decades it helped sustain our immediate and extended family, repelling waves of attacks upon it, with a little help from our dad, uncles, and their friends, of course.

In the year 2000, this famous old pub, having atrophied over time into a shadow of its former self, was sadly forced to close its doors for the last time. As a little boy looking out over the chimney pots and television aerials of Stratford, I had little inkling that, by the time our family did finally move out of the Puddings, I'd be living on and looking out over the rooftops of the *other* Broadway - that of Manhattan.

MATT JOHNSON

Taking Matthew (left) and Andrew (right) across Stratford Broadway to the forbidding Grove School. (photographer unknown)

ELEVEN IS A GOOD AGE FOR A BOY TO BE

From 11 in the morning until 11 at night, six of us toiled to do in one day what would better have been done in three: moving out of the Two Puddings. Boxing-up, lifting, carrying, loading. Up flights of stairs, pushing, pulling, heaving, dragging. Into a small elevator, round corners, along dim passageways, through a back torturing low-ceiling cellar. On and on and on. Another load on the van. Everyone squeeze on and yet another trip to the storage space.

By early evening, my biceps were no longer functioning. My hands became simple hooks. Most of my muscles had long reached the point of failure, and now I was testing the fibre that binds together the joints, the tendon and ligament tissue around the elbows, knees, ankles and spine.

But it was right that I was there at the very end. It felt symmetrical. I took one last look around the front room, a room I'd first entered as a small child almost forty years prior. There had been so much excitement then; the adults were just as excited as we children were. Our lives had suddenly changed. I remember on our first night, hearing the music wafting from below, pulling back the net curtains and poring over the nocturnal street-life below. Neon advertising lit-up the wide expanse of road and reflected in the dark puddles. Knots of pleasure seekers drifted up and down, laughing and arguing.

The Puddings became - it seems in one stroke - the notional heart of the family. It provided a natural fulcrum. It was not only a place where many of the family gathered to meet and enjoy each other's company, but it also provided employment for so many diverse members of the family. Our nans working in the cloakroom, uncles and aunts serving as managers, cousins tending the bar, second cousins preparing food, in-laws minding the door.

For almost forty years, every Monday our father would spend the day in a tiny, high-ceilinged room at the rear of the pub, meet with his two brothers, and tend to the family business. As children, we would feel privileged to be allowed into the 'office' for these meetings. There would never be enough chairs, but we would be happy to perch on the edge of one of the old iron safes lined along one wall. The floor would be piled with cartons of glasses, boxes of admission tickets, bags of change, and all the other paraphernalia that comes with running a pub. Our uncles would always make a fuss of us and ask about what we'd been doing, and they'd tease us and kid us. But we knew when to keep quiet, when it paid to just listen, as they began to discuss the more serious issues.

When men who are used to violence discuss it, they always use understatement. No one ever gets worked up and over-emotional. They talk about slapping someone, when really they mean almost killing them. A persistent, violent troublemaker is referred to merely as 'a nuisance'. They never admit to feeling nervous. It's talked about as though it's an unwanted but necessary chore. Violence, in this context, was never about machismo, never about pride or boasts.

They never made trouble to get talked about. It was all simply part of business. You were running a business, you needed to make money, and no one could be allowed to jeopardise that. If your business happened to be a haberdashery in Harrogate, you would unlikely ever need to use physical force, but if you were trying to run a pub in 20th Century East London, it was a different story. In such an instance, you were likely to come up against some of the least pleasant, most badly behaved individuals in the country. And, in order to survive, you would have to be able to repay them with interest.

There were always weapons around, though mainly hand arms, such as police truncheons, pick-axe handles, baseball bats, lengths of chain, rubber tubes weighted with lead, a vicious looking docker's hook, and a nasty thin butcher's boning knife. Whether these were ever used in battle or if they were simply taken off others and then left on display in the office as trophies was never apparent to us as children. I remember seeing a small revolver being wrapped in a cloth bank bag and placed in one of the safes. With a wink I was told that I must never tell anyone about it. And, of course, I never have - until now. I was eleven years old and I felt bigger, taller, stronger for having been made privy to at least one of the secrets of what seemed, even then, a mysterious, clandestine nighttime world.

Eleven is a good age for a boy to be.

ANDREW JOHNSON

Huge, cartoon sized safes crouched in the corners of the 'office'.
(photograph by Johanna St Michaels)

Some of the most enjoyable moments of my life were spent working in the docks. (photograph by Shirley Johnson)

THE LAMENT OF AN OLD MAN

High summer is here again. They come and go, the seasons, and when one is fairly static, no longer traveling abroad too much, there is always the sense of déjà vu because we, the average, silly human being, tends to repeat and do the same things over and over as we get older.

Most summer evenings these days I go to a lovely pub in a beautiful village in the heart of Suffolk. It's called The Angel, and it's positioned on one side of one of the most ancient squares in England. The old Guildhall - from the 16th Century - is one of the views to the left of the pub; the church can be spotted at the opposite edge of the square if you look down the hill; there's an old bakers shop and a general provisions store, all housed in mediaeval buildings on the right-hand side.

I order a glass of dry white wine and soda, put my own chair out, and sit there watching the swifts weave their joyous patterns in the sky; otherwise, I'll allow myself to be entertained by the variety of people that turn up either to drink or eat here. I thought one warm evening when it was still and quiet, just a dim light emanating from the shop and being passed by the occasional car and the odd walker, that if I were to die sitting here - now, at this very moment - I would die in Heaven. Here, in my chair, I often reflect about my life; my happiest moments, my saddest times, and the characters and events that have populated my life. And this year, with the Olympic Games arriving in Stratford, East London, my mind keeps drifting back 50 years to when I took over the Two Puddings pub in 1962.

Although by trade I was at the sharp end of the alcohol business and its destructive effects for many years, if anyone 50 years ago could fast forward and see what's happening in so many of our towns and cities today, most would be horrified and find the state of affairs unbelievable: the omnipresent drunkenness, the lewd, rude disrespectful behaviour, the urinating, shrieking, vomiting, swearing half-naked men and women out of control in the streets of so many of our towns and cities, many clutching tins of extra strong beer, the police over-stretched, being insulted by yobs and only able to warn and caution in politically correct language...

As an East End landlord for many years of probably one of the toughest pubs in that area, mainly catering for young people, I could see these future problems a mile away. I campaigned long and hard against the relaxation of the licensing hours. I had numerous letters published in national newspapers, articles in the licensees' trade paper *The Morning Advertiser,* I spoke at Licensed Victualler meetings and was quoted and supported in Parliament by Sir Bernard Braine who said he was heartened by my stance and that it made him realise how many ordinary publicans were against the move. Undoubtedly, however, at some point there will be fresh debate in the House of Commons, and no one from the government will admit to being so absolutely wrong; I argue they'll blame it on parents, schools, alcopops - everyone but themselves. They'll say there's nothing wrong with being open all day and all night; they'll claim serving strong alcohol to all and sundry doesn't pose an issue, that it's only the odd one or two that misbehave; and - oh yes - they'll claim the police have welcomed these new laws when, in actual fact, every policeman I've ever spoken to - and I've spoken to many - hates them. Mind you, they're the ordinary coppers on the beat, the ones on the front line.

Nowadays, no one remembers my one-man campaign, and so there's no point in me ever giving the 'I told you so' speech, but governments never do listen to sensible advice from ordinary people. Look at our disastrous foreign policy over the years; the Cassandras are, in the end, generally right, but it's normally too late. Yet sitting here in the fading summer light in this beautiful mediaeval village square, the troubles of our city streets could be from some distant time in the future and so I let my mind drift back once again to 50 years ago.

The tales I'm about to recount - primarily from when my family and I lived above the pub during 1962-1969 - are ultimately built on what I can remember; I have no diaries to rely on as such, although a few of these anecdotes, vignettes and pen portraits were roughly sketched out at the time. Nevertheless, the memories remain vivid. Essentially, it's a narrow view, as I haven't really consulted many people involved in those years or otherwise sought any corroboration, and it's known that time can distort the memory. But, to me, it's all as real and true as any events unfolding in the local village yesterday.

This book obviously constitutes just a fraction of the hundreds of staff, thousands of customers and countless incidents that   populated the four decades I was licensee of the Puddings. I apologise to anyone unwittingly left out although in some sections certain names and connections have been altered or omitted at request. The tales are not in strict chronological order as I have roughly divided them into groups of related subject instead, and sometimes, to put things into perspective, they do occasionally drift off into the past or wander occasionally into the future.

THE DOCKS

Before moving into the Two Puddings, I had two children, both boys, Andrew and Matthew. We were living quite happily, as far as I was concerned, in a tiny flat in Wood Street, Walthamstow. It was very cosy: we had two nice armchairs, a television set from Universal Rentals at 9/6d a week, I was starting to earn better money working down the docks, and I was also getting a fair living from the dance halls I was promoting with my brother Kenny at weekends. I liked nothing better than sitting watching Basil Rathbone and Nigel Bruce in *Sherlock Holmes* on television whilst smoking a Players cigarette and drinking R. White's lemonade.

Initially, I wasn't very keen on the idea of living above a pub; I felt I was betraying my principles. I was a leading light in the unofficial Labour movement in the docks, I was the Tally Clerks representative on Jack Dash's Strike Committee, and I was being groomed to take over the Royal Dockers Distress fund - a scheme the dockers had initiated themselves to help injured, sick or out-of-work dockers and stevedores, and I loved my job. London's docks were still reputed as the fastest turn around in the world - despite the workers resisting containerisation, which was the norm in the rest of the world. It was exciting and colourful, the ships went to romantic-sounding places; many of the dockers and stevedores were interesting characters and larger than life and many were members of the Communist party or the old Independent Labour Party - a more radical version of Labour - and were well-read in philosophy and the classics.

I've always been a voracious reader, but when I worked in the docks I was staggered at how many self-educated and literate men worked as stevedores, dockers and tally clerks. The bible, for many of them, was *The Ragged-Trousered Philanthropist* by Robert Tressell, the story of a poor, hard-working man in the decorating trade trying to earn a crust at the beginning of the 20th Century and who tries to convince his fellow workers of the virtues of socialism. After its publication, there was a lot of mystery surrounding who had actually written it, but it was eventually revealed that Robert Tressell was the nom-de-plume of Robert Noonan - a house painter - and the book was posthumously published through the determined efforts of his daughter Kathleen.

Karl Marx was a favourite. I did try to read *Das Kapital* but gave up; I found it hard-going and overly dense with facts, but I learned enough that, even now, I have subscribed to some of his beliefs.

One docker would recite and quote Congreve, Dante, Byron, whole poems and complete quotations; another man was fond of the Greek philosophers; others would talk of Proust, Kafka and Joyce. Matthew Tighe, a fellow tally clerk, once remarked that our friend John Davies reminded him of Holden Caulfield. That was when I read *The Catcher in the Rye,* and I knew exactly what he meant.

Some of the most enjoyable moments of my life were spent working in the docks, talking of life, politics and the infamy of the ruling class. It broadened my reading horizons, and I read Camus, Tolstoy, Dickens, Hemingway, Mark Twain, Mailer, Kingsley Amis, and many of the so-called 'working class' writers: Sillitoe, Stan Barstow and others. But my real hero was George Orwell, who inspired me to start jotting down my own thoughts.

At one point, I'd written a short story for our magazine, *The Tally Clerk.* The work considered the end of the world and a nuclear conflagration. According to Fred Morel, one of our leaders, who was also Chairman of the Independent Labour Party, the playwright Arnold Wesker, who he'd shown the story, really liked it.

Shortly after, there was a large anti-nuclear meeting held in the docks organised by the Committee of 100 - a more radical version of CND. At the meeting, Vanessa Redgrave spoke. She was very tall and quite beautiful, her lower lip trembling with emotion as she made a passionate speech. Ollie Williams, another of our leaders, and my friend Stevie Hegarty, both urged me to get up and speak, so I reluctantly stood to share the platform with Ms Redgrave, my cheeks burning with embarrassment as I implored hundreds and hundreds of dockers to support the anti-war movement.

Ollie used to go on all the marches, and was even arrested at one in Trafalgar Square. He was a big ex-heavyweight professional boxer and a lovely man who I was very friendly with. It was he who wanted me to take over the Royal Distress Fund, which was one of the main reasons I felt so guilty when I left the docks to become a publican.

Ollie's son Billy the 'Bomb' was a good heavyweight too. He went to America where he was managed by Muhammad Ali's legendary trainer, Angelo Dundee, and whose daughter he got friendly with - a bit too friendly, and he had to come back to England. Billy died only recently but is remembered as a fearsome fellow who made most people a bit edgy wherever he went. He'd been to prison many times and became one of the all-time great nuisances of the East End.

His dad said to me once that Billy was a 'wrong-un' when he was just fourteen years old, but I reassured him and said he'd grow up alright, but Ollie just shook his head and wasn't convinced.

A few years later Billy became a regular in the Puddings and one busy night I called 'time', and was urging people to drink up, when Billy said 'I'll get 'em out for you Ed!' and then proceeded to walk around the pub, glaring at customers whilst ordering them to drink up, frightening the life out of them in the process.

'No, no, Bill, it's alright, leave it to me' I said, which, he rather reluctantly, did.

I was greatly disappointed years later when Enoch Powell made his 'rivers of blood' speech, and there was Ollie at the forefront of the dockers march to Parliament in support of Powell. He can still be seen exhorting the crowds in old newsreels of that time.

Down the docks our hours were fluid. We could work all day and night but have the next day off. Sometimes, when the dock wasn't full, we would 'bomp on', have our book stamped and be sent home, but it was variety. If there was drink or exotic food on board there'd always be some that found its way to the gangs, and many times I'd stagger home, merry on drink, full up with food, often with several pairs of nylon stockings for my wife tucked down my trousers.

Shirley, my wife, although a full-time mum and housewife, was keener than me to move into the pub trade. She was ambitious in a different way to me: at that time I tended to regard money as unimportant as opposed to principle, whilst Shirley was practical and saw it as a way out of the poverty trap in which working class people seemed to remain stuck. No more scrimping and saving. This, as far as she was concerned, was a way out of Wood Street.

Before Matthew was born, Shirley had managed well behind the bar at the Jive Dive, a nightclub my brother Kenny had started running, and she was looking forward to a new challenge.

THE SIXTIES

The '60s was, of course, the decade when the 20th Century became 'modern'. Through the '50s, Britain was poor, exacerbated by the crippling American debt repayments that had, in return, helped to make that country prosperous. Ironically, it seemed the USA had supported Germany with massive free aid and helped that country to find its feet and create an economic miracle; the British, on the other hand, were left to struggle, more like losers of the war than winners.

Rationing lasted for 14 years after the end of hostilities, and the remnants of empire had either been discarded or handed over to the Americans. It was an era when the whole world seemed to change. It was a time of liberalisation, with women taking to the streets to set light to their bras as a symbol of equality and the right to finally have their say.

Music suddenly started to reflect young people's needs and fears, and instead of relying on our Atlantic cousins for the latest sounds, home-grown bands and singers were taking the world by storm. It was exciting and culturally respectable enough to have the Archbishop of Canterbury, William Rees Mogg and other intellectuals of the day all sitting in a TV studio with Mick Jagger discussing modern youth and its needs. It was a time when respected critics compared the Beatles to Beethoven, when clothing evolved rapidly, with designers such as Mary Quant becoming a household name, and a young Polish girl opening Biba, which cloned thousands of boutiques all over Britain.

Thin, undernourished girls with odd names like Twiggy and the Shrimp became iconic models. And Sean Connery, a Scotsman, played James Bond - the English spy the whole world seemed to love.

Young people grew their hair and smoked dope. A huge anti-Vietnam war movement grew and grew, culminating in the battle of Grosvenor Square. Satire was reborn, and the most popular show on television, *That Was The Week That Was*, broadcast every Friday. We still used pounds, shillings and pence, and swearing in mixed company was frowned upon, although characters like Kenneth Tynan were starting to push the boundaries beyond what were then 'the norms of common decency', irritating both Mary Whitehouse and Malcolm Muggeridge, who saw a breakdown of society on the horizon.

There was still a massive British car industry which, although beset with problems, did not deter most of the car-driving population from continuing to buy and drive British. London Docklands were thriving, although not with the vast financial empires and media fortresses of today; finance was still confined to the Square Mile, and Fleet Street was still 'the street of ink'. The docks were alive and bustling, with cranes working day and night, and ships from around the world queuing for berths; stevedores, dockers, seamen and ship workers could be seen everywhere in the cafés and pubs of the area.

Yet I missed most of this.

Shirley and I were working every day and most nights in the Two Puddings. Our only night off was a Wednesday. I never saw a single episode of *That Was The Week That Was*, which was televised on a Friday - and that was our busiest night.

But I saw and did more than most: I saw the best young groups (in the pub), I saw the prettiest and most fashionable girls (in the pub), and I heard all the latest opinions (in the pub).

So what I write about might seem a narrow world, but it actually wasn't. As someone famous once said, 'all human life was there'.

In those days most pubs has separate saloon and public bars.
(photograph by Andrew Johnson)

MARYLAND 2604

E. C. Johnson

"TWO PUDDINGS" PUBLIC HOUSE
27 BROADWAY,
LONDON, E.15

Maryland 2604.
Even today, all the
family remember
this famous old
phone number.
(from the Johnson
Family Archive)

'THE TWO PUDDINGS'

CALL ON SHIRLEY & EDDIE JOHNSON FOR THE BEST IN
FOOD & ENTERTAINMENT
THE TWO PUDDINGS.
27, BROADWAY STRATFORD, E.15.

Phone :-
MARyland 2604

A customer offered to provide us with free business cards.
As you can imagine, Shirley wasn't too pleased with the result!
(from the Johnson Family Archive)

Kenny and me on the door of the 'Big Beat Club' in the fifties.
(photograph by Alf Shead)

THE PUDDINGS

My involvement with the Two Puddings began when I was twenty years old. I came out of the army and, instead of going back home to Old Ford, Bow, where my heart and all my mates were, I went to where my mum and dad had recently moved - Forest Gate. It was a more salubrious area than the tiny terraced streets from which I came. Our new road was lined with trees, the houses were big, and the people living in them were what my mum called 'select'.

She didn't like it either.

I used to get the bus to Bethnal Green and the Repton Club for Boys and Girls. There I'd meet friends and, once again, feel at home. One of the older lads - who resembled the comedian Ken Dodd - was called Reggie Baker, and he was always laughing and joking, sometimes doing a little tap dance as he spoke. He started taking me and my recently de-mobbed mate Derek to all the well-known pubs, the main ones being the London Hospital Tavern in Whitechapel and the Two Puddings in Stratford. Both live-music pubs.

In those days, the Puddings had a large, arched blue neon light on its front, which could be seen from miles down the road. It stood at 27, the Broadway, sandwiched between Dunn & Co., the gentlemen's outfitters, and Stratford Town Hall.

At three stories it didn't look very big from the outside; its top floor stepped back substantially, with part of the roof of the floor below used as a balcony. It had a bottle-green tiled frontage with three large arches on its first floor, two of which housed intricately glazed windows whilst the middle one contained another, much smaller, exterior balcony. On the ground floor there were two doors, one either side of a wide metal-grilled gate. The door to the left was for the saloon bar, the door to the right the public bar. Behind the gate was a wide staircase with wooden and iron banisters and tiled walls, which led up to the first-floor restaurant and later the various dance halls and nightclubs we would run there. The 'Big Beat Club, 'Devil's Kitchen', 'Snobs' and finally 'Angel Lanes' were the various names we used for 'upstairs' over the years.

The pub itself was surprisingly large, and most people were surprised by the length of its horseshoe-shaped bar, which served both Saloon and Public customers, but which was separated by a wooden partition with a little door set in so the 'potman' - or any of the staff - could easily get to the other side. There were high stools at the bar and sturdy wooden tables and chairs scattered about the place.

There was a stage at the front of the pub in between the two entrances. At the opposite end there were 'Gents' and 'Ladies' toilets for both bars, and the fireplaces either side were always lit, from autumn through to spring, as the central heating system was so antiquated. Beyond the toilets were fire exit doors leading out to a large yard. At the back were the remains of an old Anderson air raid shelter, covered in weeds.

The pub had a very high ceiling with skylights filtering in daylight, although not enough to eradicate the need for the fluorescent lighting, even on sunny days. The walls were tiled, mainly cream with a green border; it looked quite antiseptic when the place was empty. It was floored with red and black linoleum tiles, and there was also a huge and magnificently ornate pink-and-gold leafed mirror on the wall of the public bar, which had come from a pub that had been demolished just after the war; the Mann's brewery manager had simply looked for a pub with a big enough wall as its next home.

The cellar must have been built for very short people; I had to virtually bend double when doing any form of cellar work, which made me realise the foundations were ancient. There was a beer hoist that connected it to the ground and first floor. Additionally, there was also a dumb waiter that went from the ground floor to the first floor kitchen and on to the second floor living quarters.

The kitchen itself was at the rear of the building, with large windows overlooking the yard and an old metal fire escape leading down. It was large with a huge old cold cupboard/ refrigerator that never seemed to work properly, several old cooking ranges, a potato-peeling machine that also didn't work, a fryer and a Bain Marie - an antiquated piece of equipment that kept cooked food hot. On the same floor but towards the front of the building was the restaurant cum dance hall.

The second floor housed the living quarters. A narrow wooden staircase, situated in a small hallway just behind the dance hall bar, led up to a door halfway up the stairs that ensured some form of privacy from the pub. This opened to a continuation of the staircase, which then reached a long passage at the top with a skylight allowing in plenty of natural light. There was a small toilet at the top of these stairs, and further along the passage were two bedrooms, one on each side. There was a doorway just before the bedroom on the left-hand side, which led to the rear balcony with its views across the back streets of Stratford. A bathroom, small kitchen and two large living rooms with an opening between them to create one large room completed the layout of the flat. These 'front' rooms had views over Stratford Broadway, and there was a space through the windows that you could climb onto and stand or sit within a smaller balcony.

This building - sadly no longer called the Two Puddings - has, I believe, been standing since at least 1896. For many years it was known as the Refreshment Rooms, but when a kind-hearted licensee started to put two huge Christmas puddings on a table outside during the goodwill season and handed out free platefuls to the local poor, it became known as the Two Puddings - the only pub in Britain with the name.

At one point, I did try to gain a detailed history of the building. I discovered there was a pub called the Wheatsheaf that stood on the site in early Victorian times, and the foundations do go back to the 17th Century, but during the Blitz years, Mann, Crossman & Paulin - the brewers who owned the pub - were bombed and lost many of their records. It was established that the original deeds and history of the Puddings were amongst the lost files.

Through old Post Office directories, however, I did manage to find out the names of some of the previous proprietors, such as James Smith (1896), the Davis family (1901-1906), George Benee (1908-1917), Archibald Ayling (1922), Herbert Archibald Phillips (1934) and William C. Stock (1938). The next proprietor I am aware of was Harold Stark in the 1950s.

The pub was also known locally as the 'Butcher's Shop' and was also occasionally referred to as the 'Blood House'. I tend to believe it was the tiles on the walls that reminded people of a meat shop or operating theatre, but some have a less benign interpretation owing to the occasional outbreaks of violence within its walls.

Having already been a very regular customer of the Puddings for some months, I ran a one-off dance on the first floor with a friend, Peter Aldridge, in 1953. It was a 'Tramps Ball', and met its demise in complete disarray involving the police and arrests. The band never got paid, nor did the licensee Harold Stark. As such, I avoided the place until Stark left. Harry Alden took the license afterwards and ran the pub with his wife Flo. It was during his tenure in 1956 that Kenny started the 'Big Beat Club' on the first floor and I started helping him out there on a regular basis.

The Two Puddings in the mid-1960s.
(photograph by Steve Lewis - Getty Images)

THE LANDLORDS

The owners of the property itself were a succession of breweries, leisure conglomerates, and finally global financial institutions. The brewers Mann, Crossman & Paulin were taken over by Watney's (Watney, Combe & Reid) in 1958, four years before I became the proprietor, though most of the Mann's pubs still had the same signs until the mid-1960s.

In the early days of my tenure, I would visit the brewery's head offices in Whitechapel - located next door to the Blind Beggar - to discuss pub matters, such as rent increases, which were reviewed every three years. I'd always have a good and fierce argument with Doug Blake, or whoever my area manager was at the time, but the relationships were generally excellent and any disagreements always concluded amicably, at which point we would head off to the tap room on the premises for some beer, all of which was free. Some brewery employees - both workers and management - seemed semi-inebriated all day long in those days, yet the business seemed to thrive regardless.

In the early '70s, a former publican, hotelier and estate agent appeared on the scene and sparked a highly publicised, and very bitter, takeover battle for Watney's. His name was Maxwell Joseph. He eventually won and the company shortly became known as Grand Metropolitan. In the '80s, the Thatcher Government decided to deregulate the industry and to do away with the 'tie' between landlords and breweries, and thus limit the amount of pubs the latter could own. Grand Met - which, by this time, had also swallowed the Spitalfields-based Truman's brewery amongst other companies - had approximately 6,000 pubs yet were no longer allowed to own the properties and supply them with beer. Accordingly, they cobbled together a scheme, formed a new company - the infamous Inntrepreneur - and conned many publicans, including myself, into signing 21-year leases at fantastical rent - notably full-repair leases in which the leaseholder would be fully liable for all repairs and held responsible for keeping the premises in pristine condition.

So, through devious ways and means, they became not brewers but landlords and tenants remained 'tied' as they had also merged with the Courage brewery and, as our landlords, dictated that we buy our products from them. Years later, Inntrepreneur and Courage etc. had been flogged to Nomura, a vast Japanese financial corporation, apparently one of the biggest in the world, headed in the UK by the notorious asset-stripper Guy Hands. This sounded the death knell for countless publicans and eventually forced us out of the Puddings in 2000.

THE AREA

In the '60s, Stratford was a fringe area; East London but not East End proper. That dubious honour was reserved for the likes of Bow, Bethnal Green, Limehouse, Whitechapel, Poplar, Stepney and some of the other areas that now lie within the borough of Tower Hamlets. Anywhere else was fringe and their residents were not considered quite as smart as *real* East Enders. There was a lot of snobbery involved - almost a pedigree test; the tailors not so good, the pubs not as lively, the girls not as pretty, the food not so varied.

Although it did have a lovely market at Angel Lane and some nice stores on Broadway, Stratford was nevertheless a depressing place full of factories, pubs, council houses and little streets where terraced houses abounded with a population that was wholly working class and whose amusements comprised telly, bingo and pub (in that order), despite there being three cinemas and the Theatre Royal.

The theatre was run by Joan Littlewood who worked hard for the area and managed to bring some of the best plays of the day with some wonderful actors, many of whom subsequently became famous, even world-renowned. Brendan Behan, the playwright, made his name there and was often seen staggering around Stratford after having had his full share of Guinness. But the main customers of the theatre were from the suburbs or the West End. Much to the disappointment of Ms Littlewood, very few of its regulars were local people, although the theatre bar was very popular with locals as there was usually a well-known actor or two having a drink, and they were quite lax with the drinking-up time.

Stratford borders on the beginnings of Essex, but there is no countryside, not even a field, although a small park was located down West Ham Lane, which was pleasant enough, with tennis courts and its flowerbeds well-stocked and cared for. Further west, towards Bow, there was an old 'promenade' that I used to take Andrew and Matthew to on a Sunday morning to learn to ride their bicycles. It started in Wick Lane, Hackney, passed through Stratford and ended at Beckton Sewer Works. Built in Victorian times, it was designed by Joseph Bazalgette following an outbreak of cholera in 1853 and 'The Big Stink' of 1858. It must have been quite something when it was built but, by the time we moved there, it was bordered by factories and industrial wasteland that looked something like the aftermath of a terrible nuclear conflict and, to give credence to that, during the war they'd built anti-tank pill boxes along its length, some of which are still there to this day.

This promenade was re-named the Greenway by the council in the '80s, and what is left of it runs adjacent to the new Olympic Stadium, fenced-in and patrolled by men in fluorescent jackets with walkie-talkies. There was also the canal that meandered its brown, sludgy, oily way through the area and, although lots of people learned to swim in the canal, many also drowned; it never looked particularly healthy. The infamous Carpenters Road cut through from Stratford to Bow - infamous owing to the smells, which ranged from a shocking stink, so strong you could almost touch it with your hands and emanating from the bone yard and glue factory, to the gentle, sickly-sweet perfume wafting across from Yardley's, famous for its genteel lavender and the famous 'lavender lady' adorning the factory wall. Between these two extremes were a variety of flavours, ink, chemicals and Clarnico chocolate. Some pleasant, others less so.

THE BROADWAY

The Broadway, as its name suggests, is the main thoroughfare of Stratford. It is a very wide road, four lanes of two-way traffic bisected by a small island of tranquillity, containing several interesting structures. St John's Church - a lovely old building - is surrounded by shrubs and trees with graves dotted around and, some days, if I needed some respite and sat with a book amidst the trees, even as the traffic whizzed by on either side, it could be surprisingly peaceful. In front of St John's is a monument in memory of some martyrs who'd been burned at the stake, and on the same island were some lovely old Victorian toilets, both ladies and gents. Built underground they were all brass, mahogany and porcelain, were kept scrupulously clean, and had washing facilities so that if you wanted to go out straight from work you could have a wash and brush-up for tuppence.

One of the buildings to the right of the Puddings, Stratford Town Hall, is a sturdy Victorian structure of dark stone - or so I thought until it was cleaned in the '80s and was revealed to be almost white! It is quite a grand old place with an imposing curved staircase inside that leads up to the function hall where Kenny ran his dances for many years. When West Ham amalgamated with East Ham to become Newham, the Town Hall was moved to East Ham. The fire station next door also closed and was relocated to new premises in Romford Road, less than a mile away. The firemen were replaced by council officers.

To the left was Pelican's Tailors, alongside Dunn & Co, whose famous slogan was 'If You Want to Get Ahead Get a Hat'. Ralph Pelican, the owner of the tailors, was a small, voluble Jewish man with a pencil-moustache and wavy hair. He was a good lunchtime customer, regularly drinking with Mr Patworth, the manager of Barclays, Eddie Downes the butcher, Freddie Cooper a local bookmaker, and one or two other local businessmen.

On the opposite side of the Broadway to the Puddings was Wilson and Whitworth, publishers and stationers and proprietors of the *Stratford Express,* whose journalists were our best lunchtime customers. Next to them was Barclays Bank and Royal Insurance, both housed in splendid Victorian buildings. There was an H. Samuels, the jewellers, complete with an imposing neon sign which, with the adjoining neon for Bovril, lit up the sky and the surrounding area at night. Heading westward there was Times Furnishing, where we bought some of the furniture for our flat when we moved into the pub, Berg the Tailors, Burton's men's clothing, Barnes, a wonderful piano and musical instrument shop which, when it was opened in the '50s, had Billy Eckstein, a famous Black American singer, perform the opening ceremony whilst hundreds of people turned up and the Broadway had to be closed to traffic. There were various other shops stretching as far as Cooke's, a genuine old fashioned eel, pie and mash shop, with marble-topped tables and counter, and large mahogany-framed mirrors. The eels would be laid out at the front of the shop wriggling before your eyes; you could either buy them live to take home or have them cut up in front of you - they couldn't be fresher than that. To the east there was a renowned department store on the Broadway, Boardmans, which had a huge central staircase that spiralled up towards its large, glass-domed ceiling. Upstairs they had a restaurant and tea room staffed by black-and-white-uniformed waitresses for the more genteel   shoppers who would visit the area. It was as good as any West End store. One could buy almost anything there.

In front of these buildings, stalls would line the road and would veer left into Angel Lane, a famed market, full of bustle every day of the week. The stallholders were like characters from an early London life, some of the families having been there many generations. There was also a Home and Colonial food store down there, and an old fashioned Sainsburys, where men in striped trousers and black waistcoats would serve you, and they even had high chairs for elderly customers to sit and wait for their cheese and meats to be cut and weighed before being wrapped. There was Cafe L'Ange, a somewhat poetic name for a caff - which is what it was - and a West Indian greengrocers run by a big burly man everyone called Tarzan, plus, of course, the Theatre Royal, and just off of Angel Lane, on Salway Road, was the Grove, the imposing and forbidding Victorian school Andrew and Matthew attended.

THE JIVE DIVE

In truth, the last thing I ever wanted to be was a publican:
I thought it was a thankless job with long hours and involved
dealing with customers who, all too often, were the worse
for drink. And I was right - but it was circumstances which
ultimately led to it.

My brother, Kenny, had an idea so simple; like many great
ideas, it was incredible that no one had ever thought of it before.
In all the dance halls, town halls, halls above pubs, club halls,
wedding function halls, etc., when people ran a dance they
used a band - normally comprising a trio of drummer, pianist/
keyboard-player and maybe a bass player. The stuff they played
was limited, repetitious, and often very boring. Kenny's idea was
that he would get someone to play the latest top-twenty records
over a large sound system. As far as I am aware, he was the very
first to do it and, although some dispute this, *that* is how disco
was born.

Many years before we took over the Two Puddings, Kenny
hired the dance hall above the pub, got Arthur Taylor - the man
who used to rig-up the loudspeakers for the Dockers' meetings
that Jack Dash, the unofficial Dockers' leader, used to hold - to
install a good sound system, employed an old mate (a Town Hall
Clerk called Bernie who knew all the current hits) to put the
discs on the turntable and announce the title of each song, and
he was away.

It was as though all the young people in the East End had
been waiting for something like it - the place was jumping!
It was jam-packed to the doors, and there were queues all down
the road - girls and boys waiting to pay half a crown admission.
All the top talent was played: Bill Haley, Alma Cogan,

Lonnie Donegan, Tommy Steele, Marty Wilde, Helen Shapiro, Cliff Richard and, of course, Elvis Presley. It was known as the Big Beat Club.

Me and Kenny (left) with Rocky and a friend on the door at the Jive Dive.
(photograph by Alf Shead)

In the beginning, there was Kenny, Peter Ferdinando (my brother-in-law), Johnny Bruce (a friend of Peter), and a mate of Kenny called Desmond. After a couple of weeks Desmond packed up, and so Kenny asked me to help him out. I was always restless on a Friday night anyway because I worried whether or not he was coping and, as the Puddings did have a reputation as a violent pub - even in those days - it didn't take me long to make up my mind.

Consider that I was married and Shirley was expecting our second baby; I was yet to get my Dockers book - a ticket to work in the docks approved by the National Dock Labour Board and the Union; I had a poor job, getting paid, at the time, £11 per week, £4 of which was rent and £5 going to Shirley for housekeeping, meaning I had £2 a week to get by on - for fares, drinks, and the occasional packet of fags. Working for my brother I more than doubled my money, and soon I started a club in Tottenham at the Spread Eagle and another one at the Eagle and Child in Forest Gate, and was soon out most nights doing my best to supplement my wages - and quite successfully.

The money started to roll in, so much so that Kenny bought a big old property in Forest Gate, formerly called Earlham Grove Dance Academy. He converted the ground floor into a great bar and the basement into a dance hall; it was a very imaginative set-up with bamboo and artificial plants in the bar which, for its time, was quite unusual. For the basement, he got lots of huge old posters from a friend in the billboard business and papered the place out with them; there were adverts for Oxydol, Surf, Players, Brylcreem - all top-to-bottom on the walls. It sounds horrible but it was colourful and it worked brilliantly. We named it the Jive Dive - a memorable name for an original concept that is still remembered in the area to this day.

At the Jive Dive, Shirley worked behind the bar with my sister-in-law, Anne; they were both dark and very attractive girls who were often taken for sisters. I took the money on the door, my mum was in the cloakroom, and my dad sat upstairs and baby-sat for us, even though he longed to be down with us having a fag and a drink; so frustrated that, to give himself something to do, he began making homemade burgers in crusty rolls and sending them down to us on the door! They were so nice that he started to sell them to customers as a side-line. I think they probably cost more to make than what he sold them

Bert the Builder, Shirley, Kenny's wife Anne and Norman at the Jive Dive. (photograph by Alf Shead)

My sister Doreen (left) my mum (second from left) and Shirley's mum Sue (third from right) with friends in the Jive Dive.
(photograph by Alf Shead)

for, but he was occupied in between caring for our eldest son Andrew.

The bar was successful and very busy. We had a huge following and didn't seem able to put a foot wrong. My wife, who proved to be a great barmaid and very popular with the punters, had to leave temporarily because she was heavily pregnant with our second son, Matthew, but we carried on with other staff and all seemed rosy.

The Jive Dive seemed to fulfil a real need in young people: it was the time of the 'mod', and young East Enders were, in those days, the most fashion-conscious in the world; rendezvousing in Forest Gate every weekend and going to our club, they would have a few drinks and then dance their socks off in the basement. There was no trouble and the customers were a lovely crowd. Everyone seemed to enjoy themselves.

THE SET UP

Of course, it was a situation the police watched *very* closely, and so it couldn't be allowed to last; after all, in the '50s and early '60s young people's enjoyment didn't seem to be allowed.

One Saturday we had a very gregarious, free-spending customer - an Australian - who seemed very happy and wanted to buy us all drinks, which we were glad to have and equally pleased to reciprocate. He laughed all the time. 'What a nice bloke,' we all said. After about three Saturdays, he asked if he could have a drink after time. He was still holding the glass of beer he'd bought previously, and we reasoned with him good naturedly, explaining that we mustn't serve him because it was after time and, by the same rules, he must drink up right away. He refused; he simply wouldn't let us take his glass and, with him being such a nice man and a colonial cousin, we didn't want to use any force or give a bad impression of England. As such, we were very pleasant to him whilst trying to take away his beer.

Suddenly, the doors burst open and in poured about twenty grim-faced policemen, who went on to nick us for serving after time. This so-called Australian wasn't an Australian at all but rather a London copper sent in as agent provocateur.

In due course, we had to go to court and Kenny lost his license. The police told their story and we told ours, but it was no contest: at that time, policemen, in the eyes of judges and magistrates, were above reproach. In court, the 'Australian' had the gall to smile and wave at us and say 'no hard feelings'. Well, you can imagine the two short words we said to him with as much venom as possible. Of course, it ruined the club overnight. We tried running it as a dance hall, serving only soft drinks and coffee, but it was never the same after that.

At a later date, I was told by a friend who knew all the policemen in the area that it was the licensee of the Eagle and Child in Forest Gate - a man called Ernie Halliwell, an ex-police sergeant from Bow - who had urged his former colleagues to raid us as he had the needle. He had started a rival club above his pub and, when he opened, we gave all of our customers free admittance, killing his venture at birth. It's hard to believe it could happen nowadays, but the police had so much power back then; they ran their 'manors' like personal fiefdoms, and if you didn't bribe them they would try to put you out of business.

Nowadays, the inner cities are crying out for people like me and my brother to give young people some hope, some enjoyment in their lives, and the police would welcome anyone. But, in those days, you were regarded with suspicion and narrow mindedness, and you were hated by the police for no good reason - other than the fact you were smarter and earned more money than them.

If the police had treated us less harshly for what was, after all, a manufactured crime, a setup, we possibly might not have taken the Puddings, but it was good training for what was to come. Without question, we knew we would never get any favours from our 'heroes in blue'.

THE GUV'NORS

In 1962 the 'governor' of the Two Puddings was Johnny Prentice, who was a smart, chubbyish, typical East Ender of that period, knew a lot of people and loved a drink. His wife, Chrissie, ran the food side of things, and she'd had experience running a café and so was quite good at it. He was friendly but always seemed a little sly and loved getting the better of anyone where money was concerned. He asked me to get him some cigarettes once and pushed a shilling into my hands. When the person serving the cigarettes asked for half a crown I told Johnny he owed me one and sixpence. He was indignant, responding only, 'I thought you didn't smoke,' as though it was me pulling a stroke on him. But I did like him and found him an engaging personality - although, I didn't fully trust him. Under his stewardship, the pub started to attract a lot of trouble, and almost every weekend he, or one of his cohorts, would come running up the stairs to the dance hall where Kenny and me were running our Big Beat Club and ask us to sort out the violence that had erupted downstairs. In the end I told him that he'd have to sort out his own trouble as we had to keep an eye on our own customers. I did send one of my pals to see him but Johnny said he'd get someone himself.

He then asked two brothers, George and Alan Dixon, to mind the place. They were both friendly blokes but they were impetuous to say the least. Both big men in their early twenties, George, in particular, could be very intimidating - they both started more trouble than they stopped. George used to beg me for a job on the door on the Big Beat Club but, although I did like him and knew he was game and very big, I only wanted people who could handle themselves with a bit of finesse, and I wanted customers to like them and not be worried about getting a swift right-hander every time they laughed a bit too loudly.

A couple of years down the line, the duo 'minded' the Plough and Harrow at Leytonstone for the licensee Philly Jacobs, a young Stepney boy with a flair for music. Unfortunately, however, things didn't work out quite so well for them; they were seen all over London, Philly and the brothers, driving about in the publican's white Rolls Royce; they were accused of some skullduggery that a lot of people said was a 'set up' because of their high profile; and they finished up going to prison for some time.

In truth, the real 'governors' of the Puddings were Patsy and Jimmy Quill. Patsy had been forced to relinquish the license by the Brewers, Watney Mann, as, along with his brother and a well-known Stepney man called Tommy Marks, he'd been nicked for fraud. They'd allegedly been selling cars at a cut price rate whilst receiving inflated prices from the finance company. There were all sorts of 'con' tricks like that in the '50s and '60s before computers and credit cards and all the paraphernalia of modern life made it so hard for old fashioned genuine crooks to earn a living. Although Patsy, Jimmy and Tommy Marks quite rightly got 'chucked', i.e. found not guilty, on that particular charge, they were nevertheless told to get out of the Puddings before the trial because the Brewers were extremely strict in those days and there could be no whiff of any untoward behaviour. So, Johnny Prentice was really, secretly, working for the Quills. They had previously asked me if I'd run the place but, nice though they were, I didn't fancy working for them.

When Patsy was found not guilty by the courts, Watney's were full of apologies and, because the Puddings had been so busy, they realised they couldn't afford to let such a good publican go. Patsy and his brother were very well known in the East End and had a huge following, and so they were offered the Blind Beggar which, at that time, before all the notoriety, was a terrific pub. The Quills then decided to really get rid of the Puddings as well as Johnny Prentice, and so they asked Kenny and me if we were interested. My brother couldn't hold a license due to the earlier court case, and so, albeit a bit unwillingly, I agreed, mainly because, at the time, we were frightened that any new licensee would want to run our dances in the night club upstairs themselves.

THE JUDGE

Now we had made the decision to take the pub the first hurdle was actually getting the license. Some years prior I'd been involved in a fracas outside the Kingley club in the West End. I was with two pals, Stevie Hegarty and Teddy Reeve, when, after a couple of remarks, we were attacked by a crowd of men, two of whom suffered bad injuries in the ensuing fight, one with a broken nose and jaw, the other a cracked cheekbone and broken ribs.

A Mr Harold Abrahams, who was the Art Director of the *Sunday Pictorial,* happened to be passing by, saw the incident, took it upon himself to call the police, and then followed us and confronted us at the bottom of the escalator in Oxford Circus tube station, whereupon we were surrounded by twenty policemen, arrested, and carted off to West End Central, where we were then charged with causing grievous bodily harm - or GBH in the common parlance of the day. Some months later we were appearing at the Old Bailey. Thanks to mine and Teddy's statements in the witness box, in which we both swore that he had nothing to do with it, we managed to get Stevie 'chucked': he was a pro fighter at the time, and so his offence would have been regarded as even more serious, but he genuinely was not guilty; in fact, he'd pulled Teddy away from one bloke who was lying on the ground and stopped him from jumping on him!

The judge's name was John Maude, and all the prisoners down in the cells reassured us he was a good bloke. One prisoner, as he was escorted past our cell, gave us the thumbs up and shouted, 'I was expecting a neves (seven) but I've only got a   two-year stretch.' He seemed a highly delighted old lag and had a huge grin on his face. Me and Teddy looked at each other, quite alarmed: it was December and almost Christmas - bad enough to get banged up any time, but not at Christmas!

The policeman in charge of the case, Detective Sergeant Saxby, became quite friendly over the course of the investigation, and although I never fully trusted him, he turned out to be decent - and I believe he came to like us too. The people we'd had the fight with were well known to the police and had previous form, some for violence. Saxby had gone into our backgrounds and realised we were hard-working dockers and, in his evidence, he made a point of this and stressed our previous good character. The judge spoke to us sternly but almost kindly, told us to stay out of further trouble, and fined us quite a small amount considering the original offence.

All of this was three years prior to getting a licence. I told the broker of my offence, who said I must tell the brewery, which I did. I was told to approach West End Central police station, who seemed quite happy for me, wished me all the best and all the luck, and told me they certainly wouldn't object, which was a huge relief.

I suppose West End coppers were much more sophisticated and worldly than their East End counterparts, who I had to approach next. I got a much frostier reception from them.

The man in charge at Stratford was a Chief Inspector Jones who, when I went to the station, called me into his office and then proceeded to harangue me, at times almost abusively, saying he'd seen me and my brother driving round with flashy women in his flashy Jag. It was true: Kenny *did* have a big white Jaguar and we often went out with our wives around East London, but all of our money was hard-earned and legitimate. Naturally, I couldn't put up with too much of this; I thought he was going to object anyway, and so I told him to forget it and walked out. Obviously I was disappointed, as were Shirley and Kenny, but, I reasoned, he'd only make our lives a misery once we were in the pub - or perhaps he was just after a bribe and I didn't cotton on. Either way, I wasn't the sort to kowtow to coppers - or anyone else, for that matter! - and so I accepted we wouldn't get the pub and told everyone to just forget it.

THE BUTCHER

Two days later, however, I went into the Puddings to tell Johnny Prentice what had happened, and standing at the bar was Eddie Downes, the butcher who supplied the pub with all their meat. He was a huge, fat man, almost as round as he was tall. He had a completely bald head and looked like a cartoon butcher. He was jovial, always smiling, and was always boasting about his connections with the police, bank managers, courts, and every other influence in the area. It was also said that he was a 'grass', which wasn't a very nice thing to be known for. I didn't believe he was, not in a conventional way: anybody with any sense would never tell him any secrets anyway unless it was to wind him up which, being East London, people tried to do all the time! He simply loved mixing with the local bookmaker, the local detectives and the local bank manager, all of whom congregated one or two afternoons a week and had a drink together.

He seemed excited to see me. 'I hear you're taking the pub?' he said. I explained what had happened round the nick.

'Will you still be buying the meat from me?' he queried.

'Of course I will,' I said, '*if* I get the pub.'

He laughed and told me not to worry.

I met him again a couple of days later. He described exactly the meeting I'd had with the Chief Inspector and said he'd sorted it out for me. Although they never got in touch with me, the word filtered back that they wouldn't object. The pub brokers and the brewery thought it advisable that we didn't go for a Protection Order; the Order meant one could move into a licensed premises on a temporary licensing pending getting the full license at the quarterly Brewster sessions. Consequently, we had to wait until

October 5th, which was three months away and a Friday - the busiest day of the week - and we'd have to have already arranged to move from Wood Street without even being one hundred percent sure I would even get the license! What a knife-edge to be on, and all because the police would not give a definite affirmative. I wondered if it was a cruel joke they were playing but I think, as usual, they were their usual insensitive selves and just couldn't bring themselves to be decent and straightforward.

Shirley and I spent the intervening weeks working at the pub under the supervision of Johnny and Chrissie Prentice. I quickly realised I wasn't going to learn the practicalities of pub work from Johnny, and so I had to instead rely on his bar/cellar-man or self-styled 'manager' Joe Hopson, the mascara-moustached, limping ex-greengrocer who Johnny relied on for the day-to-day running of the pub and who was very proud of the way he cleaned the pipes and kept the cellar clean. Joe told me that Johnny Prentice couldn't even change a Red Barrel keg, which went some way to explaining Johnny's reluctance to show me how to do it when I pressed him! Chrissie, on the other hand, was much more helpful, showing Shirley the food side; she'd had experience running a café and was quite competent, giving Shirley little tips, like mixing beetroot with cheap pink salmon to make it seem like the much more expensive red salmon.

October 5th came round quickly enough. I'd said all my farewells down the docks, sometimes feeling quite tearful and sad, and then it was time to say goodbye to Wood Street. It hadn't been a bad place to start married life, although it would, of course, have been better if we'd had more money. I remember we'd been so poor at one time that, in the winter, when it was dark, I'd climb over the high wall to the local coal yard with a couple of stout bags and fill them with up with handful after handful of glistening coal just so we could keep warm. But we'd been a happy family despite the setback of me being in hospital with TB for three months.

It was time to move on.

My father-in-law, Joe came over early to supervise the removal men. The kids had to be dropped off at my mother-in-law, Shirley had to go to the pub, and I had to go to court.

To everybody's relief I was granted a license! The brewery, the brokers, me and Shirley, Kenny and, above all, Johnny Prentice - who was desperate to leave, having had his fill of working for the Quills and who almost cried with joy at his salvation - were all relieved.

THE CHANGEOVER

Back at the pub, Shirley was flying about behind the bar, really enjoying it. She'd picked it up quickly and was in her element, talking to and laughing with customers as she served. She was so happy; it was as if she'd been born to do the job.

Changeover day was, and probably still is, the most hectic and confusing in any publican's calendar: you have to serve everyone, move in all your furniture, check the beer deliveries, pay money to the outgoing tenants, which had to be cash, be nice to the customers (you daren't lose any regulars), play host to the brewery officials and all the local publicans who came in to buy you a drink and wish you luck, look smart and stay sober.

It was tradition that everything happened on one day, with the changeover normally done on a Monday or Tuesday; however, because of the odd circumstances, our transition was on a Friday - normally the busiest day of the week.

But everything, fortunately, seemed to go fine. At the end of the session, the broker organised a 'silver' collection from the Brewers and various trade reps and other parties present, and they handed this, with expressions of good luck, to the incoming tenant's wife. Shirley was delighted to receive such a bonus after years of struggling with little money to speak of, and this was as good a start as any.

When we went upstairs to try to get the flat straightened out before the kids were brought home, Jimmy Quill, who, with his brother Patsy, had, of course, been one of the real owners, was sitting in our best armchair waiting for some money. We'd agreed to pay some unofficial 'goodwill' to ensure getting the pub. Jimmy and Patsy had done a good job introducing us to a reliable money lender and, at the same time, praising our qualities to the heavens to Watney Mann, so that was no problem.

Jimmy and Patsy were two of the 'faces' of Stepney. Jimmy had been a good amateur boxer, and the two of them had started a 'coal' business at an early age and branched out into the second-hand car business. Jimmy was blonde, considered handsome and dashing, and the parties he held most weekends, in an old, empty house he owned, were legendary. Patsy was considered to be the more stable of the two; wiser and more settled. But they were both very smart and well turned out, and Patsy, a good raconteur, always had a story to tell.

The removal men had to be paid, and they also expected a pint before they left, so we did what we could. We had a quick cup of tea and a sandwich ourselves, tidied up, collected the kids, and reopened the pub at 5.30 p.m. to more hordes of customers. Friday night and a pop group was playing; it was very busy anyway, and so our official 'opening' night was going to be the following Monday. We figured there wouldn't be enough room for all our friends on the Friday, but a lot came anyway. In fact, the place was packed out and the joint, as they say, was jumping. At the end of the night, whilst I struggled to check and balance the tills, the barmen played cards till 2.00 a.m. I eventually wound my way up the narrow wooden staircase to the living quarters and went, very wearily, to bed.

When we closed that night, I'd said to Shirley, 'Two years of this is about all I can stand. Two years and we're off! Take our money and leave. Finished.'

I wouldn't have believed then that I'd still be licensee at the turn of the century!

1962 and our first day behind the bar. Little did I know I'd still be licensee of the Puddings until the turn of the century!
(photographer unknown)

THE MONEY LENDER

To most of my friends, even close friends, it was a complete mystery how I'd raised enough money to buy a pub like the Puddings. What happened, though, was that the Quills, as well as selling us the pub, had put us in touch with a money lender, but we'd been sworn to secrecy. Another complication was that Kenny had to remain a secret partner because of his conviction as license holder at the Jive Dive; the Brewery, Watney Mann, would never have approved. It was particularly embarrassing because a docker friend had asked me one day to lend him a 'caser' (five shillings), and I'd said 'I'm sorry, I'm skint myself,' and a week or so later I bought a well-known pub, taking a small fortune.

The money lender - or rather the conduit through the money came - was a nice man called Jack Britton. He'd been connected to the coach firm 'Brittons', a well-known East End company. Patsy and Jimmy were obviously anxious to get the full money for the pub, and so they introduced us to their man, Jack. I suppose they knew that more experienced publicans would shy away from the Puddings as it was known as an 'aggravation' pub with a violent reputation, going back to way before the war when, in a legendary fight, a man called Billy Palmer had bitten the ear off a man named Arthur Scurry. They were both well-known villains - or perhaps tearaways would be a better word - and Billy Palmer, grandson of the great boxer Pedlar Palmer, was heard to remark afterwards, 'Arthur's ear tasted just like chicken!'

Jack wasn't the sort of moneylender you hear about all the time now; the horrible sort of low-life that breaks people's legs or throws acid over them if they don't pay up; vile, cowardly bullies who prey on the poor, deprived and poverty-stricken elderly. The way we were, we'd have broken *their* legs for not lending enough!

No one would have relished tangling with us in those days.

Mr Britton was very helpful, always willing to advise, telling us to put all our spare money in property. His money came from people who were anxious to earn a bit of interest on their dough without the tax man knowing, which was one of the reasons we had to keep the deal secret. I can't remember how much we borrowed - something like five grand which, nowadays, doesn't seem a lot, but back then was the average man's wages for five years. We were supposed to pay it back weekly over a three-year period. Kenny would join me in the Puddings office every Monday, we'd sort out our money and he'd go to the caravan site to give the man his payment. I think we managed to pay the lot back in six months and still kept a fair bit for ourselves, which was a relief for our dad as he'd stuck his house up for security.

THE BOND

When I took the Puddings, I was lucky that I had a beautiful wife with lots of personality and a lovely mum and dad who were very supportive. I was young and well known in East London and had a large group of friends.

It was a step into the unknown for me as I was a docker with a young family to uproot, but if I was hesitant no one else was: I was urged on by everyone I knew.

My main support, aside from Shirley, was Kenny. We were partners from the start. Kenny is four years younger than me and we look alike, but although he's not as tall as me, he's very well built and, as a schoolboy, had represented East London in football, cricket and athletics, and had also been Garrison champion middleweight boxer in the army, later boxing for West Ham. I remember him coming home from training with all sorts of lumps and bruises. One time he told me he'd been sparring with a young heavyweight he said we'd hear a lot more about; this turned out to be Billy Walker, who subsequently fought for the title. In later life, from the age of 25 to the present day, Kenny's great passion has been tennis. He excelled, becoming, in his age group, one of the best players in the county. One noted tennis coach told me that, if he'd been trained from an early age, he would have made it to Wimbledon. On top of this, he was the best street fighter and pub brawler I knew.

Without question, Kenny had so much energy; I might have been the thinker but he was the dynamo. Whilst I ran the Puddings he was off all over the place, promoting concerts, dances and clubs as far off as Whitby in Yorkshire and Liverpool as well as closer to home at Shoreditch Town Hall, West Ham Baths, Stratford Town Hall, The Eagle at Tottenham, and in venues in Dagenham, Harlow and Croydon. At Shoreditch, the licensee of the Crosby Head would provide the bar. The pub had a picture of Bing Crosby on their sign, and I believe Mr Crosby did actually visit the place once.

I'd envy my dad, Uncle John and Uncle Don as they used to catch the train from Euston on a Saturday afternoon to go and help run the dances for Kenny. One time, my dad actually drove them all up there only to get lost in the mountains of the Lake District. He was forced to abandon his car and somehow find a taxi to get them there in time!

Kenny also opened the Way Inn club in Mare Street, Hackney, where the Who and Diana Ross & the Supremes were amongst those who headlined for him. Most of the big groups and artists of the era - the Animals, Screaming Lord Sutch, the Kinks, Manfred Mann, the Move, Little Eva, Them, Billy J. Kramer,

I used to envy my dad (left) and Uncle John travelling the length and breadth of Britain helping Kenny promote concerts.
(photograph by Eddie Johnson)

Martha and the Vandellas, Jerry Lee Lewis, John Lee Hooker, the Drifters, Rod Stewart, Long John Baldry, amongst countless others - all worked under Kenny's aegis. Many of the big names he worked with would also perform at the Puddings or, if they didn't perform, would at least drop by for a drink.

Later on, Kenny tried to take over an old theatre in Dalston, which went on to become a famous ska and reggae club for West Indians known as the 4 Aces. He also went after the Rex in Stratford, as he wanted to put on rock concerts and old-fashioned film shows and try to bring some glory back to the famous old building. The council refused, claiming the roof was in a parlous and dangerous state. A Mr Baxter was head of planning, and so when the cinema actually did re-open a few months later in order to show Asian films, Kenny asked him why he had changed his mind and granted a license for the premises. He raised an eyebrow, gave a wry smile, and said 'orders from above'.

In partnership with Teddy Lemon, a friend and customer in the Puddings who attached himself to Kenny and became an invaluable partner and helper to him, he opened an office at 100 Charing Cross Road, which he called the Lemon B. Johnson Agency, and began managing various groups. Teddy later joined the famous English reggae musician Judge Dread as a performer and songwriter. Kenny also ran the famous Lotus Ballroom in Forest Gate, first as a dance hall and then a casino, and finally a nightclub, which finally closed its doors in 2001.

Yet, despite all of these hugely time-consuming duties, Kenny always stood in for me on my night out on a Wednesday, and was always in the pub with me on a Friday night. If there was trouble in the pub, it was always a race between us as to who was first on the scene.

THE OFFICE

Every Monday morning for almost 40 years we met in our little office at the Puddings. This room deserves a special mention. Kenny, being superstitious, never wanted it cleaned or decorated. Of course it would be swept and mopped now and again, but the ceiling was festooned with cobwebs and there were old, torn posters advertising some of our long-forgotten concerts and events hanging from the peeling wallpaper. It was the grottiest office in London - if not all of Britain! - but we loved it, or rather me and Kenny did.

It used to drive our younger brother Michael mad. When he was managing the pub for us many years later he would tidy up on the sly. Kenny's superstitions went so far that, instead of a briefcase, he carried important papers, as well as lots of cash, in an old small 'lucky' attaché case made from cardboard that he'd had since the

The 'office' used to drive our younger brother Michael mad. When he was managing the pub in the eighties and nineties for us he'd tidy up on the sly! (photograph by Johanna St Michaels)

age of fourteen. He kept it until one wet and blustery day when it finally burst its seams in a car park, scattering paper and money everywhere into the swirling wind and rain, at which point I pointed out to him that it can hardly have been 'lucky' to have fallen to bits in such an inconvenient place.

In the office we would discuss business and ideas, make sure the books were balanced, take our wages, and bank the takings. Lots of ideas came from these meetings, some of which were put into practice whilst others never got off the ground.

Kenny and I are very close, very rarely disagreeing, but when we did the language would turn the air blue - mainly from me, I will admit. The silence beyond the closed office door was profound as no one dared interrupt and ask what was wrong.

Me and Kenny counting the money in the sixties heyday of our 'office'. (photograph by Shirley Johnson)

Maxine Daniels, the brilliant jazz singer who arrived at the Puddings in mysterious circumstances.
(photographer unknown)

THE COOKS, THE CLEANERS,
THE BURGLAR AND HER LOVER

THE FAMILY

Many members of our extended family worked for us over the years, and many even went on to own and run their own East End pubs. I suppose my mum was the first and the most faithful, working in the ladies' cloakroom until she became very ill. All the girls loved her and she loved all of them. She also had her own money for the first time in her married life, as before my dad would never let her go to work. Our loyal sister Doreen also did a brief stint 'behind the door', as did Kenny's wife Anne. Our aunts Sue and Kate also ran cloakrooms for Kenny at various venues. Our uncles, John and Don, cousin Rita and her husband Billy, and our in-law Ben also worked for him at different dance halls under our dad's supervision.

Shirley's dad, Joe, would decorate for us and her vivacious younger sister, Susie, who she was very close to, helped behind the bar when she was still only seventeen. She worked in the evenings and loved it, proving extremely popular with the customers and even met her husband Alan 'Jonah' Jones there. In later years they owned several East End pubs themselves. Sharon, the step-daughter of Shirley's younger brother Peter, used to help out behind the bar when he was managing the pub for us in the '70s, and when my younger brother Michael took over from Peter in the '80s our niece and nephew Jackie and Nicky also did long spells behind the bar. My cousin, Carol Price, who has since gone on to become a local authority on the history of Forest Gate, ran the cloakroom when her mum, Aunt Flo, died; Aunt Flo had taken over from my mum when she had passed away. Later on, Carol worked for many years with Michael's wife, Claire, running the food side of the pub at lunchtimes.

Shirley's dad, Joe(left) and mum, Sue (second from right) and my mum, Ginny and dad, Charlie, celebrating at Kenny's Lotus Ballroom. (photograph by Alf Shead)

My sister Doreen (second from left) Kenny's wife Anne (right), my mum (second from right) and friends relaxing before starting work at the Jive Dive. (photograph by Alf Shead)

Even the next generation in the family seem inspired in some way by the activities of their forebears. John, the partner of Michael and Claire's daughter Jenna, now DJ's and runs nightclubs in Shoreditch and around the East End, whilst Kenny and Anne's daughter has become a successful ceramicist under the name Miss Annabel Dee and some of her work, featuring old photographs of the Two Puddings and the Blind Beggar has even been on display in Downing Street and at Sotheby's.

We had mastered a recipe for success: everyone could be trusted, we paid decent wages, it gave everyone a new lease of life, they all enjoyed it and made friends with most of the customers, and so there was very little trouble; even when there was, the young tearaways had a lot of respect for them.

THE CLEANERS

Back in the '60s, pubs with fitted carpet were as rare as ice machines, lemon in drinks, and nice, elegant glasses; they were all in some distant future. Floors were linoleum or wood and had to be scrubbed and then polished. We never had a vacuum cleaner - that was only in the domestic quarters. After a busy Friday or Saturday, the pub was a terrible mess, and so we would do our best when we closed; emptying ashtrays, sweeping the piles of broken glass into the corner, picking it all up and putting the detritus of the night into the dustbins. But it still looked as if a bomb had exploded.

When I first went to the Puddings, the two cleaners seemed nice enough women but, to my inexperienced eye, they were not industrious enough and they kept wanting to borrow money, and so I made the decision to give them notice. What a mug I was: a good cleaner is one of the hardest things to get in the pub game.

And so, being a new boy and rather green, I advertised for new cleaners in such a way that whoever answered knew they would need to be super-efficient and spotless. I was gratified with the response. 'That was easy enough,' I thought. After interviewing a few, I picked out the two I thought would be best and told them to start as soon as my present cleaners had worked their week's notice.

'I'll soon have this place sparkling,' I had told myself. But, on the day my new staff were due to start, my two seemingly eager applicants never appeared. Surely they would turn up? They had seemed keen but they never showed up. I never saw either of them again. Later on in my business life, I realised this happens quite a lot: many people are interviewed and given a job and then fail to turn up. Of course, the job was not very salubrious or glamorous; pub-cleaning was a dirty job and there was plenty of other work about.

However, with the help of Joe Hopson, I somehow coped that day. Shirley, once the kids had been looked after, came down to lend a hand. We scrubbed and polished and, up to our elbows in grime, managed to open on time. Shirley and I took turns to bath and change, and then Joe blackened his moustache and we were ready. I never actually remember Joe having a wash, but he would blacken his moustache and eyebrows and put on lots of Brylcreem; he looked okay - from a distance…

I had a regular cleaner who did Sundays only. She was a nice person, very dark in looks, and who told me she had been a film extra and, when she was a little girl, had worked on the film *Elephant Boy*, which made a star of a young Indian boy called Sabu. She said she'd met him and he was very nice. They had made most of the film in the studio, apparently, but it was a famous film in its day and one of the big successes of the Korda Studios. I persuaded her, after some weeks, to take on the weekday job, but her husband, Albert, made it quite clear that she couldn't work over the Christmas and New Year holidays as he was fed up having to cook the festive dinner himself.

Rene Terry was her name, and she was a wonderful cleaner. She worked for me for fifteen years until crippling arthritis forced her to pack up. Her youngest son, Paul, was my eldest son Andrew's age, and he used to come in and play with him and they remained friends into adulthood.

THE SINGER

My first Christmas at the pub - that of 1962 - I was still short a cleaner. Rene was, as I'd promised her husband, off for the festive season, and so I put a big notice in the window hoping to get someone in… anyone!

I have never known a pub as busy as it was that Christmas Eve. It was packed every minute of opening time. Morning and night. We just couldn't get the glasses as the potmen couldn't get through the crowds! At one point I tried to help them but could only get halfway down the pub - and even then it took ten minutes to get back behind the bar, even though I was pushing and shoving people out of the way with little or no ceremony! When we finally closed I could not believe the mess. There were mountains of broken glass, the lino-tiled floor was covered in thick mud, the debris of a mad Christmas Eve was everywhere. It was though a flood from a dirty river had swept through the pub and, as I looked, all I could think of was not the hundreds of pounds we had taken but rather how on earth I was going to get cleaned up. As well as doing all this I had to play Father

Christmas and take the kids' toys into their bedroom, and we also had to have our usual, not-to-be-missed Christmas morning fry-up. On top of that Shirley had to get the dinner on, I had to bottle-up, do the tills, have a bath, and look smart and ready to greet all my customers and most of my family who were coming to celebrate our first Christmas in the pub. Add to the panic the fact that it was also snowing heavily!

The doorbell started to ring unceasingly from 7.30 a.m. Me and Shirley were up, having had little sleep, not getting to bed till 3.00 a.m., and then Andrew and Matthew were jumping all over the bedroom at 6.00 a.m. showing us what Father Christmas had bought for them.

I staggered downstairs and opened the door of the pub. A young black woman stood outside, a shawl over her head protecting her from the snow. It was like a scene from Dickens.

'D'ya wanna cleaner?' she asked, her voice more cockney than mine. I grabbed her and pulled her into the pub before she could change her mind. I must have looked pretty desperate as she seemed startled by my response. *Thank God*, I thought. 'Can you start now?' I asked.

She was a very attractive girl and seemed unperturbed by the mess. After I explained her duties, I went upstairs and told Shirley we'd been rescued. She thought she'd better go down and see how the lady was doing. She soon came up again.

'She's cleaning the floor with her foot,' she said, puzzled. 'Go down and look.'

Down I went again and, sure enough, hands on her hips, humming and singing to herself, with her foot on the washcloth, she was attempting to clean the mud-encrusted floor with her foot.

I sighed. I felt a mixture of grief, frustration, helplessness and, above all, a sense of deep loneliness. The world was against me; no one realised how hard this new life was proving to be. And, although I knew I couldn't collapse onto the floor and kick my heels in the air and sob (it would be too unmanly), I felt like it.

I heard a voice muttering something. It was our new cleaning lady, Gladys.

'What?' I queried, not having heard what she'd said.

'D'you 'ave singers in pub?' There were posters round the pub advertising Jim Rivers and his group, The Castaways.

'Yes, we do,' I answered, distracted, and thinking of my soon-to-come impatient customers as I looked at the mess. The place looked like the pitch at Upton Park after a cup tie in a thunderstorm. 'Why? Do you sing?' I asked out of politeness whilst debating whether having no cleaner was better than this and trying to formulate a way to sack someone that had worked for less than an hour.

'Yer, 'ad me own television programme once.'

A nutcase I've got, not a cleaner, I thought.

'You'll have to come up and give a few songs one weekend,' I muttered, humouring her.

'Alright. Me name's Gladys Daniels, but me stage name was Maxine Daniels.'

I took a good look at her then and found myself shocked. Yes, it was her, Maxine Daniels, the lady with the lovely voice who could sing Jazz, Blues and pop music equally well. She'd had a spot on the *Tonight* programme and then a half-hour TV show of her own. What on earth had gone wrong?

I sacked her right away, of course, and immediately booked

her as our resident singer at higher wages than a cleaner. Her brother was Kenny Lynch who'd had a hit record, 'Up on the Roof', and she sang better than him. She could sing like an angel.

Somehow, we managed to get the pub ready for opening and Maxine made her debut on Boxing Day night. She was a huge success. In the meantime, I'd been busy phoning the newspapers - local and national; it proved to be quite a big story; it was like having thousands of pounds worth of advertising. She packed the pub out even more.

Gladys was a lovely person, although quite shy, and would try to stand at the back of the stage when singing. She had loads of fans; in fact, one man came all the way from Spain and wanted to take her over there to sing as a resident entertainer in a big hotel he owned. Television were interested and Kenny, my brother, who had set himself up as her manager, rigged her out in new clothes for an audition, but she didn't turn up. Eventually she became ill and packed up, but I used to hear about her now and again, singing at various Jazz venues round the country, until she died a few years ago. She was always highly thought of on the English Jazz scene, working with Humphrey Lyttelton amongst others, and without her hang-ups and complexes she would have been a major international star.

THE CAT BURGLAR

With Rene off for a few weeks, I was generally moaning to anyone who would listen about my lack of success at getting a stand-in cleaner, and it was then that a little dark woman with black bobbed hair and big saucer eyes - who was sitting on a stall at the bar sipping a pint of Guinness - said, 'I'll do it, I'll have a go at anything.' She was an energetic, wiry little woman, and she got stuck in and was a success. About this time, I also managed to get a second cleaner who was a younger woman, quite plump with a lot of energy.

The little dark lady, Ruby Catto, told my man Joe some startling stories. When he repeated them to me I laughed and said, 'she's kidding you up, Joe.' For example, her husband apparently liked to dress up in ladies' clothes, which he made her buy in his size and, if that wasn't bad enough, he would then make her tie him to a chair with wire, and then whip him hard about his body with a bicycle chain. This was his pleasure. Me and Shirley or even Joe had never heard anything so outlandish; nowadays, however, stories like that are quite commonplace, but in those days ordinary people were not privy to - what seemed to us - such awful secrets.

After working in the pub for a couple of weeks, Ruby asked for a Friday off. She said she'd try to come in but she might be a bit late. I told her not to worry, she had been very reliable so far. But, much to my surprise, she never came back.

The following week, Joe, in a state of fevered excitement, rushed into the office waving around a copy of the *Stratford Express*. Ruby Catto had been sent to prison for burglary! Apparently her young son would accompany her to shops or factories and she'd push him up to any open fanlights or windows as he was small enough to wriggle through and open the door for her. She had wanted the time off to go to court and yet, in the short time she worked for me, I found her absolutely trustworthy, a good cleaner and a pleasant lady.

THE FLOOD

Soon into the New Year, I was woken up at 5.00 a.m. one morning by the man in the shop next door ringing. It was part of the same building but was a lock-up shop that opened very early in the morning to sell cigarettes and sweets to the workers on early shifts. 'Water's pouring into my shop,' he shouted. 'It's coming from your pub!'

I went running down the staircase and found the dining room cum dance hall on the first floor completely flooded. The water was pouring down the staircase like a waterfall. Again, the blackest despair clouded over me, and I had the same thought that I was to have over and over again in the coming years: the pub game just wasn't worth it. The cat burglar was still on the staff then and, with the hard-working young plump girl, they scrubbed and bailed out like two Trojans. They were good for my morale and cheered me up no end, which was more than I could say for Edith and Maisie, our two posh lunchtime waitresses who marched in, stared, sniffed, and said they hoped it would all be ready for *their* customers, or for Joe Hopson who took one look and started to vigorously polish all the glasses.

The cause of the flooding was a burst water pipe, which was the first of 37 burst pipes I was to have in that very severe winter of 1962/1963. It was one of the coldest winters of the century and one I would never forget.

A sidelight to that story was that I'd phoned the brewery for help in resolving the matter and repairing the pipe and, without hesitation, they'd sent the foreman of their building department and two men down, who worked very hard to get the pub ready for opening. Nowadays, such departments no longer exist.

Another cleaner who seemed super-efficient and who told me that she was going to make the place gleam vanished after three days, never even asking for her pay. I was told that, when she saw the pub on a Saturday morning, she went home and collapsed. The doctor diagnosed nervous exhaustion with complicated complications.

A Scotswoman I had as a cleaner said she was doing the work because she was bored at home: her husband was in business, she was a director of the firm, and they had property in Devon, Ireland and Scotland. She worked very well with Rene Terry for about 3 years and they proved to be a good partnership. She also told me, with an earnest look on her face and as I was about to embark on a holiday to the Isle of Skye, that her brother and his family, whilst driving on to the ferry at the Kyle of Lochalsh, had slidinto a watery grave.

A lot of the cleaners lasted just days or a couple of weeks at most. It was hard-going, dirty work that had to be done every day. They needed to be in early and it all had to be finished by the time the first customer came through the door. Over the years, we even tried contract cleaners with machines, but they were never satisfactory. I had some good cleaners and some bad ones, but Rene was, by far, the best.

THE COOKS

When I worked in the docks, my friends, Johnny Smith and Matthew Tighe, introduced me to a fellow dock worker called Lenny Alexander. He was not the normal 'dockie'; he was tall, slim and rather refined in appearance, and also seemed to speak a little 'posher' than the rest of us. However, his main attraction was that he possessed an open-top sports saloon, a Ford Zodiac, and his mum had a café.

Whenever we had a long lunch break, we'd all pile into Lenny's car and go to his mum's café in East Ham. I've no recollection what the food was like, but it wasn't particularly memorable.

Some years later, when I was well-established at the Puddings, I was still friendly with Lenny who, by a weird process for which I was partly responsible, had metamorphosed from a refined docker into a refined crook. Or rather he was on the fringe of crime. Some people I'd introduced him to had been quite impressed by his manner. Aloofness implied a certain respectability that was a rare commodity in the area, and they thought he would make an ideal front-man for a 'long firm', which involved setting up a company, obtaining credit from suppliers, and then not paying them. They promised him all sorts of fortune if he joined them.

About this time, Kitty Cullen, our faithful and brilliant cook, told us that she was going into hospital for a hip operation. She had suffered from arthritis for a number of years and had finally decided to have the operation, which wasn't as tried and tested as it is nowadays, and so she wasn't sure if she'd ever be fit to work again.

Kit had started at the pub before the war and she had told us all sorts of tales. Of the different governors that had employed her, one in particular used to chase her round the tables when she was a young girl in the kitchen. Shirley and me found it hard to imagine her as a young girl: she must have been about sixty but she was a tall, quite a handsome woman, and no doubt would have been very attractive when she was young. We were both saddened by the news - we knew she wouldn't be back; she only said she might to soften the blow.

We regarded her as much as a friend as an employee. Her cooking was so good that we knew we could never replace her; homemade scotch eggs, pasties, home-cooked gammon hams, meat pies, steak and kidney puddings that she called 'babies' heads' because of their shape, fish and chips freshly cooked every Friday, shepherd's pies, liver and bacon, plus lovely sandwiches, all made with proper, fresh crusty bread. We had no deep freezers in those days, no frozen chips; all the potatoes had to be hand-peeled and cut into shape; the fish was bought fresh from Angel Lane and if we didn't sell it the day it was bought and cooked we would eat it ourselves or give it to the staff. But everyone loved her cooking. It was food from what now seems to be a bygone age and, what was better from our point of view, bygone wages. Microwave ovens and pre-prepared food was still something yet to be introduced. It's all made it a lot easier for the average pub nowadays, but what a sorry mess it can be: too hot, tasteless and often inedible, and the people who heat it up - who can't be called cooks - want a small fortune in wages.

We tried so hard to get someone to replace Kit. One old boy who claimed he'd been Head Chef at the Dorchester promised to revolutionise our kitchen and the food. He started by ordering enough dry goods to stock a hotel - 3 cwt of flour for a start - as well as carboys of vinegar and cases of butter, and he even banned Eugene, our younger son, from the kitchen. Kit loved our children and especially Eugene: he was only three years old and he would chat away to her whilst she was cooking and would keep her amused, but the old boy chucked him out, not wanting to be distracted. As a former Head Chef, his work had to be taken seriously. But, in all the time he was there, I don't think he cooked anything that was tasty or that we liked, even some lobster he ordered was so expensive that we couldn't sell it and, when Shirley and I, to save waste, went to eat it, the taste seemed a bit off and so we threw it all away! He didn't last long. I believe some of the flour he ordered was still in the cellar when we left at the turn of the century.

We tried out various people with not much luck, until, one day, a small plump lady came in and asked for a job. Shirley came into the office and said, 'She seems nice and she's Lenny Alexander's mum.'

'Grab her,' I said. 'She'll be perfect. She had a café.'

All our problems in the cooking department were over - so we thought. The good thing about Maggie was that she adored Eugene and he loved her. We didn't have to worry about a babysitter; he couldn't wait to get downstairs into the kitchen with her.

But as far as cooking was concerned... How she ran a café I'll never know! Shirley asked her to make some sausage rolls and some pasties to try out her skills, and when she went into the kitchen to see her progress there were sausages, mincemeat, all rolled into various shapes and sizes, flour, suet and God knows what else all over the kitchen table, some of which was mixed with milk, some with butter; the oven was turned up far too high; some of the meat was pre-cooked, some was raw and just covered in flour and water; as for her Scotch eggs... she tried to make them without taking the shell off the egg and without cooking, so when I bit into one it had raw egg and shell all mixed up with sausage meat! She tried to roast potatoes without boiling them first. Shirley did her best to help but had to spend most of her time serving in the pub. We tried eating some of the sausage rolls but some were too burnt, some were undercooked, and the pastry tasted strongly of bicarbonate of soda. We never sold any to customers, but after we'd tried them I gave the rest to the kids, Andrew and Matthew, who looked at me with hurt eyes as if I was trying to poison them! Eugene said they were lovely, but I noticed he never ate any - he just liked her looking after him. She'd sit him on the food bench and tell him stories all day.

Even her tea and coffee wasn't that good. Essentially, she was a disaster in the kitchen, but we kept her on because we both liked her and we didn't want to embarrass Lenny, who was a good friend to us. But he hadn't spoken to his mum for a couple of years because, although his dad died of Leukaemia soon after the war, when Lenny was a small boy she had started a relationship with her Irish lodger years after she was widowed and Lenny could never come to terms with it. She had another son who was quite comfortable with the situation, and she would tell Shirley all about it and would get really upset at Lenny's attitude.

We compromised so that Shirley would do most of the skilful cooking and Maggie would just make the sandwiches and wash up, which suited us at the time because Stratford was in the phase of its ugly '60s regeneration, knocking down and destroying the famous and lovely Angel Lane in the process. This market, so beloved by Joan Littlewood and her actor friends from the local Theatre Royal and held in deep affection by all the residents of the area, was being replaced with a horrible, characterless indoor market. In the process, all the old, historic offices on Stratford Broadways, whose inmates also happened to be amongst our best lunchtime customers, the Stratford Express,

Wilson & Whitworth, the Royal Insurance, Barclays bank, were all demolished and replaced by featureless concrete blocks, which proved to be a depressing feature of the '70s. So, our lunchtime trade and takings dwindled, but fortunately, the blow was softened because our evening trade - thanks to our vigorous searches for new bands, new ideas and new marketing - went up and up.

Thanks to our vigorous search for new bands our evening trade continued to go up and up. (photograph by Alf Shead)

Chief barman and cellar man Joe Hopson (white shirt) and the rest of the public bar staff on our first Christmas Eve in the Puddings. (photograph by Alf Shead)

THE GREENGROCERS

Over the years I had some wonderful staff at the Puddings as well as some that were awful and, of course, many in between. I suppose some of them were honest but, being cynical about the East End's values, I had to assume that most of them 'fiddled' a bit. I remember somebody telling me that staff will just help themselves to cigarettes and crisps and not even think of it as dishonest, which had the potential to really eat into profits after a while, as the margins on such items were very low; it was regarded more of a service to the customer to serve cigarettes, and the price was fixed as there were only two big cigarette companies that dominated the trade, which was why machines, despite the moans of customers, were considered such a good thing.

My chief barman at the pub in the early years was Joe Hopson. A former greengrocer, he came from a family of greengrocers and was considered the black sheep of a respectable family. His brother, Harry, had a stall in the road opposite the pub and, every half hour or so, he would come hobbling across Stratford Broadway, waving his walking stick at all the traffic, forcing them to slow down or stop. He suffered terrible gout and so it was an awkward journey. The wide road then was two-way, and he Harry was forced to dodge the traffic, wincing with pain, as he struggled across. He used to drink half a pint of Red Barrel and liked it in a thin, straight glass. Joe would torment him and give him a small half-pint dimpled jug, which he knew Harry hated, or he would pretend not to see him, pointedly looking for customers in the other bar, knowing full well that his brother hated to leave his stall for too long. He would be looking across the road, worrying about it, tutting away, and desperately trying to get Joe's attention. Eventually, he'd get served and have a slanging match with his brother, at which point Harry would swear never to come back and off he'd go, hobbling back across the road, painfully weaving his way through the traffic again.

He'd be back in half an hour for more beer.

On Joe's day off I made sure Harry received good and prompt service in his thin glass. Harry was very proud about being a Freemason and, on the day of his lodge meeting, he would be in early evening, all dressed up in black jacket, striped trousers and homburg hat - and very smart he looked too. Of course, it was supposed to be a secret, and if I asked him where he was going he would mumble, half under his breath, something about a   business meeting. Of course, we all knew where he was off to, but we had to pretend otherwise.

Freddie, Joe's other brother, was a terrible show-off. His stall was in Angel Lane - the area's most famous market - and he was always boasting how good his fruit was, far and away the best in Stratford, the best in London, he would contend. He would sit on a stool and brag how his house - a terrace cottage in a little side street - was the best in the area; how he and Molly, his wife, went on far superior holidays than any of the other stallholders. He always spoke in a loud voice, not to Joe or anyone in particular, but rather to address his remarks to the pub in general.

I used to buy all my fruit and veg from Harry except at Christmastime when I ordered it from Fred. Harry never seemed to mind; he readily conceded that his stuff was run of the mill. To be fair, Fred's boasts about his wares were fully justified - it just couldn't be bettered. He was the first I knew to get pecan nuts. He got me some strawberries for Christmas, flown in from California, so he told me. His oranges were sweeter and juicier than anyone else's and his apples more crisp and luscious. The first time I saw a kiwi fruit it was from him. He truly was the King of the Fruit Sellers in Stratford.

THE CELLAR MAN

Joe Hopson also had several sisters, but only one of who approved of him. She was a nice little woman, quite pretty, who had been rather flighty in her younger days, which was probably why she didn't mind Joe. He was a terrible womaniser, always the first to serve a pretty woman. He was a self-styled Ronald Colman look-a-like with a little moustache he kept well-blackened with mascara. He would shave and wash his face and hands, but the rumour was that he never - or rarely - took a bath and didn't bother washing under his arms. He walked with a limp owing to suffering with polio as a child, and apparently, on the sly, took snuff, although this he vehemently denied.

Joe was also a terrible liar. He was 60 years old but told everyone he was in his early forties. I don't think anyone was fooled by this except for his girlfriend, a sweet but naïve young girl called Susan. She believed everything he told her.

Shirley and I came back late one night and Joe was clearing up the bar while Susan waited for him. They had just moved into a couple of rooms together; apparently her mum had chucked her out and Joe had managed to get lodgings for both of them.

As we stood talking before they left, Susan said, 'Oh, Eddie, and you, Shirley,' - and she looked adoringly at my wife - 'thanks ever so much for all the plates, knives and forks and cups you've given us. That's really nice of you. Me and Joe are so grateful.'

I looked at Joe, who's suddenly started to vigorously polish the bar top, something he'd never done before.

A self-styled Ronald Coleman look-a-like, Joe was the black sheep of a respectable family. (photograph by Eddie Johnson)

He was humming to himself as if no one else was there.

'What's that then, Joe? When did I give you those?' I questioned.

He looked up from his polishing as if startled out of a deep reverie. 'No, no, she's muddled up. Don't be silly, Susan,' he said, chuckling. 'They're not from here!'

'You told me they were,' she replied adamantly, clearly firm and sure of herself. 'You said Shirley and Eddie had given them to you, you know you did, Joe.'

Joe's face reddened. He was rarely embarrassed by anything and, as he was always telling me - and anyone else who would listen - how honest he was and how he would never, ever steal anything, how he'd been honest all of his life, how anyone, particularly me, could trust him absolutely with anything - money, drink, property. Of course, neither I nor Shirley knew anything of this cutlery and crockery.

After lots of bluster, Joe said Kit the cook had suggested he 'borrow' a few things to tide him over. He was going to bring them straight back, he was so discomfited. Shirley and me had a job to keep our faces straight, but when we went upstairs we couldn't stop laughing because he was so 'holier than thou', and we just loved to catch him out.

When I told Kit the next morning she was most indignant. 'I thought we were missing some stuff. He's such a bloody liar! Wait till I see him!'

I never sacked Joe. I knew he couldn't be completely trusted: he used to pour himself a drink and, if I was in the vicinity, he would raise his glass to an imaginary customer, say 'Cheers!' in a loud voice as if a customer had bought him a drink, and down it would go. It fooled me - once. But after that we all knew it was a sham.

One night, a little bit cruelly, another one of our barmen, Jackie Bowers, gave him a half-pint and said a customer had bought it for him. Joe raised his glass, said 'Cheers!' and downed it in one and then nearly choked so badly it alarmed us all. Jackie had put a load of Joe's snuff in the glass.

All through the evening sessions, no matter how much beer Joe drank, I never once saw him go to the gents. Sometimes, when I went down the cellar to change a barrel, I thought I detected a whiff of urine. This didn't happen often as he guarded his barrel-changing job down in the cellar jealously. 'I'll do it, don't you go and mess everything up,' he used to say if anyone else wanted to go down there. When I asked him about the smell he reacted in predictable fashion: he, Joe Hopson, the cleanest, smartest, most honest, most handsome man in Stratford, beloved by all the ladies, would never stoop to such low depths as to pass water in his beloved cellar! Especially considering the fact he personally cleaned and scrubbed it, as if it was an operating theatre, every Wednesday evening!

How could I even *think* such a thing let alone say it?

He didn't fully convince me - in fact, I never believed him at all. So, one night, I quietly followed him down the rickety wooden stairs, making sure he never knew I was behind him. It was a long, very low cellar, and I had to almost bend double to walk along. It was full of the debris that a pub accumulates over many years. Apart from the cases of beer, lemonade, fruit juices and spirits stacked to the ceiling, there were dusty boxes of glasses, empty cases, stacks of papers, and accounts and invoices dating back decades belonging to licensees long since gone and probably dead. It was a cool cellar but there was no refrigeration or cold room, and it was dimly lit by a couple of bare, low-wattage bulbs. I hid behind a pillar - one of many that seemed to be holding the entire building up - and had my suspicions confirmed. I watched with growing horror as Joe unzipped himself and, with a blissful look slowly spreading across his face, proceeded to pee all over the beer barrels. I jumped out from behind the pillar and shouted at him: I swore and screamed and I nearly hit him, but bent double as it was too awkward to be angry for long. More in sorrow I sent him upstairs in disgrace.

He reminded me of a Spaniel I once had, his eyes full of remorse looking at the ground as if it was all *my* fault. For once he had absolutely nothing to say. That was the nearest I got to sacking him.

He was a pain, a nuisance, full of vanity and not particularly honest. He was all top show, mascara-clad moustache and eyebrows, Pashana hair tonic on top of Brylcreem on his head, but the fact remains he was a real character who thought he was doing his best for the pub. He was also fiercely loyal, and customers, even those that didn't like him much, told me that he hadn't a bad word to say about me or my family or the way the pub was run.

Walthamstow dog track was a favourite haunt of Joe's most Tuesdays, which was his day off. If he came in early and happy on a Wednesday morning I knew he hadn't lost much. He was always enthusing about a marvellous barman who used to serve him at the Bakers Arms where he'd drink before going to the dog track. 'He's like me,' he used to say, 'smart, quick, honest, good personality, although not quite as handsome as me.' Nothing more calculated could have put me off the man. One week I was so short staffed that, despite all my misgivings, I told Joe I'd give his man a trial.

He did have some similarities to Joe in that he had a moustache that was blackened and heavily Brylcreemed hair. He wore a white shirt, slightly grubby, frayed round the collar, a bright yellow tie, thick dark brown corduroy trousers with a heavy brown belt as well as braces. He wore heavy boots and had string tied round the knees of his trousers. His top half looked like a seedy clerk whilst the bottom half looked like a navvy. When I asked him his name he answered Fred Clunk; I almost fell to the floor, stifling a laugh. It was a name I'd never heard before but it seemed to suit him perfectly.

I put him with Joe round the public bar. During the evening he seemed okay; no ball of fire but he'd be alright alongside Joe; maybe a little slow but, I thought, he'd do now and again.

At the end of the evening I asked him how he liked it. 'I don't, not reely,' he responded in what I could only assume he considered to be a sophisticated accent. 'Hi'm more of a cocktail barman ackshally. I like a more refined crowd. It doesn't reely suit me, thanks all the same.'

When he'd gone I said to Joe, 'Don't ever recommend anyone to me again, you're no judge at all!'

Joe shook his head and said wistfully, 'But he seemed so different in the Bakers.'

When Joe eventually left to go into a supposed pub partnership with someone, he was treated very badly. His partner was a local ex-boxer, not particularly bright, and made Joe the butt of the pub they ran, bullying him and slapping him about. Joe was too frightened to leave, became ill, and was subsequently diagnosed with cancer. He died in London hospital. He was the youngest of all the Hopson brothers and sisters but the first to die.

THE POT MAN

One of the more important jobs was that of the 'potman'. There don't seem to be too many in modern-day pubs - these days, the bar staff do all those chores as part of their job - but years ago 'potmen' were always an integral part of the fabric of the business; usually a misfit, someone who didn't fit in at a normal job. Nearly all pubs had someone like that.

When a pub is as packed as the Puddings was, glasses soon ran out and we depended on a constant supply, achieved through a quick dip, rinse and drain, at which point they were ready to be filled again.

Old George was inherited. He'd been at the pub for years. A tall, thin, old man with a greasy old flat cap and a worn out pullover, he had a grey, heavily lined face and a drooping white walrus moustache.

No one knew his true age; it was estimated between eighty and ninety. The trouble was his birthday came around every couple of months. He'd go round with his old cap collecting money from customers for his 'birthday'.

He was a crafty, thieving old sod. He'd help himself to crisps and cigarettes when he thought no one was looking, and when I caught him, as I did many times, he would swear it was the first time and that he'd never, ever do it again. But when all was said and done, he'd bring the glasses in, the customers liked him, they'd buy him lots of beer and put plenty of money in his cap, and so I never had the heart to sack him. In fact, he stayed till he died.

I never did find out how old George actually was. No one, not even his family, seemed to know.

Old George was inherited and I never did find out how old he was. Not even his family seemed to know. (photograph by Eddie Johnson)

THE FLYING ANGELS

In the early years at the pub, I employed mainly men behind the bar at night. It was a very rough pub by the standards of the day, and whenever the Puddings name was mentioned anywhere in London, people - mainly those who'd never set foot in the place - would knowingly shake their heads and make some remark like, 'That used to be called "the butcher's shop" because of all the blood,' or 'I'd never let my daughter go there.' Of course, much of it was exaggerated, but even so, sometimes a bad name attracts bad people; young men who fancied themselves as tough guys would often swagger in and look round in a challenging fashion, stare at a few people and, when no one responded and just treated them as everyday blokes and nothing special, they would buy a pint and settle down to enjoy themselves.

These days, there are a lot of girls behind bars; it seems almost mandatory that there has to be pretty girls serving the drinks. But, at the same time, all these trendy places employ crop-haired, thick set, miserable looking bouncers in tight-fitting dinner jackets who stand scowling at the customers and probably cause as much trouble as they're supposedly hired to stop. The trouble is, as I've known lots of them, I can say the majority are weightlifters, which they combine with karate or kick boxing, and lots of them also take steroids which, as well as pumping up their muscles, also pumps up their testosterone levels, making them extremely twitchy and hot tempered.

My barmen and many of the doormen upstairs were ordinary blokes. Some had done a bit of boxing, some were pals from the docks. One, Don Satchell, was an ex-sergeant from the army, and when he first came to work for me and I interviewed him, he stood to attention, rigid as a ramrod. He was a stocky black-haired man with a black, military moustache, and he never lost that respectable manner that old soldiers have for who they perceive as their superiors - not that I regarded myself as superior to him or anyone else; I was an old fashioned socialist, rather uneasy with my role as a publican who, in those days, were regarded as arch conservatives and rabid capitalists.

Most of my barmen were prepared to jump over the bar and help me in times of stress or 'aggro' time as we called it. Jackie Bowers and Norman Baptiste were my two top barmen, the fastest in the East End, they styled themselves. They had the busy till at the top of the pub. Their ambition was to take more on their till than the two Scottish brothers, Bill and Terry Docherty, who were employed upstairs and always took more money because there was only one till upstairs as opposed to four down. The two brothers were also very fast, and it was a moot point as to who was really the quickest. Jackie Bowers, an ex-pro-boxer who had been championship material, was always quickly by my side in times of trouble. He was very good with really nasty customers as he would always manage to pin their arms whilst I would give them a sly dig in the ribs or on the side of the jaw to knock all the 'go' out of them before chucking them out. He boxed as featherweight, but he was at least welterweight when he worked for me. He had a real boxer's nose - flat across his face - but he smiled at customers, had nice blue eyes, and they all seemed to like him, especially the girls.

Norman was in Marine insurance and was a very particular and fastidious person. He only ever bought cashmere when he wanted a sweater, and he bought all his clothes, so he told me,

Don Satchell (foreground) Roger, Pat, Norman and Sid. When trouble started the 'Flying Angels' would leap straight over the bar, white shirts and ties flowing behind them. (photograph by Alf Shead)

in Burlington Arcade in the West End. He said the money he earned at the pub was paying his mortgage. He would never, ever get involved in any fights in the pub; instead, he would call me and would ensure he never got caught up in it. I always knew that, if I was lying on the floor being kicked to death, Norman would just carry on serving. That was fair enough: they were employed to serve beer, not to fight, and if they did help me out I was pleased, but I never expected them to or ever told them it was part of their duties.

Bill and Terry Docherty were two brothers from Paisley, near Glasgow. I had inherited them when I bought the pub, and they were both good boys. They worked very hard and cleared up well. Bill, the eldest, was always quick to stop any trouble he saw brewing, or else call Kenny and the doormen. I paid them a little more than the downstairs staff as they had such a lot to do, putting all the chairs away at the start of each session, as it was a restaurant during the day, and then putting them all out again when we closed. They both had thick Glasgow accents, which sometimes caused a misunderstanding with an order, but all in all they were both popular and were never intimidated by any of the rougher customers that went upstairs.

Don Satchell and another older man I had working for me, Sid, known as 'Slippery' Sid, were known as the 'flying angels' because, if there was any trouble, it seemed they would leap straight over the bar to nip it in the bud, almost in tandem, their white shirts and ties flowing behind them. Sid had been a greengrocer, stall holder, film extra, ex-seaman and had done most things in life, it seemed. He was about five-eleven, slim and rangy with curly blonde hair, and a sly, lop-sided grin that the women seemed to love.

THE AFFAIR

One Friday night, Sid, who was happily married with two children, started to talk to a young girl, attractive, aged about nineteen, who came in with a crowd of people. She seemed to take quite a shine to Sid, who was getting on for forty. I joked with him about it.

'She seems to like me,' he said. 'I'm taking her out next week.'

I looked at him, incredulous. 'What about the missus?'

'It's only a laugh, nothing serious, no one will ever know,' he answered.

A few weeks went by. The girl came in a few times whilst Sid was working. He spoke and laughed with her a bit, and I never thought much more about it until one day, a big, old-fashioned-looking man in his fifties came to see me. He wore a tight-fitting suit with a tie and a cloth cap. He told me his name was Frank Grimstead and he was an ex-speedway driver quite well known in the field. He introduced himself very earnestly and started to ask me about Sid and Sid's background. It turned out he was the girl's - Beryl's - father, and he wanted to know if my barman was a decent bloke and if he'd been 'around' a lot.

'I mean,' he said, 'she's only nineteen and this Sid, he seems alright but he's nearly thirty!'

He seemed a nice man but there was no way I could grass on Sid, and so I prevaricated. 'All I really know about Sid is that he's honest,' I said, 'but about his private life I know hardly anything,' which was a half-truth. Of course, I knew he was married - happily, I had thought - with a family.

Mr Grimstead looked at me intently, trying to judge the truth of my answer, but he walked away with doubt in his eyes.

When Sid came in next I questioned him. Apparently things had drifted on and on. He'd took ten years off his age, hadn't told her or her dad he was married. Beryl was Mr Grimstead's only child, a widower, and wanted a big white wedding for the apple of his eye.

Sid was starting to get really worried.

About a week after the father, I had another visitor, an attractive, brown-haired lady, soft and gentle in demeanour who looked at me with sadness in her eyes. It was Sid's wife. She asked me what was going on with him. 'Why are you working him so hard? All these extra hours... He's hardly ever at home now. Or is he taking someone out and telling me lies?'

I answered her in the best way I could; I couldn't tell her the truth but I hated telling lies to such an obviously nice person so, again, I prevaricated and told her Sid was doing a bit more because I was short staffed. I promised I'd ease some of his sessions off and, whilst I was at it, I added that, no, I didn't know if he was seeing someone else but that I wouldn't have thought so. I don't think she believed me.

From being something mildly amusing, this was shaping up to be tragic.

Some days later, Mr Grimstead marched in again - and this time he was raving. His face was crimson, he had an axe tucked under his raincoat, and he wanted Sid now. He said he wanted to kill him. I managed to calm him down and said I didn't know his whereabouts, which was true: Sid had taken some time off to try and sort things out. He had finally plucked up the courage to tell Beryl that he was married but had promised her he'd seek a divorce. She had told her father and also told him Sid's true age, and so he wanted to kill him or at least give him a good beating.

When I next saw Sid he was contrite and crestfallen. He and Beryl had gone down to Southend for a few days to get away from his wife and Beryl's father. It was winter and had been snowing heavily. They both went to the pier and walked to the end, snowflakes covering them both. They had stood looking out to sea, holding each other close for warmth, and had contemplated jumping into the icy sea and ending it all. They just didn't know what to do.

Sid looked at me as he was telling me all this, and tears started streaming from his eyes. 'I love Beryl,' he said, 'but I really loved my wife too and now she's going to divorce me.'

I consoled him as best I could; it was a situation which, like so much in life, had no answers. But, as things turned out, Sid got his divorce and in time he married Beryl. They had a child and, as far as I know, led fairly normal, happy lives.

Sid, having patched it up with Mr Grimstead, carried on working for me for a while and rented a house locally. He eventually left because he got a full-time job working for a fruit machine company. He'd go round all the pubs and empty their fruit machines. The trouble was, he became sorely tempted. I'd always found him honest, but apparently the sight of all that money eventually became too much for him. He started to keep a third of all the takings and soon got into a position where he daren't take a day off. He couldn't go on holiday, he couldn't be ill. They thought such a lot of him they wanted to promote him to Area Manager, but he didn't dare accept because all his fiddles would come a tumble. He even nicked some old fruit machines, installed them round his house, and invited people round to parties to play them.

One terrible day Sid slipped and broke an ankle. He wasn't

sure it was broke because he never had time to go to the hospital. Beryl only had limited first aid knowledge, but strapped it up as best she could, got him a crutch, and went out on his rounds with him. He staggered, in dire agony, from pub to pub. At the end of the first day, when he finished his round, he knew he needed to go to hospital, where they x-rayed his ankle and confirmed it was broken. He was mortified but, of course, still couldn't take time off. He soldiered on with his crutches.

His governor, Manny, a little ginger-haired Jewish man from Whitechapel, was overcome with emotion: 'Siddy, Siddy, my boy,' he said as he hugged him. 'If all my workers were like you who knows what I would achieve?'

The irony wasn't lost on Sid, who gave Manny a lop-sided sickly grin. 'Don't worry, Manny, I'll just carry on.' Of course he couldn't, and Manny agreed that maybe Sid could do half a round, but Manny wouldn't be so heartless as to let Sid do it all.

Sid knew the game was up, and so he fled with Beryl. Overnight they were gone from their little terrace house in a Stratford side street. They borrowed a lorry from one of Sid's many spivvy acquaintances and blew the coop, taking even the fruit machines with them! They finished up in the outskirts of London in Hertfordshire. He'd kept in touch with Don Satchell, the barman he was friendliest with and who later told me all this. Manny initially wanted to take him to court and get the police involved but in the end decided against it - it might have given his other workers ideas.

Beryl, I was told, was thoroughly relieved it had all finally come a tumble - at last they could now draw a line under this episode and plan a new life together.

THE GAMBLER

Dan was another barman who had a lovely wife but who used to meet, on his day off, a woman who was a lot older than him. She was a heavily made up and quite a plain woman, but they would go off every week to a seedy motel in Romford Road where Dan would rent a room for the two of them which they would use till about 1am, when he'd go home to his wife in Poplar. The woman, I presume, would go home to her husband. Everyone, including me, thought he was mad, and no doubt, like most of my barmen, he actually was.

The man was also a terrible gambler. One day he came into my office and blurted out, 'I've got to leave.' He looked ashen.

'Why?' I asked.

'Bobby Ramsay's been here and said I've got to pay some money to a bookmaker that I owe.'

Dan was visibly shaken. Bobby Ramsay was a well-known tearaway, crook and ex-boxer, who had been one of the self-styled 'King of the Crooks' - Billy Hill's henchmen - and was closely associated with the Kray twins. He was quite feared in East London.

I'd heard he'd been in the Puddings but I hadn't seen him or I would have had a drink with him and he probably would have spoken to me of the problem. I wasn't so concerned about Dan's debt but annoyed that Ramsey had marched into the pub and chased after my barman without consulting me - it wasn't polite or diplomatic.

'Don't worry about Ramsay,' I said. 'You carry on working, I'll make sure he doesn't bother you here again.' I got in touch with my old friend JD, who assured me Bobby Ramsay wouldn't show his face in the Puddings again.

I never found out if Dan paid his bookies' debt, which was of no concern to me, but he was certainly never again harassed for it in the Puddings.

THE FIDDLER

Pat Carmody, who mainly helped Joe Hopson in the public bar, was like a stage Irishman; thin and wiry with sticking up hair like Stan Laurel, his face red and craggy. He sometimes spoke 'cockney' but at other times had an Irish brogue. He was born in the 'Emerald Isle', as he called it, and he liked his drink.

Before he worked behind the bar he'd done some painting and decorating in our flat. He got on well with Shirley and even better with the kids, telling them stories of an Ireland full of Leprechauns, lemonade trees and sherbet hills, and glasses that were forever filling up with your favourite drink. They loved him.

He was a quick barman, which is what I liked in the Puddings - until he had a drink. I eventually sacked him when, as he was putting a fresh vodka up on the optic, he left his finger pushing the dispenser so that the whole bottle emptied whilst he stared at it, pop-eyed, a look of utter bewilderment on his face. When I shouted he dropped the lot on to the floor, sending vodka and glass everywhere. Trying to clear it up, he cut his finger.

Some weeks later I received a letter from a solicitor on behalf of Mr Patrick Carmody. They were claiming £250 on behalf of their client as, owing to injuries received to his finger, i.e. a bad cut whilst clearing up on the pub's behalf, he could no longer play the violin properly. This was, of course, the first any of us had ever heard about Pat playing the instrument, and although I wanted to dispute the case - in court if necessary - my insurance company insisted on settling up. Despite all this, he still walked into the pub when he was paid out and insisted I have a drink. He was a likeable rogue, but he never got near my bar again.

THE LAUGHING BARMAID

Shirley hired a barmaid to help her lunchtimes, as well as Joe Hopson, because, as the pub got quieter during the day, I started to have a bit of time off, at which time I'd maybe play a bit of golf or go and look at property. We had the idea in mind that living in the pub indefinitely was not going to be our end plan and so I would often have a drive to North Essex or Suffolk to look at cottages, etc. Shirley's main help then was a tall, wise-cracking girl called Rosie Doughty, who had a well-known brother Bill, known as 'Brusher'. He was often in the pub, always drinking and doing deals with various burglars, safe breakers, robbers, call them what you will; a mixed bag of acquaintances, anyway. She was so proud of Bill. He was a big, well-built, good looking man aged about 40, who had lots of romantic affairs. She used to tell us all sorts of stories, one in particular of when he was going out with an older, very rich lady who, when he tried to end the relationship, hired two huge bully boys to give him a good beating. They knew 'Brusher' quite well so they told him to get done up in bandages so they could collect the money and they would share it with him. When the rich old lady saw him lying horizontal and motionless on his bed, head and large parts of his body wrapped up in bandages, she was full of regret and rushed to him, sobbing and crying, and swearing her undying and unconditional love. Of course, he was able to spurn her advances with dignity with right on his side and managed, with a little tear in his eye, to tell her he could never ever love her again after the terrible thing she'd done to him.

Rosie, who was attractive and very popular with the customers, was married to a tall ex-guardsman known only as 'Mac', but she was discontented with him. He was a hard-working man, honest and good, but Rosie was attracted to the villains who were the companions of her brother, Bill.

But she loved a good laugh, and when I played practical jokes on people - as I often spent my time doing - she loved it. I once told a gas meter reader that the wooden stairs down to the cellar, where the meter was, were out of order and so he'd have to go down in the lift. Well, the 'lift' was the little beer hoist that only had room for six crates of beer, but the man just about managed to squeeze into it and I closed the shutter on him and then quickly ran down the cellar stairs, I then slowly winched it down by hand, opened the door of the hoist and, with a perfectly straight face, helped him climb out. He gave me such an old fashioned look, probably thought I was completely mad, and I went back up the stairs whilst he got on with reading the meter. Rosie, meanwhile, had fallen onto the floor, helpless with laughter.

She stayed working in the pub for quite a while until she ran off with one of her brother's mates, leaving 'Mac', who shortly after became ill and then died quite suddenly.

It's odd in life because Kit, Maggie, Rosie and many others became close friends and an integral part of our lives whilst they were working for us. We'd talk to them every day, exchange confidences, and generally treat them like family, and yet, when they left and we moved, we exchanged Christmas cards for a while and then never saw any of them again. This has happened

Shirley with the wise-cracking barmaid Rose Doughty (left) who loved joining in the practical jokes I played on tradesmen and customers. (photographer unknown)

to me so many times in different pubs: people become close friends, they weep and swear undying friendship whenever I've left a pub, but very rarely does anyone keep in touch in the long-term.

THE RUEFUL MAN

Midway through the '60s, Alec Rew started to come into the Puddings. He never drunk much alcohol; he'd usually buy a coke or a soft drink. He was a big chap and had a round face with tin spectacles that made him appear owlish and scholarly. I got talking to him because he loved science fiction and which, at the time, I used to read a bit. He lived with his dad, had a part-time job in the laboratory at West Ham College, and said he wouldn't mind doing a bit of 'potting', which was collecting glasses. Apart from a couple of interludes, he stayed at the Puddings for the next thirty odd years. During this time he was chief 'bottler up', babysitter, bouncer, barman, bar manager... He had aspirations to be an artist and was a good sketcher: when babysitting, he would draw cartoon characters and monsters for the kids. They loved it when he was looking after them.

One night when he was 'on the door', there was a fracas between some women. One, a large black girl who acted quite tough, seemed to be the instigator, and she had laid into a couple of smaller girls. Alec was the first on the scene and there was a bit of a melee going on. Michael, my younger brother, and Mel, one of the other 'bouncers', had managed to throw some of the girls out. It was always dimly lit upstairs and the music was quite loud, and the incident seem to pass without too many customers noticing. Michael, who was back at the bar and about to start his drink, heard what seemed to be a distant strangled cry for help.

'Help! Help me! Somebody help me!'

Mel gasped. 'Look! Look over there!' And there, in the far corner on the floor, were two large bodies writhing around, arms and legs entwined, the black girl on top with her teeth sunk deep into Alec's flesh, who had his arms wrapped tightly around her to stop her punching him. My brother and Mel managed to pull the girl off and throw her out and help Alec to his feet. The main thing that was hurting was his pride but Alec also had to visit the hospital to receive attention for the bite wounds.

One of his interludes was after I had a row with him over his lateness. He'd met a girl in the pub and was becoming very unreliable; he'd have lots of late nights and didn't seem able to get up early. I was getting more and more exasperated. We had a row and I sacked him. I didn't see him for a few weeks, and then his father came in and told me he'd robbed a garage at knife point along with two other desperadoes. Soon after, a couple of middle-class type men who'd just passed middle age, both wearing trilby hats and suits under tightly belted raincoats and looking like detectives in an old-fashioned black-and-white British film, waltzed in and introduced themselves as Alec's uncles. They asked me if Alec was a good enough risk for them to stand bail at his forthcoming trial, and also if they should go as character witnesses. 'We hardly know him,' they sniffed. 'He's our sister's child.'

Alec's Mum had died when he was quite young. I said what I could to persuade them to stand bail and to testify in his favour. The two uncles must have thought he was a bad risk because they never showed for his trial and he received eighteen months in prison.

Another interlude Alec had was as a ticket collector on the London underground. He had that job for about three years and seemed to like it but, for some reason or another, he returned to the fold and was back behind the bar at the Puddings. Soon after, he started to take one of the lunchtime girls out. She was a tall, willowy, very attractive blonde. Her name was Viv and she was very popular with the lunchtime customers. For many years she and Alec seemed very happy together until one day she met someone else and left him. Alec was devastated for a long time but he carried on working with her in the pub and they remained friends. Her son, who Alec had adopted, remained living with Alec whilst Viv carried on doing his washing and cleaning and made sure he cooked properly for himself.

As the years went on, Alec got burlier, had his hair cropped short, and grew a beard. He still had a somewhat owlish look but he looked a bit tougher and meaner. He always carried a little cosh in his back pocket, but despite this it didn't stop him getting mugged and robbed when he was doing a stint at Stubbs, a rival club in Romford Road belonging to Jackie Mansworth, an East End bookmaker, where Alec's main duty was putting the takings into a night safe.

THE SPY

During the last stages of our time at the Puddings, Alec left to become a security guard at a factory, mainly working nights. He had become increasingly exasperated by the behaviour of our chief 'potman' and live-in caretaker, Tom Easy, another man who'd helped us for many years. Tom, who ended up living in our old flat above the pub, would spy on Alec and report every move he made to my younger brother Michael who, by that time, was running the pub but not living there. As a result, Alec decided that, after all these years of service and because the writing was on the wall for all of us with the new owners of the building, he'd leave before being shoved out as we eventually were.

Tom Easy, a small, unsmiling man with staring eyes and a beard, was a hard worker who wouldn't talk to anyone but Michael. If Kenny or me asked him anything, he would simply look to Michael before answering. If my younger brother gave a barely perceptible little nod he would then respond to our question. Everyone knew when Tom was coming because, well before he came into view, you could hear the clinking and clanking of the dozens of keys, which opened every single door and lock throughout the entire building and which he kept permanently on his person, dangling from his belt hooks. I suppose this may have handicapped his spying activities somewhat. He regarded himself as my brother's aide-de-camp; Kenny and me, in private, called him the Adjutant.

When I was running the pub I knew him as a customer. He would be in every weekend, listening to the groups, always propped up at the bar, usually alone. As I used to run up and down frantically serving, he always seemed to be staring intently at me, his eyes following my every move, trying to attract my attention for some service, but when I came over and asked him if he wanted a drink he'd say, 'No, I've got one.' He started as a potman but progressed to caretaker and general handyman, being loyal and ever true to Michael, faithfully keeping an eye on everyone else right to the bitter end.

Bob the 'Muppet', another long-serving and loyal staff member, was an eccentric but very fast barman who formed some sort of unholy alliance with Tom against Alec. But, on one occasion, Kenny and one of our customers, Bobby Fourway, rather cruelly arranged a boxing match between Bob and Tom in the pub during closing hours. Encircled by hordes of drunken, cheering customers, the pair were stripped to the waist, wearing baggy shorts and over-sized boxing gloves, and, at the sign for the fight to begin, viciously went for each other. After two violent rounds, Bob the Muppet signalled that he'd had enough. Tom never said much, just had a look of quiet triumph in his eyes as he looked towards Michael for the expected miniscule nod of approval.

When Alec finally left, Tom would clean the pipes and Bob would do his bar sessions, but Alec was missed terribly; he was part of the family.

Our midweek early evening customers were a poor lot, always rooting around for change in their pockets or huddled around the fireplace for warmth. (photographer unknown)

THE COLONEL

He'd come through the door of the public bar wearing an old cap and a shabby double-breasted black overcoat, walking like a slowed-down version of Groucho Marx, with one hand thrust deep into his overcoat pocket.

'Good evenin', Guv'ner,' he'd grunt. 'A lemonade please.'

'No Guinness tonight?' I'd enquire.

'No, me dad's put the block on 'em. Too many late nights,' he'd answer, his face screwing up like a sunny, wrinkled, russet apple, one eye closed in a parody of a wink. The colonel, as he was universally known, was sixty-five years old then, so I was told, but he looked a lot older. Stratford was his universe and his trade, so he'd tell me, was night-watchman, but he hadn't had a job for the past two years.

Nobody knew how he got the name Colonel, but he'd always been called that and always would. Harry Woods was his real name, and he was my most regular customer. When I first took the Puddings over, I was green as the grass of early summer. I was told by the previous tenant and other various well-intentioned people to bar him. I made a half-hearted attempt to do so but, in the ensuing argument, during which he informed me that all the resident layabouts of Stratford who were found daily in the snooker hall on the corner of Chant Street had signed a petition to get him reinstated last time he was barred, I came to rather like the old chap. I suspected, however, that they had all signed the petition to keep him out of the snooker hall rather than to convey their admiration of the old rogue.

In all honesty, I'm glad I didn't bar him: there were many lonely mid-week nights when he was my only customer, and he would regale me with tales of old-time fighters and of the times he himself had fought men who were later in the championship class.

He suffered with a bad foot, and it was evident that he was often in extreme pain. 'What caused it?' I asked.

'Done it during the war, in the army.'

'What war was that then, Colonel?'

'The last war!' he said, as if it was obvious.

'How old are you then, Colonel?'

'Sixty-five,' he answered and went on to explain, 'I was in both wars, the first World War I was a Stoker, first class, in the Royal Navy. The last war I was in the army.'

'What regiment?' I asked.

'Pioneer Corps,' he answered with a touch of pride and near reverence.

'So, your bad foot… Were you wounded in action?'

'Nah, I got it playing football. I get a little pension, though.'

He'd tell me of all the villains he knew and sometimes, after first checking over his shoulder and then looking all around the otherwise empty pub, he would whisper close to my ear of the 'Guv'nor' who, according to him, controlled the underworld.

When I'd ask the 'Guv'nor's' name he'd wag his finger, screw his eyes up and give a knowing leer. 'Aah, you don't talk about things like that!'

When he was on the 'borrow' he'd show me papers and official looking documents referring to an impending claim for some accident or other. Apparently he had these accidents quite regularly and achieved some notoriety over them. Soon after I had taken over the pub, one of his claims paid up. For the next fortnight he was at the pictures every afternoon. He liked Pat

Boone best, followed by Cliff Richard. He drank rum and black every night, treating everyone in the public bar, including the taxi driver who came at 10.00 p.m. every night to take him to Rowton House, a charity hostel in Whitechapel, where he'd managed to book a room; apparently it was quite hard to get in there, and the way the colonel spoke it was as good as the Savoy Hotel.

'Ooh, it's smashing up there,' he'd say. 'They don't disturb you in the morning, you know. They let you lay in till ten o'clock.'

But, alas, his money never lasted long. The first signs were when the taxi stopped, then he'd go back to Guinness, and finally he'd shuffle in, his face all glum, and he'd call for half a bitter so we all knew he was skint or, as he would say, 'boracic lint'.

He had a large family of ten daughters, two sons, and innumerable grandchildren whose photos he'd carry about. Even the little ones called him Colonel. His wife, whom he often mentioned - always prefixed by, 'God rest her dear soul' - had died a few years before, yet none of his children seemed to love him enough to give him a permanent shelter, and he had no fixed home.

He'd drift, when the pubs closed in the afternoon, to the snooker hall. He'd go to Lyons Corner House tea shop for a cup of tea and a bun and then, on half-past five on the dot he'd be at the pub doors for opening time. There he'd sit, huddled, if it was winter, in his overcoat, round the fire. He had no regular job but sometimes sold flowers for one of the stallholders. At Christmas, all of the stallholders at Stratford Market would club together and pay him to stay up all night watching their stalls which, at that time of the year, they'd leave out along the main road.

Sometimes I used to look at this poor old man who had nothing to live for except what is past, and think that, although he'd served in two world wars, he was nothing but debris, had nowhere to lay his head, couldn't afford a drink, had no regular food, and yet was surrounded by wealth. It seemed as if no one cared. The colonel disappeared from my life sometime in the '70s - he probably died around that time - but, despite my enquiries, no one knew what had happened to him.

THE PIMP

In these early days, a shabby looking couple were always at the door at opening time during the week, along with my other early evening regulars, the colonel, 'Dodger' Mullins, an ex-crook, well-respected in his time but now an elderly little man with white hair, and Johnny Gibbons, a builder, who was often called Johnny Lee as he was married to a lady from the Lee family, who were flower-sellers in the market. Johnny was born in Ireland, and though he'd lived in England for many years, he still had an Irish accent. He was a builder, and my only weekday evening regular with money.

In the winter, when the evenings were dark and cold and the fire was glowing in the public bar, this couple would sit huddled around it with the colonel whilst Johnny Gibbons and 'Dodger' would stand at the bar. 'Dodger' would always insist on pouring his own drink; a Mann's brown ale, shaking the bottle first so that it had a nice foaming head on it.

The shabby couple were the youngest of my five regulars; I would guess they were in their mid-thirties but, to my eyes, because they were so poor-looking, they looked older - at least in their forties. He was slim with dark, greased hair and a pale face.

His movements were always quick and a bit jerky, almost as if he had lots of nervous energy. He was known as Benny. She was also quite slim with fair, wispy, mousy hair, her complexion red and rather blotchy. She wore very little make up, just a smidgen of lipstick. They were collectively known as Benny & Esta and were rarely seen apart. Outside of pub hours they could be found in the snooker hall or Lyons Corner House tea shop, where most of my regulars seemed to go, along with Joe Hopson, my bar manager. They were both extremely friendly and polite, almost humble, when they ordered drinks. A few pleasantries would be exchanged with Joe whilst he was serving them, or the colonel would declaim the latest gossip or tell them about a film he'd seen in the afternoon at the Rex. But mostly they would sit very quiet, not saying much to anyone or each other.

After an hour or so sitting, making their halves of bitter last as long as possible and only exchanging an anxious word or two now and again, a tall grey-haired man would come in, looking quite confident. He would wish everyone a good evening, buy himself a drink, and then ask Benny and Esta what they wanted. Benny's demeanour when he saw the man would lighten up considerably; Esta would still sit quietly, but Benny would go to the man and say hello, then order a pint with a whisky chaser for himself and a half-pint of bitter and a whisky mac' for Esta.

It was normally the same man, quite a bit older than them - probably in his sixties. Now and again a different man would come in, but it was always the same routine: they'd say hello, buy the couple a drink, and go and sit with them. Benny would be getting merrier and merrier, laughing, coming to the bar with the other man's money to order more drinks, whilst the man - whoever it happened to be - would edge closer and closer to Esta, whose attitude, apart from a very slight smile now and again, wouldn't change. The man and Esta would then disappear, leave the pub, and be gone for half hour or so.

I must have been so naïve because it was some weeks before I realised that Benny, who was married to Esta and had children with her, was selling his wife for sex. He was her pimp. Looking back, it was no wonder they were so polite and rather nervous. I was quite shocked, as was Shirley; they were quiet, and though they were poor, they were so ordinary looking that it was hard to fathom. What they were doing was not strictly lawful as it was a form of prostitution and women of the night were not allowed to ply their trade in pubs. I suppose I was guilty in as much as I didn't discourage them, but they were never any trouble and I quite liked them; besides, I would have felt very embarrassed at having to tell them they were not allowed in anymore.

After a while, I noticed they had become very friendly with another lunchtime customer. He was called Dave and was a dustman from Stepney. He'd finish work quite early and started to meet them every afternoon. As he had a regular job he always seemed to have plenty of money for drink. At first he was just a drinking friend, but then he started to join them early evening and he became a customer of theirs - he would disappear with Esta now and again, and so I assumed that's what he was - but the relationship seemed to alter in a strange way, and they became a sort of ménage a trois, although I couldn't quite work out what their relationship was. Undoubtedly, he was Esta's lover, but he also became a fellow pimp with Benny because other men would still come in but they would now have to buy all three of them drinks before they disappeared into the dark with Esta, leaving Benny and Dave sitting together.

I can't remember the last I saw of them; I believe they stopped coming in the pub soon after it had its first major refurbishment. I abolished the public bar, making it all one big bar, bought a lot of highly coloured plastic furniture, bright red, blue and yellow banquettes, and put up coloured lights everywhere. I bought pine furniture and a new highly polished wooden bar top. I lowered the ceiling with enormous plastic mock wooden beams and I installed new red lino tiles that had to be polished. I really thought it looked wonderful. Most of the customers loved it. The previous owner, Patsy Quill, remarked to me on the opening lunchtime that it was the best looking pub in London.

Customers flocked to the pub like seagulls - we were packed every night and taking a fortune - but Benny and Esta seemed very quiet; they said it looked very nice but their congratulations were muted. Instinctively, they felt alien to the place, knew they wouldn't fit in with this brash reflection of what was to be known as the swinging '60s, and along with most of the other regulars of the early years, they drifted away. I was too young to realise what I was destroying. These people were the true fabric of the place, just like the huge, magnificently ornate gold-leafed and carved mirror, the wonderful high ceilings, the fireplaces, lovely Victorian tiles and fretwork - all relics of a bygone age that could never be recaptured.

THE CHRISTMAS PARTY

Compared to most pubs of the era, we didn't have many public bar regulars. We had a dart board of sorts but it was rarely used, and we had what they called Russian billiards, a long narrow table that used small cues and billiard balls and 'mushrooms' in front of holes, and that was only played occasionally. Our lunchtime regulars were mainly saloon bar types that worked in offices and came in for a bit of lunch, the journalists from the *Stratford Express* were a lovely crowd who provided lots of steady custom, but they would look at the menu, choose the cheapest item - shepherd's pie, for instance, which was about eight pennies - and wouldn't spend a huge amount on drink either.

In the evening we were a 'music' pub, and everyone came from far and wide for the entertainment. These were the main source of our revenue. A young and vibrant crowd didn't seem to mind the prices or how much they spent, and so we always put the prices up a bit on music nights to help pay for the band. With that in mind, we essentially had hundreds, maybe thousands, of regulars in one way. However, the usual pub regular that pops in every evening for one or two pints we were sadly lacking in - it was just the nature of the pub.

The ones we did have - those that were in, unfailingly, every day - were a poor lot, rather seedy, always rooting about for change in their pockets or bags. In winter they would gather round the fireplace, huddled for warmth. Most of the pubs in the area wouldn't serve them or made them feel so unwelcome that they stayed away. Shirley, my wife, was such a friendly type who enjoyed talking to most people and she made them all feel a little bit special by greeting them with a smile and asking how they were and taking an interest in their daily lives. She always said to me that if you take the trouble to chat with them they're a lot more interesting, in most cases, than all our 'office' type regulars who came in for the cheap lunches. Perhaps because we'd been so poor ourselves recently we sympathised more with them.

For the first time in our lives, we were both earning what we considered to be plenty of money, and when people from our background had money, they were inclined to want to share it. So, in the lead up to our first Christmas in the pub, we decided to have an afternoon party for our public bar regulars.

We asked the colonel, Benny and Esta, 'Dodger' Mullins, another two couples whose names escape me but who were notable by always having a little 'whip round' between them before they came to the bar, and finally Johnny Gibbons who, although he had money, was such a nice man and quite generous to the others that we couldn't leave him out just because he was better off than the rest.

I put champagne on ice, whisky, gin, rum and plenty of beer out on a long table. Shirley laid out a magnificent buffet: cold-poached salmon, a big cooked turkey with lots of stuffing and cranberry sauce, some of our home-cooked ham, pickled herring, gala pie, potato salad… it looked a treat. They came in wearing clean shirts and ties; the ladies had on their best frocks. They were all on their best behaviour and seemed quite shy - unlike how I'd ever seen them before.

Joe Hopson was in charge of serving, and I had a talk with him beforehand telling him not to be his overweening conceited self which, although it impressed Benny and Esta who always flattered Joe in the hope of getting a free drink, irritated 'Dodger' and enraged the colonel, who once tried to whack him with the cue from the Russian billiards, narrowly missing him but instead smashing a brand new Red Barrel cowl. When he saw me he shamefacedly denied it after Joe's accusation, yet at the same time was telling me how sorry he was.

I put on some old records of Bing Crosby, George Formby,

Gracie Fields plus some Cliff Richard, as I knew he was the colonel's favourite. They were all drinking and eating and being very nice to each other and to Joe. They were full of gratitude to me and Shirley.

Johnny Gibbons, who was the only one who had money, insisted on buying a couple of bottles of champagne - not only for the party but one for us. In his slight Irish accent he thanked us. 'All these years I've lived in Stratford, no one has done this sort of thing for these,' he said, nodding towards the others who were busy drinking and eating and taking turns to dance with Esta. 'In fact, most pubs do their best to get rid of them.'

As they got drunker, the colonel started snarling at Joe and Joe sneered back. Benny and Esta argued for the first time I'd ever seen. 'Dodger' told Colonel to behave himself, and then started to confess to some of the villainous things he'd got up to, including robbing a greengrocers at Upton Park, who'd kept lots of money hidden under his mattress. He and his co-robber had gotten away with thousands in pound notes and ten bob notes. The trouble was, they were all old-fashioned notes, long out of date, recalled by the Bank of England twenty years before the crime. The greengrocer had been too nervous to take it the bank because it was all untaxed and, of course, 'Dodger' and his partner were stuck with them. He did sell me a few of the notes at cost price; I bought them out of curiosity.

As things were heating up, it was opening time. I told the customers that drifted in to help themselves as there was plenty of food left. Eventually, the party guests all staggered out about eight o'clock, well drunk, arm in arm, singing old songs, and having a knees-up along the street. The exception was Johnny Gibbons, who never seemed to get drunk no matter how much he drank, and who stayed till closing time, staunch, lifting one glass after another to his lips, never moving from the same position at the bar he always occupied.

Shirley and I enjoyed the afternoon as much as anyone, and I don't think it did our image any harm. In fact, it was the talk of Stratford, and lots of people came in and thanked us, including the colonel's daughters.

We held the party for a couple of years afterwards, hoping to make it an annual event, but after the renovation we carried out on the pub the early evening atmosphere subtly changed, it was never quite the same again and our regulars gradually drifted off. Johnny Gibbons still came in but the others never felt as comfortable.

Apart from Johnny, they were all pretty sad cases, all with a hidden history that might have been pretty dramatic or maybe mundane, who knows, but it was a nice feeling to be in a position to bring some pleasure into their quietly desperate lives.

THE SNAPPER

Quite a few of the photographs in this book were taken by Alf Shead. Alf was a lovely man and the main photographer at Trafalger Square who, as a sideline, took photos of the customers in various clubs and pubs he visited and would charge them for prints. He became a regular at the Puddings every Friday and Saturday, and so he must have earned a reasonable living from it. We had a little arrangement: I'd commission him to take photos of my family and friends in the pub and in exchange I'd pay him a modest fee, allow him to ply his trade in the pub plus buy him a couple of brown ales when he arrived and before doing his rounds.

I'd take Andrew and Matthew to see him sometimes in Trafalgar Square and, through the judicious sprinkling of bird seed, Alf mastered the knack of getting the pigeons to land wherever he wanted them to - on heads, arms, hands, shoulders - and would then snap away with his Leica. He'd often take me to a little café in nearby Villiers Street, and we'd have a cup of tea or coffee. One day he showed me a lovely picture he'd taken of the Queen Mother. He said he'd tried to get her to sign it through one of her aides, and she did, but on the very strict understanding that it was his personal property and would not be re-sold. He said he wanted to give me a copy, too, unsigned of course. I'm far from being a royalist, but I agreed just to please him. He turned up at the pub with the photograph the following week, all framed and nicely wrapped up, but then demanded fourteen quid! I later gave it to David Edwards, the ex-manager of our neighbouring pub, the Swan, and a very keen monarchist, for his birthday, and as far as I know the Queen Mum still has pride of place above the grand fireplace in his living room. Incidentally this image is now in the collection of the National Portrait Gallery.

ALF SHEAD PHOTOGRAPHER. VAL 1298

TAKEN AT 'BIG BEAT' CLUB

OVER 'TWO PUDDINGS' PUB. E.15

ON...

Alf Shead and I had a little arrangement; I'd allow him to ply his trade in the Puddings in exchange for photos of my family and friends in the pub.

THE BOUNCERS

The boys looking after 'upstairs' for Kenny and me in the '60s included Peter Ferdinando, JD, Johnny Bruce, Billy Mynor, Georgie Turner, Johnny Jags, Tony Mead, Tommy Kemp, Georgie Mills, Davie Storie and many others in later years. They were a great bunch. Unlike many of the aggressive, steroid-enhanced bodybuilding thugs you find on the door of many nightclubs these days, this lot were very tough but very fair. Johnny Jaggs was 5'10" tall but built like a bull. He was a docker and was very strong. He took pride in his ability to fight anyone without ever using a tool, although he did brandish a bayonet once when completely outnumbered and confronted with a hostile crowd at the Stratford Snooker Hall.

Tony Mead came from across the river in South London to work for us. He eventually emigrated to the States, and owned several properties and a yacht at San Francisco harbour. He unluckily got involved with the 'mob' and lost his fortune. He was found dead in a remote hotel room in his early forties. His wife Patricia remains a good friend of Kenny.

THE PATROLMEN

Johnny Bruce was an old school friend of Peter Ferdinando. He worked on the door upstairs for us for many years. He was loyal, always around, and always willing to help us out. Johnny wasn't very big, but he was strong, brave, and never ran from a fight. He was pretty quiet, until he'd had a few drinks, that is, at which point he'd start arguing with Rocky Bob and invariably end the evening by punching him.

As a pastime, he and Peter would often don peaked caps and uniforms and patrol the night-time streets of East London

The boys 'upstairs', Johnny Williams, Tony Mead, Peter Ferdinando, Johnny Bruce, Tommy Kemp, Kenny, Billy Myner (kneeling) and friends. (photograph by Alf Shead)

The long arm of the law. Johnny & Peter often prowled the streets of sixties East London dressed up as policemen. (photograph by Alf Shead)

in the black Wolseley 6/110 owned by Peter, which was identical to those used by the Metropolitan Police. To complete their new identities, they even managed to obtain a flashing blue police light, which they would temporarily rig to the roof of the vehicle before setting off for their evening's entertainment. They would regularly follow cars, pull them over and give the occupants a thorough dressing down about this or that before sending them on their way. They carried out this caper for many months and thought it was absolutely hilarious. I'm not certain if they ever made any arrests though!

THE DOPPELGANGER

One of our best customers 'upstairs' was Johnny Williams. Johnny had arranged to take a short break in Jersey with Peter and Johnny Bruce. He'd actually told his wife he was going on a business trip whereas, in reality, he just fancied a few days away from London for a boozy weekend with his mates. Johnny was traveling ahead of Peter and Johnny and, on the flight over, had got talking to a very attractive young lady seated next to him. They got along so well, in fact, that upon arrival he immediately cancelled his room in the hotel he was staying at with Peter and Johnny and booked himself and his new-found friend into the most sumptuous five-star hotel on the island.

As they were excitedly carrying their bags into the elevator, the over-zealous hotel porter noticed that Johnny bore more than a passing resemblance to Roy the 'Weasel' James of the very recent Great Train Robbery. Before he'd even had time to undress, Johnny was arrested and thrown into a cell for seven hours whilst a policeman who knew the 'Weasel' was flown over from London to identify him.

Meanwhile, the press received a tip-off that one of the Great Train Robbers had been arrested in Jersey, yet upon discovering the mistake led the next morning with the front page headline - and with accompanying photographs of the two love birds - OOPS! IT WASN'T THE WEASEL BUT JOHNNY WILLIAMS AND HIS GIRLFRIEND ON HOLIDAY!

The hotel, as an apology for the distress their jobsworth had caused, treated Johnny and his new lady friend to endless bottles of free champagne - not that this would have been much consolation to Johnny's wife!

THE CHIN

One of our more eccentric customers was a failed music hall comedian, whose name was Johnny Ross, better known as 'Chinny' or Johnny the 'Chin'. He used to wander around the East End cleaning cars, a bucket in one hand, pork pie hat tilted forward over his eyes, his big chin jutting forward. He was a familiar sight to everyone: stall holders, publicans, park keepers, dustmen, street cleaners, char ladies - they all knew Johnny. He was also referred to as 'Trinder' due to his likeness to Tommy Trinder. I personally used to think he looked more like Fernandel, a famous French comedian and actor.

He was always bemoaning his lot, he'd once appeared on the radio in a show called *Discoveries* run by a famous Canadian called Carroll Levis. It was very popular, a precursor to the Hughie Green show *Opportunity Knocks* and the present-day *X-Factor* format, and he'd done quite well.

I'd seen him on stage when I was young at the Granada cinema in Barking Road when a friend of mine, Peter Aldridge, who first christened him Johnny the 'Chin', got a party of us together to go and cheer him on. He was the variety act they sometimes used to put on between the 'B' picture and the main attraction. He got lots of applause and was, I thought, very good. His main platform comprised the East End pubs that always had a bit of music plus a comedian. His most memorable joke was when he announced that he was going to sing a well-known song backwards, whereupon he'd turn his back to the microphone and sing. It seems a bit weak now but, at the time, watching him was hilarious. Another of his routines was to ask some heckler in the crowd to come and stand next to him 'to make me look healthy'.

Johnny 'the Chin', a failed music hall comedian who wandered the East End streets with his trusty bucket and sponge.
(photograph by Eddie Johnson)

His career - what there was of it - took a sharp downward curve when he got involved with some 'wronguns', as he put it, and finished up doing three months in jail. He blamed that and his short marriage for his lack of success in 'show business'. He was married for just two weeks before his wife walked out on him, and he used to mention her quite frequently over the years. He hated her with a venom that I'm sure she didn't deserve.

Early on in his career he knew Max Bygraves quite well, and following his short spell in prison, he went to see Max to ask if the more famous man could give him a leg-up to boost his faltering career. He said that Bygraves' attitude changed completely when he knew Johnny had been 'inside', and made it quite clear that they could no longer be friends as any association with an ex-con would harm his, Max's, career.

He had a spell working as a docker, a much-prized job in those days and one that was not easy to get. To obtain your 'ticket' or 'dockies brief' it had to be handed down. I'm not entirely sure, but I think his father may have been a dockworker or maybe it was an uncle, as in all the years I knew him he never mentioned a father. He spoke of his mother a lot, though; in his eyes she was saintly, the dearest and closest thing to his heart, and when she died it affected him deeply.

He seemed to have found his level wandering the streets cleaning cars. He was quite proficient - he'd clean a car satisfactorily and never charged too much - but he would moan prodigiously if his customers never added a pound or two to his price. The trouble was, as soon as he acquired a few pounds, he'd be in a pub. He was a heavy drinker and he wouldn't stop until he was penniless. He'd show remorse and sometimes a black eye after these drinking sessions, and he would swear on his life, the bible, or anything else to hand, that it was his last drink. 'Never again, I just can't handle it anymore.'

It was during one of these remorseful periods that I offered him a job as a 'potman'. After a lot of 'humming and hawing' and laying down various conditions, he accepted. He was a tremendous talker and knew a lot about the music hall and various artists for whom who he had great respect. He could be interesting and quite fascinating, talking about some of the great names, some of whom he'd met. One of his proudest moments was when he met Stephane Grappelli, the great French violinist, co-founder with Django Reinhardt of the Hot Club de Paris. He was also a tremendous patriot and would go every year to the Cenotaph on Remembrance Sunday. He would tell me of the elderly men with their bowler hats and rolled umbrellas who would march with straight backs and stern expressions. 'True Englishman. White, every last one of them,' he would say with pride. He was a very racist man.

For a long time he seemed okay and was enjoying himself. He seemed to be able to have a few drinks without getting greedy for more, and my dad and Uncle John used to have a drink with him when they came in every Friday night. They were both very kind to him. My dad was always slipping him a pound or two, and my uncle gave him a couple of nice suits and a Crombie overcoat.

I was short of bar staff, as always, and so I asked if he'd be interested in doing the odd session on quiet nights behind the ramp. He told me that he'd always been interested in that side of the bar, and so I put him with 'Slippery Sid' as his mentor. The night he started was very quiet, so I told Sid to let him do all the serving if possible.

About 9 o'clock that evening, who should walk in but Reggie Kray with a blonde girl and another chap. I bought them all a drink, which Sid served us after a frantic look from me conveyed the message, 'Don't let Johnny serve us.' Reggie asked if we served cigarettes - we did but only out of the machines - and so I asked the new barman to get them for him, thinking no one could mess up a simple job like that. When Reggie walked in I could tell Johnny Ross was nervous, but I didn't expect him to get into such a state putting money in the cigarette machine but, somehow or other, the packet came back all mangled with the cigarettes bent and twisted up, which he sheepishly passed to Reggie, who looked incredulous at the squashed up packet of fags. I grabbed them and quickly went to get another packet.

Unfortunately, whilst I was getting them, the Kray twin asked for another drink but, by the time I got back to the bar, I could only watch in horror as my new barman was, prior to serving, furiously shaking a Snowball - a popular mixture of lemonade and advocaat, as though it was a bottle of cough medicine that had to be shaken vigorously before being taken. I couldn't stop him in time and, as he opened the bottle, the entire contents shot up like a fountain and all over us - but most of it seemed to land on Reggie, who was soaked. There we all stood, smothered in the sickly yellow liquid, and there was Johnny Ross, his face a mixture of fear, apprehension and dumb stupidity, staring at me with his mouth open as though gasping for air, frightened to look to the left or to the right.

I asked Sid to get some clean tea towels and apologised profusely, but Reggie seemed to see the funny side of it and we all stood laughing. It was to his immense credit that, considering the reputation of the Kray twins, Reggie was just the same as everyone else in an embarrassing situation: he was man enough to take it and shook off my protestations about dry cleaning any of the clothes.

I decided that night - after telling Sid off for not watching him more closely - that Johnny Ross would never make a barman, and so he went back to his 'potting' job. He was alright at that until he started to drink heavily again, at which point we persevered for a while until one night in the dance hall upstairs, when he punched a customer for no apparent reason other than the fact that he was black. This was the final straw and we chucked Johnny out and told him never to come in the pub again - either as a customer or an employee.

After that I would hear stories that he spent a lot of time 'slagging' me and Kenny off, and I would see him now and again in some pub or another, but tried to ignore him.

He was an unfortunate East End character really, of which there seemed so many, who, because of drink, upbringing and no father, blame the world on their circumstances. He became very bitter because of his lack of success, but he could also be so nice. He had once spent Christmas Day with me and my family, and he was so appreciative and grateful and drank only a moderate amount that he was a pleasure to be with. He was colourful and made people laugh with this stories and jokes.

I like to think that he's still alive, wandering the East End from Mile End to Stratford, moaning about the Labour Party and the state of Britain, pork pie hat tilted forward, bucket and wash leather swinging from his hand.

THE SLICE

Another of our customers, who was a mate of Johnny Ross, was 'Hoppy Chasser' Chapman, real name Ronnie Chapman. He was a small-time crook, ships painter, ex-sailor and, at the time, matchmaker and secretary of West Ham Boxing Club. He was a shortish man with a pronounced limp, the result of being run over by a bus when he was young, cutting short, so he said, a promising boxing career. He had a bad scar down one side of his face, the result of a knife fight, and he spoke out of the side of his mouth. He always wore a trilby hat and most people seemed a bit nervous of him, although I thought he was a lovely bloke. He used to drink Red Barrel.

He limped in one day, hat on the side of his head. 'A pint of Red please Eddie'.

'Would you like a slice of lemon in it, Ron?' I said. Apart from his two brothers, Bill and Curly, I was the only one that called him Ron. I expected him to laugh but he took me seriously. 'Slice of lemon? Nah, leave off,' he answered.

'It's all the trend now, Ron. Everyone's drinking Red Barrel with a slice of lemon in it.'

I fully expected him to laugh and dismiss the suggestion with a friendly 'Fuck off!' but instead he said, 'Alright then.'

After a couple of pints, just as he was going, I asked him how he liked the slice in his drink. ''ansome,' he said, 'I'll always 'ave that.'

About two months later I was having a drink with Alan Wheeler, a local publican mate, when he said, 'You know that Chasser Chapman, 'e only asks for a slice of lemon in 'is beer every time 'e orders, and a lot of other customers are 'aving it an all. 'ave you tried it?'

'No,' I said. 'I don't drink much beer.'

'Well, I 'ave,' he said, 'in me light ale. It's quite nice.'

Briefly around the East End and down the docks you could see big tough dockers and road workers ordering pints of beer with a slice of lemon floating in it. The trend didn't last long.

THE STREET FIGHTER

Another regular was 'Sprat' Hardy, a friend of 'Chasser', and far from the sprat of his nickname. He was a powerfully built man with a pencil moustache. He always wore a broad-brimmed 'Stetson' and drape suits with wide padded shoulders. He was known as a fearsome street fighter. In the mid-1950s, some years before I took the Puddings, me and a pal, Peter Aldridge, rented the dance hall above the pub and styled the night, 'Tramps Ball at Cell Block Eleven'. We hired a four-piece band, and both sold as many tickets as we could and kept the proceeds.

Everyone turned up in old ragged clothes. There were very few women in attendance and, after lots of drinking, the affair degenerated into a fairly good-natured melee. Clothes were ripped from people's backs, suits were shredded, even shoes were hurled out of the windows. The band, manfully playing a mixture of Jazz and palm court orchestra, was pelted with muddy turfs from the nearby churchyard and the landlord was forced to call the police. Peter Aldridge, his brother Alan and me, decided at this point to depart rapidly.

Arrests were made, Freddy and Ginger Hammond were stuck in the police wagon, Georgie Hatton was also arrested but gave the coppers twenty quid and they let him walk, but 'Sprat' Hardy put up a struggle of such Herculean strength that it took all of ten policemen to eventually cart him away.

The next day we all met in a café not daring to go near the Puddings as the governor, Harold Starke, as well as the band, had not been paid, nor would they ever be. Everyone was laughing, all relaying their particular experience and commenting on what a great night it had been - all except for 'Sprat', who was utterly glum and had a dazed look in his eyes. Not only had his clothes been ruined and his Stetson hat lost, but he'd also received a heavy fine and, back at the station, the police had chucked him into a cell, unleashed two vicious Alsatian police dogs to follow him into it, and bolted the door. Freddie and Georgie Hammond said the screams were bloodcurdling. He went before the magistrates covered in blood and bite marks, hatless for once, and wearing clothes hanging from his body like strips of rag. The magistrates looked at him and decided he must be a very bad man indeed and fined him accordingly.

THE CONTORTIONIST

Bobby Goss was a small, prematurely balding man. He had a dark visage with a fierce unsmiling face that needed shaving twice a day, and his drink - consistent over the years - was gin and bitter lemon. He worked 'in the print' in Fleet Street, and so earned plenty of money and had lots of time off. Somebody once called him 'Rocky Bob' and the name stuck, which is how he was known throughout East London. He had a tendency to argue and to speak his mind, regardless of people's feelings. Normally, at the end of the night, his mate Johnny Bruce would threaten to bash him up and did actually punch him from time to time out of sheer exasperation at the constant arguing.

He was one of our best customers. He was also a contortionist. Rocky's party trick, that caused amazement whenever and

The contortionist Rocky Bob (foreground) Joey Toye (centre) and me. (photograph by Alf Shead)

wherever it was done, which was most Sunday mornings, was his ability to touch his right shoulder with his left shoulder. It defied all the rules of human anatomy. He would stretch his arms straight in front, bring them together so that they crossed, and his shoulders either side would somehow curl over his chest until they touched. It was as if he was boneless.

Rocky was such a regular, like many of them, that if he never turned up over the weekend I'd phone him up and ask what was wrong. He offered to let me have a doctor's note if he ever had time off.

THE MYSTERY MAN

Sunday morning there was usually a crowd of regulars, as many as twenty, all drinking together. Always on the fringe of this company was George, a stout, red-faced, smiling fellow, he'd be talking to Rocky or Lennie Clark or Bobby Fourway. I noticed after about six weeks that he never bought a drink. Everyone, maybe not in every session, bought a drink, always when it was their turn. Not so with George: he never, ever put his hand in his pocket. Never bought a drink once. I pulled Rocky up one time.

'Here,' I said, 'your mate, George, he's so tight he can peel an orange in his pocket one handed. Tell him, will you, that he's got to buy a drink at some point?'

'He's not my mate,' said Rocky, a little indignant. 'I don't know the man. I think he's Lennie Clark's pal or maybe Billy Newell's.'

I proceeded to ask all the group, one by one, and no one knew where he'd come from. No one had ever seen him until six weeks prior when he'd first come into the pub. The following Sunday I 'ready-eyed' everyone, told them whatever happened not to buy George a drink.

He came in as usual, stood on the edge of the crowd, smiling, laughing at the jokes, waiting for someone to get him his usual light ale. Everyone was affable to him, but no one made a move to the bar. His face grew even redder than usual until eventually he asked if any of us wanted a refill. Twenty empty glasses shot forward and he paid up.

He still carried on drinking with us Sundays, but in future he got his round in like everyone else.

The man no one knew turned out to really be called Frank.

The famous Soho 'face', Daniel Farson with Shirley's mum on our opening night. (photograph by Alf Shead)

THE MAGIC DOOR

Daniel Farson was a hugely famous Soho face in the '60s, and I was surprised when he showed up on our opening night. He was a television personality famous for his interviews, and a journalist and author who claimed to know the true identity of Jack the Ripper. He'd written a play about the famous music hall star Marie Lloyd and presented a programme on television that showcased pub acts and was one of the most popular shows of its day. His father, Negley, had been equally famous in an earlier age as an author, traveller and adventurer, and so I was very pleased to see him. He seemed a very friendly man; affable and approachable. My mother-in-law was thrilled to meet him, too, and delighted when she had a photo taken with him. He told me that he was also opening a pub the following week - a big old pub called the Newcastle at Millwall, but he'd changed the name to the Watermans Arms, which he thought was more appropriate. He said he'd made a lot of alterations and planned to put on variety acts featuring many of those he'd made famous on his television show.

We hadn't left the pub for a week since we'd arrived, and the place was beginning to feel like a prison. As a new publican, I thought it was my duty to never leave the premises. Shirley, after the lunch session, would go upstairs and see to the kids - she hadn't even had time to go out shopping, but as all our food was delivered, we lived off the pub stock: the meat courtesy of Eddie Downes, the fruit and veg through Harry Hopson, fish from Mitchell's, and groceries and household stuff from a little man called Arthur who owned a little shop in a Stratford side street that had very little passing trade, and so he was happy to deliver. This all seemed lovely - at first - but we were now starting to feel a little stir-crazy, and so when we received a hand-delivered invitation to attend Farson's opening, we were quite excited.

Kenny was arriving early to mind the pub. Shirley had contacted an employment agency run by a lady called Millie, who'd promised us a trustworthy babysitter who was highly recommended. In the event, Millie herself turned up after the highly recommended babysitter let her down. She did, however, find us someone to look after the kids during the day, Pat Doodens, who proved to be a good childminder, even though Andrew had confessed many years later that he and Matthew had tormented her unmercifully and led her a merry dance, but she had never complained to us.

After saying goodbye to the kids and arranging the time of our return with Kenny and Milly, we went with friends Johnny and Barbara Smith and Mary and Johnny Pearson. When we arrived it was packed to the doors with a mixture of well-known characters from the show biz and art worlds; Americans including Billy Daniels, Jan Sterling and the Clarke Brothers, and Shelley Winters, who was accompanied by film icon John Derek. There was the famous painter Francis Bacon who was with his Soho friends Alan Hall, David Edwards and Jeffrey Barnard, and then Arthur Mullard, Queenie Watts and her husband Slim, as well as Lionel Bart and a host of actors from TV. There were plenty of East End faces as well, including Patsy Quill and Tommy Hoadley and their wives, Ronnie and Maureen Gilbert, Roger Lovatt, the Careys, Curly King, the Murphys, the Aldridges and the Pooles from Canning Town… I seemed to know all of them! It was a great night and the entertainment was worthy of the best cabaret, complete with well-known jazz singers and music hall comedians, all giving their best.

Farson, looking elated, wore a broad smile on his face most of the evening. He asked me how I was enjoying it.

'I'm loving every minute,' I replied.

Swearing me to secrecy he leaned forward and whispered conspiratorially in my ear, inviting me and Shirley to a party afterwards at his house in Narrow Street, Wapping. 'You can bring a couple of friends,' he said.

I really was loving it, as was Shirley, and we had the feeling that, as publicans, we'd now been handed the keys to a magic door that opened into an exclusive wonderland where everyone welcomed you in warmly and drank to excess. It was, of course, nothing more than an illusion, but until recently we'd been living in our tiny flat in Wood Street with very little money and then suddenly we were plunged into a maelstrom of music and celebrity. It was as if we'd been instantly elevated to a higher status.

Farson's house was very impressive: three stories of spacious rooms overlooking the River Thames. Originally a waterman's hostelry - which is what inspired the name change for the Newcastle - it was furnished with antique and ancient furniture, and huge overstuffed settees and armchairs. There were tables full of drink, and he had the staff of the Lotus House, Edgware Road - at the time, the most famous Chinese restaurant in London - walking amongst the guests with trays, all serving spare ribs, deep fried prawns, dim sum, chow mein, pork balls, crispy duck, rice, and prawn crackers. Everyone helped themselves. Patsy Quill and his wife Cusher had turned up, too, and were enjoying it as much as we were.

Shirley was sitting on a sofa between Rollo Gamble, a famous TV director and producer, and Francis Bacon the painter, and was making them laugh with her stories when I suddenly realised the time. I shouted across the room to her, 'What about the kids? It's nearly two o'clock!' How we drove home I'll never know - this was before the days of the breathalyser, and everyone at that time would drink and drive. In actual fact, though it seems reprehensible now, lots of people used to tell me they could drive better after a few drinks!

We staggered in to the pub. Kenny and Millie were both standing there with long faces and their coats on.

Kenny pointed at his watch. 'Where have you been? What time do you call this? We've been worried!'

I couldn't be bothered answering and instead just stumbled on up to the bedroom to sleep off the drink. I believe Shirley muttered her apologies, paid Millie, and locked up.

Patsy Quill phoned me the next day, indignant: Daniel Farson had suddenly turned on them. In a towering rage - during which he didn't mince his words or tone down his language - he accused them of being gate-crashers, thieves, ponces, East End scum, and raved about how dare they sit there on his furniture, in his home, eating his food and drinking his drink. 'Get out at once!' he had apparently screamed, his face purple, saliva dribbling down his chin. Patsy had thought he was going to have a fit! Apparently, this was par for the course for Farson: when he'd had too much to drink he would turn on even his best friends and accuse and harass them endlessly for no good reason.

Quill had his revenge some months later when Daniel came staggering into the Blind Beggar paralytic drunk, demanding drink. Patsy grabbed him by the seat of his pants and hurled him out onto the street.

Nevertheless, Farson was an interesting and charming man when sober, although he was a terrible nuisance when drunk. Consequently, he had to have a minder with him most of the time. I knew one of them quite well - Alan King of Forest Gate, a rugged and respected character who told me that the trouble with Dan was that, when he got drunk, it was all the big, mean-looking dockers and sailors he liked the most. Apparently, the bigger and tougher they looked, he said, the more he fancied them, but unfortunately most of them certainly didn't like him, and so Alan had his work cut out. Farson would always send his minder ahead into a pub or bar to get his drink and he would then follow a few minutes later; I suppose that was to stop a re-occurrence of the Beggars incident. Previous to Alan King, his minder had been 'Mad' Teddy Smith, a well-known homosexual and one of the Krays' 'firm'. He'd disappeared in mysterious circumstances sometime after the Boothby/Kray affair in which he had a prominent part, and for many years his disappearance remained a mystery, although, reputedly, Reggie murdered him.

I suggested to Farson, in one of his sober moments, that we set up a syndicate of half a dozen pubs and share our acts. At the time, Maxine Daniels was working for me, and I used to employ quite a few guest singers. However, the really good ones were becoming increasingly difficult to get hold of: he was very enthusiastic about my idea but, every time I went to the Watermans to discuss plans further, he would end up getting extremely drunk and try to persuade me to stay behind to talk about it over further drinks. I always made my excuses and left, and so the plan never got off the ground.

At his suggestion, I did take Maxine Daniels over there one night to sing. He was going to pay her quite generously and his pub was packed. I asked him to give the Puddings a boost by getting his compere to mention that Maxine sang at my place every weekend. He had no objection to this and said he'd do just that.

His master - or, rather, mistress - of ceremonies at that time was a big blowsy singer called Kim Cordell, who could belt out a song and had quite a voice. She was on television a lot and had a reputation for being hard-swearing, outspoken and rough.

I was with Tommy Morrison, Leslie North and our wives at the bar, and Tommy's wife, Betty, asked Shirley to go to the ladies with her. As we were drinking, above the sound of the music I suddenly heard screaming and Betty came running out of the toilet, ashen-faced and trembling. 'Quick, quick, Eddie,' she yelled, 'Shirley's fighting with Kim Cordell!'

Shirley, powdering her noise, had overheard Kim Cordell bellowing in her loud, belligerent voice. 'Who's he think he is, coming down here, telling me to advertise his fucking pub! Well, he can fuck off!'

My wife, quickly realising that I was the subject of this derision, had, without further ado, replied with, 'That's my husband you're talking about!' and gave her a swift wallop. It was Kim Cordell who was screaming, and though she was a large woman and Shirley was slim and petite, the singer was frightened out of her life and climbed back on stage and gave me the plug I wanted. Although my wife was very pretty and had a very kind nature, she'd also grown up a tomboy on the streets of East London and was quite strong. Everyone liked her, but if anyone spoke ill of her family or tried to hurt them, she became a ferocious ball of fury.

Daniel Farson eventually lost all his money in that pub. Packed most nights, he was paying a fortune for entertainment and, despite celebrities such as Tony Bennett, Shirley Bassey, who sang 'I Who Have Nothing' when heavily pregnant, Claudette Colbert, who replied 'Yes, I'm often told that,' when a customer remarked she looked like Claudette Colbert, Frankie Howerd, Lionel Bart, Judy Garland, Dirk Bogarde, Joan Littlewood, Billy Daniels and countless others, his money was just draining away.

Everyone was fiddling him: his bar staff, the delivery people, the draymen, his own cellar man. It became the talk of the area. He'd pick up with some rough customers and they would take his hospitality - and whatever else they could steal when he was drunk! - and disappear into the night. I tried to warn him whenever I saw him but it was hopeless and, because of his struggles with alcohol, it was a dot on the card he was going skint.

When he eventually sold up and salvaged what he could, he forsook the East End, the area he had embraced and took to his heart. He left feeling disillusioned with the people who he thought were the golden-hearted cockneys and open-handed working class people of yore, those that he could trust and love and who would love and take him to their hearts in return. Alas, he realised it was all a mirage and that, whilst on the surface they were jolly and welcomed him, it remained that all they wanted was to get something out of him and were, in reality, grasping and cunning, and their jollity was false. To really know East Enders, you have to be one and, unless you are, your trust must be withheld.

Farson moved to his father's old house in Devon, apparently a beautiful place in a lovely unspoiled area, where he got some peace, and carried on writing and doing some television work for Westward TV. I saw him a year or so before he died. He'd put on a bit of weight, wasn't very drunk, was very affable and charming, and seemed more content with his life than ever before. He said he remembered me well.

THE WODGE

Suddenly I was earning more money than I'd ever dreamed of. I always had a wad of notes in my pocket, which was a lovely feeling; a nice, thick wad tucked into the back pocket was very comforting. There were no credit cards back then, and so everyone carried cash. A fiver really meant something in those days and was actually still quite rare. It was said that if you wanted to get served quick in a crowded pub just wave a 'blue one' in the barmaid's direction. It was pound and ten bob notes that made up the average 'wodge'.

I started going to Wood's, the tailor of Kingsland Road, Hackney, who made suits for the Krays and many of the other faces and sportsmen of the East End. Once I had three suits made in quick succession, all dark blue, all with a stripe, all the same shape. Shirley was exasperated. 'What's wrong with you? You keep choosing the same material!' It was like a memory block: I'd go there, look at all the material, finger it, stroke it, look at it in the light outside, think how beautiful it was, and then pick it, once again, for yet another suit. I used to think Mr Wood looked at me a bit quizzically but he never said anything. I said, in future, she would have to accompany me.

Shirley, in the meantime, was enjoying her own spending spree. In those days, Whitechapel was the place where all the smart, well-off East End women went: Medway's for shoes, Merlin's, Spalter's and Mahler's for women's clothes... These shops had the most beautiful suits and dresses - mainly from Italy and France. Clothes that seemed unobtainable elsewhere. There was Harold Conway's for curtains and lace and, in the same area, a shop with nice children's clothes. There was no Mothercare at that time, and Shirley would hunt down shops that sold fashionable clothes for adults and children as they were quite rare in those days. Shirley was like a bloodhound on the trail; she'd read all the trendy magazines like *London Life,* which had a brief reign in the '60s.

Anne Wheeler (left) Shirley and her younger sister Susie (right) in the Puddings on a busy Saturday night. (photograph by Alf Shead)

She ordered furniture from Harrison & Gibson and had our flat on the top floor of the Puddings decorated by a Polish craftsman, recommended by one of our pub customers. This was much to the disgust of her dad, a self-employed builder and decorator, but it was to her design and she wanted to really be able to tell the person who was decorating what to do. She knew her dad would do a nice job, but he had a habit - particularly when it was for family - of not getting the right coloured paint or the exact wallpaper if he could get materials a bit cheaper (from a crooked assistant he knew that worked at Young & Martens, the local builders merchants). When the flat was decorated, we had a party and invited all our friends. Teddy Reeve and his wife Sheila told us it was the nicest decorated, best furnished place they'd ever been in. There were similar comments from most of our guests.

It was as if we couldn't stop. In the '60s, young East End publicans with successful music houses were a bit like the Arabs of the '70s and the later money dealers and traders of the '80s and '90s; not quite so wealthy of course, nor quite so flash, but we didn't care as we earned our money legitimately, working very hard, catering for a young, noisy, sometimes violent set, and so we felt entitled to spend it how we saw fit. No one told us there'd be hard times ahead so what did we know?

Financially, I was an illiterate. Insurance men used to come knocking on our door and would sit and explain endowments, investment portfolios, share opportunities, etc., and I could feel my eyes glaze over, the words coming out of their mouths starting to jumble up in my mind as I struggled to comprehend what on earth they were talking about. All the time I'd be nodding my head sagely, acting as if it all made perfect sense.

We only had one night off a week, Wednesday, and normally we'd go to the West End to some smart restaurant I'd always longed to visit. We were two of the original 'foodies', I suppose: I would sniff out restaurants nobody in the East End had heard of. There was no Fay Maschler to tell Londoners where to go in those days; very few people in our circle went out just to eat. Restaurant criticism, where it existed, was in its infancy. I used to buy *The Good Food Guide* when it was edited by Raymond Postgate, the doyen of all critics, and I would carefully peruse and choose, Ecu du France (no longer), The Empress (alas, no longer) the Coq d'Or (now Langans brasserie, which I became very fond of when it opened, and when the flamboyant, white-suited Peter Langan was host), Jules Bar (gone), Quaglino's before it was altered to become part of the Conran empire, and whose chef, Mick Harper, was a friend. Mr Chow of Knightsbridge where, at various times, we dined on neighbouring tables to the glamorous Ava Gardner, our future Prime Minister Ted Heath, film director Otto Preminger, and Hollywood's James Stewart and his wife. The Carlton Rib room, the Savoy, the Dorchester, the Ritz, Claridge's, Scott's Oyster Bar, Wheelers (before it was a chain). The Caprice, when it was relaunched, was our favourite, and we once sat at the adjoining table to Jean Muir, the fashion designer famous for her 'little black dress' and who Shirley was a fan of.

We managed to go to all the finest and best places, and all I could think of was how cheap they seemed. We'd have lots to eat and drink (pre-breathalyser) and still have change from a tenner! When a new hotel opened with all the fanfare and publicity that accompanied it in the '60s, we were generally there within a week. We were regulars at The Royal Garden in Kensington for a couple of months, and I remember parking in their car park and flashing a 'Man from U.N.C.L.E.' secret service pass at their security and they would let me park, all smiles and deference. I'd borrowed the card from one of the kids' games, which proved quite useful. In addition, the Lancaster Gate Hotel opened a Mirror Room restaurant that we loved for a few weeks.

Weekend mornings I reserved for the kids, Andrew and Matthew. On Saturday, whilst Shirley looked after the pub, I'd go up the city; it was lovely and empty at that time. We'd visit the Monument, St Paul's Cathedral, the Tower of London, Madame Tussauds, the Embankment. It was easy to park and very quiet in the '60s. It was as if you had the city all to yourself at times.

Sunday morning I'd take the boys over Victoria Park to the boating lake or to the old 'promenade' towards Bow to ride their bikes, or we'd go to Petticoat Lane Market and buy pickled herrings served from a barrel and wrapped in newspaper, so we had to be careful that the oil never spilled on our clothes. The beigels (most people these days erroneously use the American spelling of *bagels*) I bought from a little old Jewish lady, dressed as though she lived in war-torn Poland, which were served from an old Hessian sack. I'd queue up at Marks, the famous old deli in Wentworth Street. Mr Marks, a talkative gentleman in his sixties, would always serve me himself, offering up slices of smoked salmon, saying '*This* is the quality you want, I can see that you appreciate the best.' He would wink at me and stage whisper, pointing to the cheaper salmon, 'You don't want *that*, that's for people who haven't got our taste.'

Of course, I'd buy the dearest, 7/6d a quarter, as opposed to the more inferior fish that was 5/- a quarter, and felt as if he was doing me a favour. I don't suppose I'd have known the difference.

We also bought hot latkes - Jewish potato cakes - which were Matthew's favourite. We'd get back to the pub before it opened for lunchtime, the pickled herrings for the bar and the rest - the smoked salmon, beigels and cheesecake - for our tea.

I know this must sound as if we did nothing but enjoy ourselves and spend money, but there were many times I felt very depressed and wished I'd never left the docks and our simple life in Wood Street. I'd feel this way because of a number of reasons: continual fights, aggravation, stress. But, on the other hand, compared to today, it still amazes me how much profit there was in the pub trade in those days.

Although the beer tie, which meant we were restricted to Watney's products, was strictly applied, I never dreamed of breaking it, nor did anyone else I knew. The rents were so low - I think a fiver a week - and the brewery was very happy with the barrelage. During the latter part of the '60s, the Two Puddings became Watney Mann's Number One pub for beer sales in East London, which also took in a good part of Essex. That was some feat in those days: most pubs had a good solid customer base; my only rival at the top was the Bell in Walthamstow, which had a town hall and a college next door, and subsequently received the trade of thousands of students as customers. At one point, our yearly barrellage reached a high point of 1,800 which, at 36 gallons to the barrel, totalled 518,400 pints. We roughly worked on an official figure of fifty percent, but it was more like sixty percent unofficially, and so if we took £1,000 a week, our gross profit was £600. Wages and rent and all the other expenses came to about £200, and so me and Kenny were earning £200 a week each. A clever accountant ensured we paid the minimum of tax and so, when you think the average wage was less than £15 per week, it really puts things into perspective.

At today's prices, taking into account food, wines and spirits, turnover would be over £3 million a year, and bear in mind that was *without* a late license or all day opening. I was earning far more than the Prime Minister, and when you take Shirley's food money - which was about £50 a week profit - you begin to get an idea of how well off we were in those days.

We knew how to earn, we knew how to spend, but sadly for us, what we didn't know was how to save.

THE WINE MASTER

I can't remember the first time I tasted wine. For my generation, it was some exotic liquid that the French and Italians drank, or it was VP wine - a fortified drink that was imported from South Africa and sold in off-licenses to make working class alcoholics satisfyingly drunk for a handful of change. I may have tasted it at weddings when everyone stands to toast the happy couple, although I believe, even then, it was most often sherry or even light ale for the men and Babycham for the ladies.

By the late '50s and early '60s, wine started to get mentioned more often. I was an inveterate reader of the quality newspapers - mainly *The Observer* - and I loved reading the restaurant reviews. These were not yet common to all newspapers and, as well as the food, the reviewer would discuss and recommend or criticise the wine.

Raymond Postgate, despite his impeccable left-wing credentials, was a connoisseur of fine wine as well as a noted gourmand and, in our little £4 a week flat in Walthamstow, whilst my wife cooked us economy meals of stuffed hearts one night, boiled bacon and pease pudding the next, I would read aloud to her the wonderful delicacies being served at Ecu du France in Jermyn Street, the Gay Hussar in Soho, the Savoy Grill, the superb fish at Sheekey's, the wonderful beef carved from the trolley at Simpsons, the Parisian fare at Madame Pruniers in St James, always accompanied by fine wines Chateau Latour, Mouton Rothschild, Chateau Petrus, Chablis, Pouilly Fuisse, Meursault or Puligny-Montrachet. We would then discuss which venue we would go to first when, one day, as we surely would, we had enough money.

The first time I ordered wine was in the early '60s, our fortunes having improved somewhat by then. I took Shirley to a pub in the city - quite a posh place it was, and we sat, slightly self-conscious amidst the dark oak panelling and red upholstered chairs. We hurriedly ordered the only dishes we recognised - a prawn cocktail to start and grilled plaice, new potatoes and petit pois as a main course - being somewhat intimidated by the waiter, a non-smiling beetle-browed character with a strong French accent who, despite the place being half-empty, seemed somewhat impatient. He also handed me a heavy leather-bound book which was the wine list. I knew it was red wine with meat and white wine with fish but, after browsing the list, I could spot only one wine that looked vaguely familiar - Sauternes. I ordered a bottle.

'Certainement m'sieur,' the waiter said, one eyebrow slightly raised.

'Lovely wine,' we said as we toasted each other, 'bit sweet, though.' Shirley said.

I agreed but never said anything, not realising until months later that it was a dessert wine.

As time went on and we went out more and more, like everyone else we knew, we would order a bottle of Liebfraumilch called Blue Nun, making sure it was nice and cold. This was so easy - we ordered it with everything we ate: steak, fish, whatever. Blue Nun was the choice of the common man.

Later, when we became more discerning and started to talk to other wine enthusiasts (you were known as an *enthusiast* in those days), I started to realise the difference between Bordeaux and Burgundy; I used to state airily, 'You can't beat a Bordeaux or Claret for red wine or Burgundy for a white,' and I would name the valleys and the areas from where various growths originated. I would query a Chablis: 'Is it Premier Cru?'. If the waiter said no I would wave it away. I really thought I was an expert and, as all of my friends knew even less than I did, no one ever told me otherwise.

One year we went to Bulgaria for a holiday. It was a time when currency was restricted and we were only allowed to take a certain amount of money abroad. I become very friendly with a Scotsman called Geoffrey Hume, who was very proud that he shared the same surname as Sir Alec Douglas Hume, who was the current Prime Minister. He was an amusing and very worldly man with a nice wife and five lovely children who kept our own kids company throughout the holiday. We became very fond of them. Geoffrey suggested we go out one evening to a hotel that had a reputation for fine cuisine and so, with another couple, six of us sat at a round table with spotless white linen, sparkling cutlery, and wine glasses.

Geoffrey suggested we try the Bulgarian wine. 'I hear they produce some fine wine here,' he said in his soft Scottish burr.

'No, no, Geoffrey,' I said, slightly patronising, 'we'll stick to the French wine. That's the best. You know, Geoffrey,' I continued brightly, 'I do know a little about wine. It's such a complex subject, but did you know there are only sixteen Masters of Wine in England?'

'Aye,' he answered. 'As a matter of fact, there's only five of us in Scotland!'

Of course, rather deflated, I slid back down in my chair and let Geoffrey get on with ordering the wine, and lovely it was too. That was the end of my days thinking I knew anything about the subject.

The last couple of decades have seen wine consumption increase so enormously that there are very few families who don't have a bottle or two with their meals on a regular basis. Pubs now sell it by the type - some of it quite good quality. From selling no wine, pubs have made a notable leap during the past 20 years, before which they sold simply red or white served in tiny glasses as if it was medicine. And sometimes it tasted like it.

The growth of wine bars caused a big rethink for our beloved inns. Nowadays, most places give a decent choice, all served in a proper glass at the right temperature, and we can all quite knowledgeably ask for a Chardonnay, a Merlot, a Pinot or Cabernet without causing consternation behind the bar.

And, thanks to Premier League football stars and their wives, we all know the famous marques of the Champagne world, names like Krug, Dom Perignon, Laurent Perrier Rose, and Louis Roederer Cristal so beloved by rappers, though I doubt many of them could tell the difference between an ordinary champagne like Mumms or Moet or a bottle of Lucozade. But, it's their money. Plus, of course, we see it sprayed all over the place from the winner's podiums when anybody wins a Grand Prix - and what a waste that is!

France was the acknowledged king of wine producers, from champagne to the finest white Burgundy and the unaffordable, sublime famous reds of Bordeaux. But modern growing techniques, young marketeers, aggressive salesmanship and clever bottle design has witnessed growth - not only from the New World, Australia, Argentina, America, Chile and New Zealand, but also from Spain and Portugal, Hungary and Bulgaria. Nowadays, almost all countries with some warmth in the climate produce very quaffable stuff. Even India has entered the fray.

But, despite all the colourful language used to describe it, phrases such as 'blackcurrant with a peachy undertone', 'a tart and citrusy zest of lemon' or 'a hint of gooseberry and sour pears', I have still not developed a decent nose or taste for wine. I still cannot tell much difference between a Beaujolais Nouveau and a Nuit Saint Georges. I've been to wine tastings galore - I know the correct face to pull, how to gurgle it around before spitting it out - yet I still cannot tell much difference. But I pretend.

Now, when I go to a reasonable restaurant, I'll just order a dry white house or a house red and, if the food's okay, I'm usually pretty satisfied. I wonder what my old friend from the Bulgarian days, Geoffrey Hume, would say. Just an amused glint in his eye, I would imagine. As for me, much as I'm fond of a drink, I try to remember my Shakespeare: 'O God, that men should put an enemy in their mouths to steal away their brains!'

THE TAILOR

At some point I decided to change tailors. A lot of East Enders in the know were saying very good things about 'Jeremiah's' in New Road, Whitechapel. The proprietor, Jerry Anderson, was a very skilled tailor and also very friendly and we hit it off straight away. He soon started visiting the pub and Shirley got on so well with his lovely wife Betty that they became regular companions on our nights out. Every Wednesday we'd visit the West End to some new restaurant or other, taking turns to drive.

One memorable occasion we went to the Beefeater Mediaeval Banquet at St Katherine's Dock by the Tower and Jerry got so drunk he started a bread fight that quickly degenerated to the point where the entire banquet hall were hurling bread rolls and food at each other. Shirley's sister Susie and her husband Alan were with us on this occasion and after we staggered out of the hall, Jerry, Alan and me then proceeded to climb down into the harbour and steal a rowing boat. The three of us were roaring drunk and singing sea shanties as we attempted to row out of the dock and off down the river Thames, whilst our wives looked on in horror. The security guards, who eventually caught us and made us give the boat up were, in retrospect, extremely kind and understanding.

Jerry went on to expand his tailor shops and at one time had 4 or 5 of them, all doing well. We remain friends but I try to keep him away from the bread rolls!

THE BINGO BOYS

Just before we moved into the Puddings, my mate Teddy Reeve had become quite well known throughout Stratford, along with his pal, Tommy Morrison, for running bingo nights at the local snooker hall, just along Broadway from us on the corner with Chant Street. They were a startling success. As Kenny had cashed in on the lack of dance facilities for youngsters, Teddy had realised older people loved to have a little gamble, and all the bigger halls, mainly ex-cinemas, were yet to start operating. Later on, as we had our queues threading down the Broadway past the town hall, waiting to come into the Puddings, Tommy and Teddy had their lines of people three or four nights a week waiting to get into the Regal Billiards Room, to give its full name. Their prizes were quite good, reflecting the huge attendance.

The only moans came from the regular snooker players, who were deprived of their beloved game, on which they gambled heavily, for a few nights a week. Frankie Sims, who ran the Snooker Hall's tea and snack bar and was used to selling the odd meat pie and occasional cup of tea in between playing snooker, suddenly realised he had a great little business on his hands with these bingo nights, and so he had to keep well-stocked with cakes and buns as well as plenty of hot sausages and saveloys.

Teddy had been a stevedore in the Docks - a job that was in the family: his father was Harry Reeve, who'd been light heavyweight champion of Great Britain in the 1920s, a time when being British boxing champion really meant something, and had also been a docker. Tommy also worked in the docks but as a ships painter. Both were well-paid jobs if you applied yourself, but suddenly in the Bingo Hall they were earning sums

Several nights per week The Regal Billiards Room on Stratford Broadway became a hugely successful Bingo Hall. (photographer unknown)

that could only have been dreamed of in the docks.

During the Cuban missile crisis, when Kennedy confronted Kruschev, lots of people were convinced World War Three was about to kick off. Tommy said: 'Just our luck, we're finally starting to get a few quid for the first time in our lives and a war's going to start!' He laughed as he said it but he, like many of us, was genuinely worried.

They were both big men - six foot tall. Teddy had blonde, wavy hair, was very muscular, and no one would relish having a row with him. Tommy was older, about 40, was big but more overweight than muscular. His hair was mousy and thinning on top, and his face was red and a little splotchy. He had rather a small head but used to have his suits made with extra wide shoulders which accentuated its smallness. He had caught the tail end of the war and had served in the army, seeing some action in Italy. He was jovial and warm, and had an engaging personality that endeared him to both me and Shirley. I had worked with him and Teddy some years prior, helping to paint Leadenhall Market in the city, and I loved listening to his tales of London in the immediate post-war years: the black market and the spivs, Jack Spot, Italian Albert Dimes and Billy Hill 'King of the Underworld', who, with his wife Aggie, ran the Cabinet club in Soho. Then there were the Upton Park Mob, Porky Bennett, Teddy Machin, Jackie Reynolds and 'Woodbine' Georgie Woods... He knew them all, legends in that part of London - long before the Kray twins came along.

THE LOST WEEKEND

Tommy always came in the pub for a drink on his break from the bingo, and one night he mentioned that he'd never been to Paris and would love to go. And so we arranged to go with our wives. I'd been in the Puddings for about a year by then and, although I'd had a holiday in Devon in the summer, I felt I needed a break before the Christmas rush, and so we decided we'd go for an extra-long weekend in October, which would coincide with Shirley's 27th birthday.

Naively, I didn't bother to book a hotel as 'Chasser' Chapman had recently taken West Ham Boxing Club there to box a Parisian team and, according to him, we only had to mention his name at the hotel they'd stayed at and we'd be in - welcomed with open arms.

Tommy's wife, Betty, got on well with Shirley. She was a bit older than us, the same age as her husband, and was a slim, fair-haired girl with a very pretty face and nice figure. Her and Tommy had five children, and Shirley was amazed at how young and well Betty looked.

We were all quite excited as we drove to the airfield in Kent. Tommy seemed quite apprehensive about flying, and though he said he'd flown when he was in the army, I began to suspect he'd never been in an aeroplane before.

Once we arrived in Paris, we struggled with our bags all the way to the recommended hotel, but they were full up and the concierge simply waved us away. When I mentioned 'Chasser' and West Ham Boxing Club, he waved even more contemptuously and said in fractured English, 'I don't care, even if Floyd Patterson the champion of ze whole world, is your best friend, we 'ave no room! Finito! Au revoir!'

So that was that.

All we could do was treat it as a laugh but, after dragging our baggage around for another hour with no luck at all and with Betty dying for a cup of English tea, we'd stopped laughing. Eventually, we found a lovely little hotel in a side street off the Champs Elysee. I loved it because it had one of those glass-encased brass and wrought iron Edwardian lifts so redolent of Paris, and it smelt of freshly brewed coffee and had a faint whiff of Havana cigars. We were truly abroad. I'd been to Paris before but none of the others had, and they found it mesmerising. The shops, bars, pavement cafes, Montmartre, Pigalle, the Eiffel Tower... It all seemed so glamorous compared to London: the coffee tasted better than any coffee I'd ever drank before;

the very smell of the streets infused us with energy; the croissants - which none of us had even seen before - were so delicious I just couldn't stop buying and eating them. And every minute we seemed to spot something exciting, so unlike our own dreary, grey capital.

After lunch and a hefty few glasses of wine, I was feeling a bit sleepy so, when Betty suggested we go to the pictures, I readily agreed, thinking that I could have a quiet doze in the dark. It was a bizarre suggestion, really: a bright, sunny day in Paris and we decide to go to the cinema for the afternoon. But we'd all had a few drinks and it seemed like a good idea at the time. It was a John Wayne cowboy film with Maureen O'Hara, a comedy in English with French subtitles. During the performance, Tommy and Shirley were absolutely shrieking with laughter, so much so that everyone else in the cinema was looking at us with irritation. This was very unusual as Shirley wasn't that fond of comedies or westerns and rarely, if ever, laughed out loud whilst watching a film. Me and Betty were getting a bit irritated ourselves and kept trying to shush them up, but it was no use, so eventually I managed to get them to leave.

Outside, whilst having a coffee, we met a well-spoken English chap who told us he lived in Paris. He asked if we'd like to go to the best-known nightclub in the city, the 'Crazy Horse' - apparently world-famous although, at that time, none of us had heard of it. We duly went along.

All I can remember is that it was pitch-black inside, and we stumbled and fumbled our way to our seats and managed to order drinks whilst talking to the torch shining into our eyes. From the darkness, we gradually started to see the dancers and strippers.

It left absolutely nothing at all to the imagination. It was a high-class strip joint - although Betty and Shirley both disputed the 'high-class' bit - and, after a lot of muttering and words like 'disgusting' and 'shocking' plus a few swear words, Tommy and myself were both dragged out of the place. I personally was quite relieved; I was too frightened to look at the girls in front of Shirley: although it was pitch-black I knew she would have sensed me looking.

As late afternoon turned into early evening, things became more surreal. We carried on drinking more and more, got a taxi to take us to a 'respectable' nightclub, emphasising the *respectable* in my broken Franglais and sign language to the driver, and he dumped us at a far more blatant strip joint than the 'Crazy Horse'. We were charged an astronomical sum for champagne and, again, Tommy and I were dragged out by our outraged wives.

In no time at all, it seemed, it was two o'clock in the morning and we were sitting in a bar on the Champs Elysee drinking cognac, but every drink Tommy had somehow slipped through his hands. He must have smashed about ten glasses. How the proprietor put up with us I don't know, I suppose he just kept adding everything to the bill. Our drinking continued at the hotel until the early hours. Just before I went to sleep I wondered why, although very merry, Betty and me hadn't been so uproariously drunk as our respective spouses.

At breakfast I felt pretty rough, but Shirley looked as white as a ghost. 'What were you drinking that I wasn't?' I asked. 'I've never known you so drunk.'

'Purple Hearts,' she said with a wan smile. 'Tommy gave me

some. I thought everything was so great, I just couldn't stop laughing! I felt so depressed at leaving the kids that he handed me some and said they'd cheer me up.'

Purple Hearts were a popular drug at the time, and were known to contain a mixture of amphetamine and barbiturate. Tommy had eaten lots at the airport to combat his nervousness at flying.

It was the first time we'd ever left our boys, Andrew and Matthew, and Shirley's older sister Jose and her husband Tommy were looking after them for a few days, but I hadn't realised she was missing them quite so much.

That day we didn't drink as much, just toured Paris looking at the sights. In the evening I asked the concierge to recommend a nice restaurant. 'Not a nice restaurant,' Tommy interrupted. 'The *best* restaurant! We want the *best* restaurant in Paris!'

The concierge looked at me with one eyebrow raised slightly. I nodded in agreement, 'Yes, the *best*, please.' I cringe now as we must have seemed like typical 'Essex Boys' before the term was invented.

The restaurant we went to was called Michael's. If it wasn't the best it must have been amongst the top ten. It was wonderful; all mahogany and brass with Edwardian lighting and deep plush carpet. The banquettes were of dark red leather, the tablecloths crisp and white, the glassware and cutlery softly gleaming in the low lights. The waiters wore white aprons and black waistcoats; the menus were four-foot high; the wine list was thirty pages long. Tommy made great play at looking at everything, but I was quite overwhelmed by the sheer luxury of the place and so I just let the Maitre d's recommendations govern my choice, and

Betty and Tommy Morrison (left) Shirley and me, enjoying our 'lost weekend' at the Moulin Rouge. (photographer unknown)

Shirley and Betty did the same. It was a gorgeous meal. The bill was astronomical but we didn't care, we were just so happy when we staggered out into the night.

No visit to Paris would be complete without going to the Moulin Rouge, of course, so off we went. It was, to our eyes, a gaudy and exuberant place. We drank, as always, nothing but champagne, and when the girls were dancing the Can-Can and whooping and shouting and kicking their legs in the air, I could almost see Toulouse Lautrec sitting down the front sketching the dancers. We all enjoyed it, although with slight reservations from Shirley and Betty as all the girls were topless, which was still a novelty for the English.

When we left, we made our way to the Pigalle area. I'd been told that Chet Baker, the famous American Jazz trumpeter, was playing there. He'd had lots of publicity recently because he'd been caught smoking marijuana, as everyone still called it in those days. Artists and musicians of America's counter-culture - especially black Americans - loved working in France and particularly in Paris because it was such an enlightened society in comparison. A scandal in the uptight ultra-religious America would be regarded as a mere peccadillo in this city.

Tommy and Betty were walking down an alleyway ahead of me and Shirley, when suddenly a man charged straight at my wife, threw a bag at her feet, and leapt upon her. She screamed. I was in a complete state of shock but I grabbed the man and tried to pull him off and started to punch into him, but he just wouldn't let go. I was aware of Tommy and Betty clinging to each other, and dimly wondered when he was coming to help me, but they were both too shocked and seemed completely bewildered. As I was struggling, a car suddenly screeched to a halt at the top of the narrow alley and four men leapt out, ran towards us, and they jumped on us too. I naturally started to fight with them all - punching, head-butting, scratching. I remember biting the man who was holding Shirley, right on his neck. I also put one of the other men on the ground with a right hander, and then we were all in a heap on the floor kicking, punching, wrestling. Our companions were still frozen, though, watching from the sidelines, clinging to each other like two statues.

I really thought we'd been attacked by a gang of robbers but the explanation - ascertained only after much shouting, waving of arms, and flashing of badges and identity cards - was that the first man was a thief who was being tailed by the police in their car. He had suddenly realised this and, I don't know if they had guns, but he had become very frightened about carrying stolen goods and had flung his arms round my wife to save himself from harm. They were very apologetic as they brushed us down after slinging him in the back of their car, and that was the reason they gave, in their broken English.

As they were about to drive away Betty suddenly came to life and shouted to the police not to forget the bag. 'Ah, oui, merci,' they said with a grin. I actually wasn't going to say anything - at least not until I'd looked inside the bag, as it could have been stuffed full of jewellery or large denomination bank notes!

We gave up on going to see Chet Baker, rationalising that was quite enough excitement for the night, and so we headed back to our hotel. Tommy was quite subdued - I think he felt bad that he'd not dived into the fray. But, to me and Shirley, after the initial shock, it was more of a lark and was all in keeping with the romance of a weekend abroad in a new and exciting city.

The next day we were going back but before we left we had a final look around Paris. I noticed the mood in the streets was quite sombre, and there were big billboards on all the newsstands announcing something 'Morte', which I knew was something to do with death but I couldn't translate the rest. I asked a waiter what it all meant.

'Today we are burying our little sparrow'. Edith Piaf, the great French chanteuse, had died and that day was her funeral. I didn't know much about her then but subsequently bought her records, read her life story, and became a great fan.

THE DEBT

Back at the Puddings I continued to see Tommy and his wife Betty, who still came in the pub on a regular basis, sometimes with Teddy and his wife Sheila, who was a great friend of Shirley's. But Tommy suddenly became quite ill and we were all very concerned. He also started to borrow money, not just from me but from all his friends, as I found out later. He started to lose weight, his complexion was turning yellow, he seemed frantic and desperate for money, and he'd fallen out with his best friend, Teddy. I remember he had to meet 'Bogie' Tibbs - the uncle of Jimmy Tibbs, a well-known boxer - in the bar, and I came down and had a drink with them but I couldn't suss out if he was borrowing more money or paying some back. He told me at the time that he couldn't sleep and that he'd drive through the empty streets of London at three in the morning in his green Mercedes. He said he enjoyed it as there were no people about, but it was plain that money worries were stopping him from sleeping, though he never explained why he needed the money.

Soon after, having been refused dialysis because he was forty (it was for the under forties only in those days), Tommy died. Tragically, he never reached his forty-first birthday.

Tommy had a big funeral because he was a very popular and well-known character in the East End. There were lots of people there who could have helped him out, but no one knew what his financial problems were about. Some years after he'd died, I was told it was probably connected to the Kray twins. Apparently, they'd approached Tommy and Teddy and asked their advice about running Bingo at a place they'd acquired at Custom House, and they wanted to know how to set it up and if the Stratford boys would consider running it for them for a good percentage share. Although Teddy was doubtful, it didn't seem a bad deal at first: no outlay on their part, the twins to pay all expenses, staff, etc. What could they lose? As such, after a few weeks they'd managed to get things moving: they'd sorted out staff, arranged suppliers for all the bits and pieces. The club was going to be called the Wickergate, yet the Krays still hadn't made a move towards decorating, and no money was forthcoming for equipment. All seemed in limbo. After a couple of phone calls, Teddy and Tommy went to Vallance Road to meet with the brothers. Tommy's whole attitude was one of apprehension. The brothers were sitting in large, wingback armchairs and, as he was talking to them, he knelt by the chairs, treating them like royalty. Teddy spoke to him quite sharply. 'Come on, Tom, get up,' and then went on to complain to the twins about their lack of action or co-operation.

'What we've decided to do,' Reggie had said, with Ronnie all the while sitting in his chair, not saying a word, staring unsmiling and intently at Tommy, 'is let you two keep the club. What we want is a oner each a week and you can 'ave it.' This was no generous offer; it was a con-trick to frighten them into paying a wage - a very high wage - whilst they ran a club they didn't want, had no interest in until they'd been asked for advice, and for little or no profit. Teddy shook his head, literally turned on his heel and walked, and Tommy followed shortly afterwards.

It wasn't long after this incident that Tommy started to borrow and became ill at the same time. It seemed the only logical explanation to Teddy, me and many others was that they must have had his money because he died penniless.

I missed him terribly when he'd gone. He was a good customer, a good friend, and a good man, always laughing and joking before the last terrible months of his life. He was kind to all and would always treat the colonel and Dodger and anyone else round the public bar.

I am so glad we had that wonderful weekend in Paris together.

Me, Kenny and Harry Mansworth in the Puddings on a Saturday night.
(photograph by Alf Shead)

The young people of Stratford worked hard all week, supported West Ham
on Saturday afternoon and were found in the Puddings most weekend
nights. (photograph by Alf Shead)

THE GOOD TIMES ROLL

THE MUSIC

In the years following the war, London was a drab place, masked in a predominant colour of grey. There were bombsites everywhere - most cleared of rubble, some used as car parks, yet very little effort made by the government or councils to build on them. Of course, we'd suffered all sorts of shortages; clothes and material goods, as well as food. The country was still anaemic following a bitter, drawn-out conflict, costing many thousands of lives, and had, during the latter part, depended increasingly on American aid (which, paradoxically, seemed to drain our economy whilst boosting theirs).

America also played a large part in our entertainment. The films of Bob Hope, Abbot & Costello, and the Bowery Boys cheered us up, whilst Humphrey Bogart set about destroying our enemies' espionage activities. In the field of battle itself, John Wayne and Errol Flynn reigned supreme, taking on the Germans or Japanese with equal brio, always winning with consummate ease - and, of course, with no apparent help from our country.

Britain's answer to these heroes was John Mills, Vera Lynn and George Formby.

Much of our music was shipped in from across the Atlantic, too, as our home-grown talent - singers such as Dickie Valentine, Lita Roza, Ronnie Hilton and Matt Monro, and bands like Ted Heath, Oscar Rabin, Lou Preager and Sid Phillips - all seemed bland copies of their American counterparts; we never seemed to have our own voice. The main reason was probably owing to the shared language, but everyone seemed star-struck with anything American when I was growing up. Me and my mates would hang around the only record stall we knew - Solly's 'down the lane' - every Sunday, lapping up Frank Sinatra, Ella Fitzgerald, Kay Starr and Stan Kenton, amongst many. This music just seemed more vital than ours, and there would be crowds of girls too, and so it was always a good place to chat them up and take them for a coffee at Ziggy's Cafe.

When we took over the Puddings, the British music scene had been slowly twitching into life for a few years. In the late '50s, the coffee bars of Soho had been the scene of a popular skiffle group movement, with musicians like Lonnie Donegan, Wee Willie Harris, Tommy Steele, Joe Brown and Johnny Kidd slowly establishing themselves. Cliff Richard and the Shadows, Marty Wilde, and others were also making an impact, and there were lively young girl singers seemingly appearing from nowhere, such as fourteen year old Helen Shapiro. So a head of steam was building up, and more and more of these new acts were climbing up the 'Hit Parade'.

Then, in 1963, the Beatles exploded. They not only conquered England and Europe, of course, but flew across to the USA and knocked Elvis Presley - the erstwhile untouchable 'King' - off his perch.

All of the biggest American musical acts who had dominated were suddenly, almost overnight, relegated. And it was no fluke either. To the chagrin of many Americans, the boys from Liverpool were quickly followed by the Rolling Stones and many others. For my generation - most of whom had been longing to see this happen - it was wonderful.

Whilst I busied myself running the pub, Kenny branched out into the music business, both managing and promoting some of the most exciting acts of the day. In those days, the young people of Stratford worked hard all week, supported West Ham United on a Saturday afternoon, and most weekend nights were found in a packed Puddings listening to ear-shatteringly loud pop music played live.

With Kenny's help, I booked different groups and singers every week; some were wonderful, some not so good, some went on to bigger things, such as the Who, the Crazy World of Arthur Brown, the Kinks, Screaming Lord Sutch, the Nashville Teens. David Essex appeared on our stage, and it was obvious the youngster had a raw, magnetic quality and, within a few short years, he realised his potential too.

Many singers and bands used to drop by just to have a drink and listen to the music. I remember standing at the bar one evening and having a drink with Clyde McPhatter, who was a lovely man. When I asked him, half-jokingly, if he'd mind giving us a song, in the most charming manner he did, staying on our stage for over half an hour and thrilling our regulars who, until I told them, didn't actually realise who he was. His stripped down version of 'On Broadway' - a song the Drifters had recorded long after he'd left the group - sent shivers through the entire building.

Rod Stewart was another regular who was often found in the pub by himself checking out the new bands, at least until one night, when a star-struck member of a support group announced over the PA that everyone in the audience should give Rod a big round of applause. This embarrassed him so much that we didn't see him again!

I also remember having a nice drink with a very young Van Morrison who was playing with his group Them at the town hall next door for Kenny, who'd sent Van and his band into the pub to have a drink in the interval. We had one of our best and most regular headliners playing, Sean Buckley & the Breadcrumbs, and young Van was quite impressed with them. He was a pleasant, thoughtful young man, and I enjoyed talking to him about his ambitions and fears for the future, and he said he hoped he could eventually write songs with some meaning. It's pleasing to me now to see that he's still going strong and seems to have more than realised what he hoped to achieve.

One Sunday night, Jerry Lee Lewis, the legendary Rock and Roll pianist, was appearing at West Ham Baths for Kenny. Lewis's career was at a low ebb in the '60s. The press had given him a torrid time on a previous tour in the '50s when they discovered he'd taken a child bride of fourteen - which was perfectly legal in the state he resided in. He'd been mercilessly booed wherever he played. I asked Kenny to bring him in the pub for a drink as I'd wanted to meet him. I told our customers he was coming and the place was packed, buzzing with anticipation. But the only person to appear was his minder, a very friendly young chap called Peter Grant, who I had a drink with and who later became very famous in his own right as manager of Led Zeppelin. He was a bit of a hard case who, during later years, was reputedly never without a loaded revolver on his person. He explained Jerry Lee was feeling very nervous because of the abuse he'd suffered in London some years before, and so, at the singer's request, he'd left him sitting alone in the back of a big American limousine parked outside. Some of our crowd went outside though and surrounded him, waving, shouting and gently rocking the large automobile backwards and forwards in an effort to force the 'Killer' from his lair. Jerry Lee did wave back, quite nervously, but understandably made no effort to climb out. We were all disappointed, but I can't say

I blamed him: the crowd we had in that night were nice enough, but they did look quite intimidating. Even Peter Grant confided that he didn't know how I coped as the atmosphere was causing him to feel a little on edge too! But that night, Jerry Lee's performance at West Ham Baths was said to have been 'blistering'.

Don Arden was another music manager reputed to be a tough guy, and I remember my friend Boater telling me one day that Charlie Kray had asked him to go and sort some problems out for Arden - apparently, he was being seriously threatened. Boater laughingly explained it was the easiest money he'd ever earned as the people who were terrifying Arden were lightweights and, after a quick word in their ear, had simply ran off.

Little Stevie Marriot came in the pub one day to see me, and asked if he could rent the hall upstairs for a week to rehearse. I agreed on the condition it was afternoons only. He brought his Small Faces in every day. They'd order a bottle of Scotch and twelve bottles of coke, head upstairs, and then make such a racket that I received complaints from the fire brigade next door and all of the surrounding offices. I charged him eighteen pounds for two weeks, but he ran off without paying. I believe the rehearsal was for 'Itchycoo Park', which was a small masterpiece, and so I forgave the debt.

Some of our bands were so good I couldn't get downstairs to see them fast enough. When the music was this strong it inspired us all: we would work harder and faster and, it seemed, at the tempo of the music. It got so loud sometimes that we, along with the customers, through the thick, smoke-filled air, would have to shout at each other at the top of our lungs to hear each other!

Some of our regulars would drive all the way down from the North of England for our music nights. (photograph by Alf Shead)

When the music was strong it would inspire us all. We would work harder and faster and, it seemed, at the tempo of the music.
(photograph by Alf Shead)

At the end of a session - and, of course, after a few light ales - we all felt as though we'd been to a great party. Most of the bar staff said they enjoyed working as much as if they'd been customers. They had all their drinks bought for them, listened to great bands, *and* they got paid!

It seemed that every young man and woman wanted to join a group and play in a pub, preferably the Two Puddings. I used to hold auditions on a Monday - a traditionally quiet night - but it was very hard telling some of the boys and girls, with their mums and dads watching, that they weren't quite good enough.

We never had a jukebox in the early years, but I installed a 'Cinebox' instead. This was many years before MTV was even thought of, and was an invention that died almost as soon as it was born. In fact, I never actually saw another one anywhere. It was a machine, larger than a jukebox, with what looked like a small cinema screen perched on top. There were sixteen records to choose from and an accompanying film was shown for whatever song one picked. There was Little Eva on a big steam train singing 'Locomotion', The Drifters performing 'Up on the Roof', amongst others. The trouble was, they only changed the films every three months. A song would become a hit but, by the time the film was made - a long process in the '60s - the record was way past its 'Six-Five Special' sell-by date. At first, customers would crowd around as it was such a novelty, but it soon wore off, ceasing to raise its rent, and so had to go.

Sometimes, I had a DJ, the best of whom was 'Frantic Frankie' Morgan, who'd be accompanied by two girls - very lovely to look at - who would gyrate wildly either side of him on the stage whilst he spun the discs.

But nothing pulled in the crowd like live music.

Some Wednesdays, which was my night off and when Kenny ran the pub, there was a band on with sixteen musicians, including two singers. They crowded the stage to its edges. Everyone loved them. The cost was horrendous, of course, but my brother loved them so much he subsidised their wages out of his own pocket.

We'd had posters made, billing ourselves audaciously as 'The Greatest Pub in the World!' Our rivals didn't like it, but nobody disputed it. One Sunday morning, Tommy Morrison came rushing into the pub in a state of excitement. 'Quick! Quick! Come over the road now! The Beatles are shooting a film down Angel Lane! We all rushed over there as fast as our legs could carry us to try to meet them and invite them back to the Puddings and, sure enough, there they were - The 'Fab Four' making a promotional film for their new single 'Penny Lane' - but we were only just in time to watch them disappear into a rival pub, the Salway Arms, a small family-run establishment where they apparently enjoyed a pint with the locals.

Later that week, a huge placard was placed in the window of the Salway, which read, 'We may not be the greatest pub in the world, but the greatest group in the world drink here!' A perfect riposte, I thought, to our boasting.

Incidentally, as far as I know, that film was never shown to the public, although maybe these days it could be found on YouTube.

The music of that time was not just part of the magic - it *was* the magic. All the clothes, fashions, trendy eating houses, new film scene that gave British film makers fresh respect, Carnaby Street, pirate radio, the boom in tourism, and London being viewed as the most exciting city in the world, it was all down to the music. The very pavements seemed to pulse; the blood in our veins seemed to race. *Time Magazine* devoted a whole issue to London, the 'Swinging Capital of the World', and the phrase stuck.

It really did seem to be wonder time for a while.

THE PICTURES

The cinema has always played a major role in the life of my family. My mum loved films, and I grew up loving them, too, as do most of my family and many of my relatives. My youngest son, Gerard, became obsessed with them almost as soon as he could talk. Along with Peter Ferdinando's son, also called Peter, the pair of them have become quite a successful team in recent years. With Gerard directing and Peter acting, they've been picking up critical acclaim for their gritty, black-humoured brand of London-based films. They must have been inspired from living above pubs and listening to all the family tales over the years. Peter's older sister Emma was also an actor and in the '70s appeared on British stage and television as a child star.

Shirley's brother-in-law Alan Jones and his son Jason are another pair that have always been obsessed with films, so much so that Alan even became a successful 'extra' in the '60s and '70s, appearing in a wide variety of films such as *On The Buses*, where, much to my children's amusement, they could spot him for a split-second hopping off a Routemaster. He also appeared in *The Day of the Triffids*, although it was harder to recognise him this time as he was dressed up as one of the man-eating plants! I also took the boys to visit him on-set during the making of one of the Fu Manchu films of the mid-1960s, but despite appearing in dozens and dozens of films, he found it hard to make the leap into speaking parts.

***Birthday boy Sam Shepherd (centre left), star of the recently rediscovered
cult film Bronco Bullfrog, celebrating upstairs at the Puddings.***
(photographer unknown)

One of our regulars in the Puddings who did make the leap was
Sam Shepherd, and he became a star overnight. He took the
name part in a famous independently made film called *Bronco
Bullfrog*. It was directed by Barney Platts-Mills, the son of the
QC, John Platts-Mills, who had defended the Kray twins. Barney
had shot a documentary about Joan Littlewood's improvisatory
theatre workshops in Stratford, which subsequently inspired him
to make the film starring the local youths Littlewood had been
working with. It was filmed in and around Stratford, and
brilliantly captured the atmosphere and youth culture of the era.
It premiered at Mile End Odeon, where Sam sat next to Princess
Anne, which made him a household name for a week or so.

Sadly for Sam and the other actors, however, they were
instantly blacklisted by Equity, the actors' union. Despite the

film playing in Cannes and winning some rave reviews and even picking up a Writers' Guild award, Barney Platts-Mills was referred to as a 'maverick' director for not playing by the rules Equity had laid down. So much for independent cinema!

For many years, Sam worked as a barman for me, he was good and fast and a lovely lad but never managed to get back into acting, which was a real shame. *Bronco Bullfrog*, although a forgotten film for decades, was recently re-released and rediscovered by a new generation, and the BFI even issued the DVD as part of their Flipside Series, which is dedicated to unveiling the hidden history of British cinema.

I'd often thought that many of my customers and associates would have made the perfect inspiration for a film, and perhaps a few more of them did make their way to the big screen after all - in one guise or another.

I used to really enjoy talking to the reporters from the *Stratford Express*, who were great customers; it's incredible how, for such a small newspaper, so many of them went on to become famous in their field. Roy Greenslade, Editor of the *Daily Mirror*, Roddy Gilchirst, Managing Editor of the *Daily Mail* and *Mail on Sunday*, Jill Palmer, Medical Editor of the *Mirror*, Trevor Bond, Sports Editor of *The Sunday Telegraph*, Alan Shillum, News Editor of the *Daily Mirror*, Ken Chandler, Managing Editor of the *New York Post*, Tony Clifton, Investigative Reporter for *The Sunday Times*, Luke Casey worked on the *Tonight* programme for years, Pat Connors became editor of the *East End Advertiser*, whilst Peter Faulkner reported on boxing for nearly every national newspaper in the country. And many others besides.

One young *Express* reporter who I was very friendly with

was Barrie Keefe. I would wind him up a bit, mainly to get some publicity for the pub. I once kidded him that I was heading off to South America to look for 'pirate treasure' on a remote island called 'Katrak', and he wrote a big story in the *Express* that featured a picture of me on the 'eve of travel'. I had to put up with the consequences, though, as even the police believed it - and consequently thought I was richer than I was! But it generated a lot of interest in the pub. I was very pleased for Barrie years later when he received recognition for a story of his that was turned into a hugely successful film, *The Long Good Friday*. Peter Faulkner told me that Barrie based a lot of the characters on JD, Sykes, Boater, Kenny and me, and the stories we used to tell him. Barrie also told me himself that Shirley inspired the role that was played by Helen Mirren in the film. He'd even wanted to use the Puddings for the pub scene in *The Long Good Friday,* but when it came to filming, many logistical problems made it impossible.

Another young customer I was friendly with was Peter Hayden. Although by this point I was no longer living above the pub, I still came back most Fridays and Saturdays to keep an eye on things and have a drink with friends. Peter had disappeared for several months, and I had assumed it must be due to the fact his father - an Irish plumber - had charged me an exorbitant fee for some dodgy work in our bathroom, and about which Peter felt pretty embarrassed, but he'd actually been in the south of France making films. It was mainly advertising stuff, such as the 'Martini' advert, which involved going up in a hot air balloon, but it all sounded pretty exciting. During this sojourn, he'd met, and become very friendly with, Martin Scorsese. Peter was a charming, fair-haired lad with plenty of Irish blarney, although his accent was East London, and so it didn't surprise me he'd made friends with the director.

When he returned to the pub to relate his adventures, he started enthusing over a film Scorsese had just made, *Mean Streets*. He told me the director had given him, Peter, the sole distribution rights for Britain, and he invited me to a private showing in Soho's Wardour Street. When I arrived at the screening theatre, a small fifty-seat affair, Hayden was waiting with a tall, leggy, rather beautiful brunette. He introduced her as Stefanie, told me she was a model for Patrick Litchfield and was featured in *Vogue* that very month. I was, of course, duly impressed. He then sat us together in the front row and walked out. I'd recently started to smoke cigars again and, as the film was starting, I offered her one, jokingly, but she accepted it without turning a hair. There we were, two people who had never met, sitting side by side in an otherwise completely empty cinema, watching an American gangster film whilst both smoking large King Edward cigars. It was all quite incongruous.

Peter returned when the film finished. 'Did you like it?' he asked. 'Isn't it just like all the Stratford boys? "Naughty Boy" Crispin? Frankie the "Whale" and all the rest?'

It was true - there was certainly a lot of resemblance to the characters, thieves and layabouts who haunted the local snooker hall. I was a bit annoyed with him, though. 'Why did you leave us like that, two strangers? It was embarrassing!' I said.

'I've seen it too many times and I thought you'd like some company,' came his explanation, given with an exaggerated wink. Of course, I daren't mention to Shirley I'd had the company of a beautiful young woman with whom I'd sat in the dark all afternoon.

Scorsese obviously went from strength to strength whilst Peter meanwhile asked me to write down material for a film idea he wanted to produce about the villains and gangsters of the East End, but I only saw him once more, when he staggered into the pub one night, again with Stefanie, both seeming worse for wear and falling about because of drink, drugs, or both, I don't know. I didn't particularly enjoy their company. Apart from a phone call to tell me he was now dating Susannah York and that he'd be bringing her into the pub on his next visit to discuss our film project, I never heard from him again.

Another Puddings customer and friend who *did* get to finish a film about London villains was Bill Curbishley, brother of my late-friend Alfie and older brother of Alan, the football manager. When Bill became manager of the Who, this opened up a whole new world for him, and, amongst other things, he produced the film *McVicar*, starring the group's singer Roger Daltrey as the intellectual hard man and constant escapee, John McVicar. Shirley and me, along with Alfie and his wife, Pat, were invited to the world premiere in the West End. We both wore tuxedos - Alfie's was white - and our wives looked glamorous enough to be film stars. We climbed out of the taxi outside the cinema and were innocently walking towards its entrance when, to our surprise, there was sudden frantic cheering, clapping and shouting, and then, just as suddenly, an eerie silence. No one in the large crowd knew who these four people were, walking along the red carpet. It was very embarrassing.

After the film - an exciting but noisy thriller - we went along to the Arts Club, a beautiful, huge, period house in Mayfair. The place was packed and had a fantastic atmosphere. Bill introduced me to Adam Faith, one of the film's stars, and to

American actor Roy Scheider, plus I bumped into lots of old boxers and East End faces, such as Billy Walker and Henry Cooper. Alfie and I left our wives to mingle with the celebrities and managed to find a little room where we could enjoy a quiet drink and a catch up. And who should wander in to join us but Ian Hendry, an actor famous for his fondness for drink. He was a charming man, and we thoroughly enjoyed his company, but it was many hours later before we were finally able to escape as he insisted on ordering bottle after bottle of champagne every time we tried to leave. By the end, Hendry could barely even stand, yet I still managed to drive us all home, if not quite sober, quite capable, or so I thought.

McVicar also featured another of our best customers 'upstairs' over the years, Billy Murray. Billy was a very promising amateur boxer born in a tough part of Canning Town. He overcame his difficult background to become a highly successful actor and film producer. Early in his acting career, he appeared in some classic British films of the '60s, such as *Poor Cow*, *Performance* and *Up The Junction*. In later years, he established himself as a regular visitor to England's front rooms, with leading roles in TV series, such as *The Bill* and *Eastenders*. More recently, the younger generation have become familiar with him as the voice of Captain John Price in *Call of Duty: Modern Warfare*.

Although in his early days of visiting 'upstairs' he and Kenny had some differences from time to time and the odd skirmish would ensue, they became and remain great friends, and still meet occasionally to enthral others with tales of their youthful derring-do. Billy is very loyal to his roots.

THE HAMMERS

Football, especially when played by West Ham United, was also a big factor in our lives. Andrew, my eldest, was obsessed with them, and drove Shirley and me mad with his continual references to Bobby Moore, Geoff Hurst, and Martin Peters. They were a great team to support in those days because their football was a joy. Ron Greenwood, their manager, had a philosophy that they should be entertaining, that skill must not be sacrificed for the dour and boring defensive game that was prevalent in a lot of English football. Even when they lost, it was with more style than any other club - not for nothing were they referred to as the 'Academy'.

One of our best ever nights was when the Hammers won the FA Cup in 1964. We were so busy on that Saturday night I don't know how we coped, even though I'd sent out an SOS and got as many extra staff as I could. It was all hands on deck.

The sheer joy of everyone in the borough was so intense and, in one way, unexpected: people danced in the streets, danced on top of cars, kissed and embraced complete strangers, and drank and drank and drank. There were no licensed late-night venues then, but people carried on partying in their homes and in the streets. All the roads of the entire area seemed to be full of revelry. In the pub that night, the band had to play 'I'm Forever Blowing Bubbles' every other number, but everyone was nice to each other and there were no fights. I can't remember the takings, but it was a record for the pub, and our beer sales had never been so high.

I was also expecting an extra busy Sunday because the club's victory parade was due to pass the pub at 12.30pm. I had one of our top bands, the Washington DCs, playing, and I laid on extra staff. All my family turned up - my dad, Uncle John, father-in-law Joe, brother-in-law Tommy - and every friend I had in East London came along, all hoping to get a grandstand view of Bobby Moore and his heroes. The side streets and main roads were absolutely thronged with masses of men, women and children. It was shoulder-to-shoulder outside and, because of the crowd, Stratford's Broadway had shrunk to just enough room for the team bus to drive along. All other traffic was either diverted or simply stopped, with the occupants getting out of their cars to watch the spectacle. Every customer was outside on the Broadway, including me and my family, except for Shirley who, in between preparing the Sunday roast, sat outside on the flat part of our roof and watched from there. The crowds stretched in all directions. Kenny and I had Andrew and Matthew on our shoulders, and we waited and waited. What I hadn't anticipated was that the roads would be so clogged that, instead of the expected 12.30pm arrival, it was almost 2pm before the bus, slow as a snail, hove into view following an almighty roar from the crowd. It was the loudest cheering in East London since the end of the war. It was an open-top bus, and the players were waving and smiling to everyone, although I noticed that a lot of them were blowing kisses and waving in the direction of my roof. It was Shirley they were waving and smiling at! It was on this day she became a real West Ham fan.

The trouble was the pub was empty till 2pm when we were supposed to close. After a lot of urging by my customers - 'Surely on *this* day of all days the police won't nick you?', I remember Terry Murphy saying - I did stay open an extra hour, and a lot of men went home very late for their Sunday lunch. We took another small fortune, and if I could have stayed open

West Ham's FA Cup victory parade through Stratford Broadway in 1964. If you look closely you can see Andrew and Matthew on the shoulders of Kenny and me. (photographer unknown)

all day I would have paid for my summer holiday, the staff bonuses, and all of our new clothes for the year. It's hard to comprehend nowadays when everything seems so lax quite how strict the police could be, especially towards me and Kenny. I was on a main road in full view of everyone, and I did take a chance, but it was a happy, glorious day - one that remained in the memory of all who there.

Winning the FA Cup was a tonic the area desperately needed. The euphoria lasted for many weeks afterwards.

Generally, if the Hammers had a good season, we seemed to have a good year. We always took an extra few bob if they won. The West Ham fans - and most of my male customers were Hammers supporters - all seemed nice people. There *was* hooliganism in those days, but it never seemed to affect the pub. They were all good-natured, if a bit boisterous, after a win. If they did get a bit out of hand, a few words from me would always calm them down.

Andrew talked incessantly of West Ham and their Holy Trinity of Moore, Hurst and Peters. Just before he was due to start a new school, he had to go into hospital to have his appendix removed, but he caught an infection and was quite ill and was off school for six weeks.

I was friendly with a rather fat, jovial, blustery customer named Eddie Green. He was the spitting image of TV's Monty Modlin. He was also Booby Moore's wife Tina's stepfather, and ran Bobby's sports shop at Upton Park. When Andrew was recovering and on the mend, Eddie insisted on taking us both round the football ground. Of course, Andrew was 'over the moon'.

It was a weekday, so not a lot was going on. During the tour we met Clyde Best - one of the first black footballers in Britain - and Eddie introduced us to the physio, the ground staff, and an ex-goalkeeper, and Andrew was taking it all in avidly.

We followed, Eddie led, and barging into the physio treatment room there, completely naked and looking - quite rightly - very annoyed was Geoff Hurst. Andrew's eyes, already wide with excitement, almost popped out of his head. Eddie Green, not noticing Geoff's annoyance, blithely went ahead and introduced us.

Andrew, at the time eleven years old and looking quite pale and thin after his illness, couldn't take his eyes off the footballer who had hastily gotten dressed. After Geoff had greeted Eddie Green, rather curtly, he shook hands warmly with me, and then proceeded to talk to my son in the nicest, most charming way. He asked him all about his own football prowess, what he wanted to do when he was older, gave him an autograph, and couldn't have been nicer. I thought then - and still do - what a wonderful sportsman Hurst was and, like my son, I became a fan.

Over the years, I'd often take the kids to Upton Park to watch the team in action. A lot of the West Ham players were also regular drinkers in the Puddings or went to our nightclub upstairs. They were a really nice bunch of lads and never caused any trouble at all. Harry Redknapp even met his lovely wife Sandra there. But, in these days of paparazzi and continual media monitoring, I suppose the modern-day player is not really allowed out so regularly or conspicuously, especially to pubs as raucous as the Two Puddings was.

One of my barmen, Ivan Foot, who became my accountant many years later, said he was friendly with a seventeen year old playing for West Ham, and that this kid was so good it wouldn't be long before he was in the Hammers' first team and was also a certainty for England. I told Ivan to bring him in to meet me, which he did. He was a smart, well turned-out young lad who only drank soft drinks. He seemed more studious and shy than his teammates. His name was Trevor Brooking and, over the coming years, he would often drop in for his customary glass of cola or ginger beer. After I was no longer living above the pub, I would still see Trevor now and again, and he always greeted me warmly by name, even though he'd now become very famous, playing for England. A few years after he'd retired I went into a well-known men's fashion shop, JG's in Loughton, whose owner was a friend of mine, and Trevor was in there. My friend Jimmy started to introduce me but I interrupted saying, 'I know Trevor,' and went to shake hands with him and ask if he still saw our mutual friend, Ivan, but he just looked completely blank, stepped backwards, and said he didn't know an Ivan and had never met me before, and even when I mentioned the Puddings, he insisted he didn't even know the pub! Maybe seeing someone out of context threw him off or, more probably, being such a well-known person and having to cope with meeting thousands of people over the years, maybe he just didn't remember people from his past, but it seemed quite odd and I felt quite embarrassed in front of Jimmy.

Someone who hasn't forgotten me is Alan Curbishley, who was often touted as a future England manager, and I often met him when he was younger and still playing football. Whenever I bump into him he's always friendly and greets me warmly, as does Frank Lampard senior, another former customer and great player for West Ham. Later on, I became good friends with Mark Ward and his attractive wife Jane. He was a lovely lad and a superb player for one of West Ham's best teams since the glory days of the '60s, and was often touted for England. Shirley and I used to go to their house in Loughton where Mark would cook us his delicious speciality Steak Diane.

The Puddings even had its own football team, captained by Kenny. It wasn't in a regular league but was made up of customers and friends who, after a hard Saturday night's boozing, were prepared to struggle out of a warm bed early Sunday morning and play over Wanstead flats. Afterwards, they'd head back to the pub for cheese and biscuits, pickled herrings, and yet more booze. Our opponents were mainly other scratch teams from local pubs. Once a year, Kenny would switch sides and we'd play his Lotus nightclub, with his side mainly comprising security staff. They only had one man behind the bar there, the rest were girls, so Kenny was obliged to play for them, which meant I had to turn out for the pub. Despite great rivalry and the Lotus 'Bouncers' being big, mean, bad-tempered and strong, our overall skill was generally too much for them, and we often managed to hand them a thrashing.

One memorable match was Newham Publicans versus Newham Vicars. This was in aid of charity and was held at the Macmillan Stadium, Canning Town. Harry Redknapp was the referee, and our team had former boxing champion Joe Lucy as one of our leading players, as well as ex-boxer Terry Murphy and another ex-Hammer, Brian Dear. The vicars proved surprisingly strong, enthusiastic and brave, and actually scored first, but it was Kenny scoring a clever hat trick and raising cheers from the crowd that achieved a win for the publicans with a score of 5-2.

Football served us well over the years. It was only later that landlords would be forced to close up rather than allow hordes of drunken football supporters take over their pubs. Thankfully, we never had that problem then.

In these modern times, sport seems to dwarf anything we had in the past. Boxing has lost a lot of popularity, but football is now the biggest thing on the planet for many people - and, consequently, pubs have to choose between being a 'Sports Bar', with the attendant large screens, bouncers on the door, ticketed events, and large licensing fees to Sky, or a 'normal' pub showing Emmerdale Farm on an old telly in the corner and serving the odd sandwich. The 'sports bar' sells huge amounts of lager and take lots of money, is male-dominated and aggressive in atmosphere, with many of them, when not hosting sports events, having comedy nights with non-PC comedians spouting near-racist or anti-feminist jokes, which all the 'lads' love. If this is the future, take me back to the past!

THE QUIET HERO

Two years after West Ham won the FA Cup, England won the World Cup. Another bonanza, but this time nation-wide. The streets, all over the country, were full of people dancing and cheering. It was a huge boost for everyone, most notably Prime Minister Harold Wilson, as many people reckoned it helped Labour win the next election. Pubs were mobbed as people who hadn't even been out of doors for months came out to drink. The country received a massive fillip, and London itself felt like the centre of the world in 1966.

Norman, who was one of my most trusted barmen and never told a lie, swore to God that, shortly after we opened, in the early evening on the *very* day that England won the World Cup, and when everyone in the country was still recovering from the draining intensity of that emotional, roller-coaster final, who should walk into the pub, order a pint, and quietly drink by himself whilst leaning against the bar but Jack Charlton. He was unaccompanied and so unassuming that Norman was struck dumb, and felt too shy to congratulate him on England's victory.

Over forty years later, I was fortunate enough to meet 'Big' Jack socially, and asked if it was true. He replied, 'God knows!' But I *was* in that area though as I'd arranged to meet a mate from Leytonstone, but I couldn't say for sure where I went first or where I finished up.' I believe the story is true because it is a

'Big Ed' with 'Big Jack', who was spotted enjoying a pint in the Puddings a few hours after winning the World Cup with England in '66.
(photograph by Joanne Brooks)

matter of record that Jack left his team mates to go and celebrate with his own mates as his wife Pat was heavily pregnant and hadn't made the trip down the London to be with the other players' wives. It was also typical of Big Jack, as he proved to be his own man so many times - both as a player and a manager. These days, of course, he would be mobbed - that is, if he'd been allowed to leave the main party in the first place.

Today, everything is so micro-managed, right down to the tiniest detail. A player of that status, on such an occasion, would not be allowed out of sight without his bodyguards and agents following him, even to the toilet, demanding payments for photographs and autographs from all and sundry. In the unlikely event we ever did win another world cup, you can guarantee David and Samantha Cameron (or whoever) will be right up front, closely followed by the likes of Ken Livingstone or Boris Johnson, all sharpened elbows, all claiming their share of reflected glory. In comparison, it all seemed so natural and spontaneous back then.

THE RING

Back in the '40s and '50s when I was growing up, my generation didn't go into pubs so much. Going dancing, to the pictures or to youth clubs was what most youngsters did. There were no nightclubs for our generation, no drugs, and very little drink. Many of us belonged to a club - mainly boys' clubs, but that was the way it was in those days.

The most popular activities were boxing and football, but most sports seemed to get a look in, including running at various distances, table tennis, and swimming. Most of these clubs had a full membership.

I belonged to Eton Manor first. It was named after Eton College, whose old boys came to the East End to help the poor. It was boys only and you could only join between the ages of fourteen and sixteen. You had to go in front of their committee to be 'vetted', and once a member you had to keep up your attendance and do a minimum of activities and training, otherwise you were up before the committee again. Our secretary was a serious looking man called George Jackson. I never once saw him smile, and so it was nerve-wracking to stand before him and the committee. Because of the abundance of clubs, most of the boys I knew did boxing training, even if they never kept it up in the long-run.

A few of the clubs were the Crown and Manor, Brady Street Boys' Club, Hoxton Manor, Fairburn House, the Fisher, and West Ham Boys, which was solely boxing and who Kenny boxed for. These clubs were such a big thing in boys' lives. Eton Manor seemed the best equipped; they had the boxing, table tennis, and indoor activities at Riseholme Street in Hackney. The gym had four boxing rings and plenty of punch bags and punch balls, lots of trainers, and produced many amateur champions. Their outdoor grounds, the Wilderness at Temple Mills, was a huge space - must have been 30-40 acres - enclosed by a high wall. It had football pitches, cricket pitches, cricket nets, squash courts, a little swimming pool known as the 'splash', a canteen, and even had a little stadium with stands for the main football team. Its remains now lie buried beneath the new Olympic site.

The Repton, on the other hand, was much more free and easy. They had lots of female members, a lovely, friendly secretary called George Dessert, and a little gym, albeit with only one ring and limited equipment. They played records in the tea area, and they held dances sometimes. And yet they produced just as many - if not more - champions than most.

I think some of the clubs may even still be going but, of course, youngsters have such a huge choice nowadays that memberships have dwindled, and youth clubs are under-funded and not as disciplined as they once were. It was a wonderful local resource, and something that's badly missed today.

Boxing might be a minority sport now, but up till the '50s and '60s, it was flourishing. I - and practically everyone I knew - did some sort of boxing. It was a popular sport, and many of the boxers had huge followings and, like today's footballers, were quite celebrated. Men such as Ron Barton and, later, Billy Walker were often in the tabloids as much for their looks as their ability. I was very friendly with a lot of well-known boxers over the years, many of whom were regular customers in the Puddings. Bobby Davies, Phil Lundgren, Terry Murphy, Billy Walker, Patsy Gutteridge, Roy and Danny Enifer, Ronnie Redrup, Terry Gill and Terry Brown all came in the pub quite regularly. Davie Sammons, a good heavyweight, and his pretty wife Hannah had their marriage celebrations in the Puddings, and Shirley and I became such close friends that we regularly spent our nights off with them, one of our favourite haunts being 'Annie's Room' a jazz club run by Annie Ross and Kenny Lynch. Ronnie Gilbert, a mate from the docks and another ex-boxer turned fairground prize-fighter, also became a regular who, along with his wife Maureen, became good friends who we spent evenings out with. Robbie Cameron, who I've known for many, many years, was a champion amateur boxer and along with his wife Betty, remains a good friend to this day and, as they now live fairly close to me in Suffolk, Robbie has become a regular golfing partner.

One afternoon another mate from the docks, Terry Lawless and his wife, Sylvie, came in seeking my advice. They'd decided they wanted to become publicans. At the time, Terry had a couple of 'swag shops' in Leytonstone, which were doing quite well. He had started to devote a lot of time to boxing, and he seemed to think a pub would give him more time. I really must have had the 'ump that day, though, as I soon disillusioned both of them. I gave them a litany of what was wrong with such a role - the continual fights, long hours, aggressive customers, the difficulty of finding reliable cleaners or bar staff - and, as a result, they decided the hospitality business wasn't for them after all. Terry went on to become a very successful boxing manager, looking after several world champions, including Maurice Hope and John H. Stracey, as well as Frank Bruno. They seemed a lovely couple to me. When his boxers first turned pro', Terry never took a penny from them. He and his wife, Sylvie, looked after them like a mum and dad; she cooking them big steaks and generally keeping a watchful and motherly eye on them.

Sammy McCarthy came in the pub occasionally, and although not a regular, I was always delighted to see him. He won the British featherweight title in 1954, and was known all over London as 'Smiling' Sammy. One of my favourite people of all time, he was - and is - a true gentleman in all of its meaning.

THE BABY FACED ASSASSIN

Another one of my favourite people - and another ex-customer of the Puddings - was Terry Spinks. After winning an Olympic gold medal, and under Sammy's guidance, he also became a British champion. Shirley and I went out with Terry and his wife, Val, a few times, and he was recognised everywhere we went, never turning anyone away, always having a little chat or giving an autograph. Spinks became quite ill many years later, and was in a bad way in hospital, when his cousin, Rosemary, who had worshipped him when she was a schoolgirl, went to see him and was so shocked that she and her husband Terry took him into their home, where they cared for him until he died in April of 2012.

I remember them popping in to see me at the Woodman near Ongar - a pub I owned at that time - and, after reminiscing for a while as we hadn't seen each other for many years, I was shocked to find out that, since winning his title at Melbourne in 1956, Terry was the *only* British Olympic gold medallist who had never received any sort of recognition for his exploits. This seemed an absolute disgrace to me. Nowadays, it seems that anyone who wins anything at all in Britain is showered with so many honours their legs buckle under the weight. Can you imagine the honours that will be bestowed upon any British winners at the grotesquely over-commercialised games of London 2012? Yet Spinks had gone all the way to Melbourne, as a last-minute choice, and had shocked the boxing world with his grace, skill, and superb boxing ability to win the flyweight title - and all at barely eighteen!

I ran a big charity night at the Puddings for Terry. Lots of old fighters came, including Bobby Neill, Sammy, of course, the Lazarus family, Ronnie Cooper, who fought for England in the

1948 Olympics and who still spars up with anyone who dares look at him, Brian Hall, Billy Walker, Terry Murphy, Charlie Magri, all the Bowers family, and many, many others.

Tony Banks, the late-Labour MP, came and gave me a bottle of Houses of Parliament whisky to auction. Tom Johnston, the famous cartoonist of the *Daily Mirror*, came and gave a drawing to auction. Kenny Lynch, the entertainer, an old friend of Spinks, also dropped by. The night was a huge success and raised quite a lot of money.

Afterwards, I wrote to many MPs, including Tony Banks, and to many newspapers and appropriate awards committee, the letters forcibly expressing my dismay at the disgrace of it all. I even nominated Terry to the awards committee myself. Various noted sportswriters eventually took up the cudgels on his behalf and, while on holiday in France, completely by chance, I met prominent Labour MP Tony McNulty, who promised he would try and do something for us.

A momentum started to grow and, after a lot of pressure and lobbying, Terry was *finally* awarded the MBE in the year of the millennium. It somehow seemed appropriate. He had a big party celebrating that and his birthday at the York Hall in Bethnal Green, for which many thousands turned up, but unfortunately they couldn't all get in! Wembley Stadium would have been a better venue. Who finally approved it no one knows but without my campaign he may never have been honoured.

Although it's denied by everyone, including Rosemary and the family, I firmly believe Spinks was never given an honour because of his association with certain East End people. Terry never, ever turned down any plea to help anyone or any charity. Until the last months of his life he would turn up to give prizes at all sorts of events connected with boxing and never asked for a penny. Once or twice, the Krays asked him to boxing functions. He innocently had photos taken with them - they loved their photos being taken with celebrities. It had all seemed perfectly harmless to Terry, but I believe the powers that be take note of such things and act accordingly. Nothing else makes much sense.

Terry, despite his medical condition, with the devoted help of Rosemary and her husband along with Sammy McCarthy, still went to the London Ex-Boxers Association until the last few months of his life. Up until the end he still seemed to me the same baby-face cherub who went to Australia in 1956 and stunned the world by winning his gold medal with style and verve at a time when Britain badly needed a boost.

The Mayoress of Newham, Terry Spinks and me at our Puddings charity night for the champion boxer. (photograph by Leslie R. Brand)

Tommy Christian, JD, Kenny and Peter.
(photograph by Alf Shead)

THE DEVIL'S KITCHEN

THE FIGHTS

Life in the Puddings wasn't all spend, spend, spend. Despite the obvious financial rewards, the stress and aggravation used to get me down. In fact, just writing about the violence, even after all these years, still makes me feel a bit depressed, and is the least enjoyable part of reminiscing. Yet it was a major part of life in the Puddings, and so it's important at least some of the characters and incidents involved are mentioned, as well as some general background on the subject.

In the '60s, the crowd in the pub was young and very lively, and although violence and drunkenness wasn't as generally widespread across Britain's towns and cities then, there was certainly enough of it in and around East London to keep us occupied, especially at weekends when our nightclub above the pub was in full swing.

Because the Puddings had some notoriety, we'd often have to deal with various nuisances showing up, trying to enhance their reputations. Recently, I was going down memory lane with Peter, Kenny and Michael, and we were amazed at just how much trouble we did have to deal with when we added it all up. Peter also mentioned that, when he was managing the pub in the '70s, he became friendly with a policeman who confessed that, whenever trouble broke out in the Puddings, the police would just watch it from the safety of a shop doorway on the opposite side of the Broadway as they were too nervous to come over and break it up themselves! Only after the trouble had been dealt with by the Puddings' staff and minders would they wander across and make their appearance.

THE GANGS

During the war - and for almost a decade after - the Black Market thrived owing to the strict rationing imposed on Britain until 1953 and for ten years after that. As a result of various 'export drives' and the scarcity of foreign currency, luxury goods were in very short supply. In these conditions, crooks and thieves thrived; it provided an opportunity beyond their dreams. Every area had its gangs, comprising thieves, burglars, safe-breakers, etc., many of whom were deserters from the services and who therefore couldn't get a straight job even if they wanted to. The Upton Park Mob seemed to control the Plaistow, Canning Town, Stratford areas, and they had some notorious heavies, such as Porky Bennett, Teddy Machin, Georgie 'Woodbine' Wood, Jackie Reynolds, etc. Their headquarters was the 'Queens' pub in Green Street, not far from West Ham's football ground.

There were the 'Elephant Boys' from the Elephant & Castle, a gang that 'Mad' Frankie Fraser was associated with. North London had the 'Angel' team dominated by the Nash family. The self-styled governor of all these was Soho-based Billy Hill, who had heavies like Bobby Ramsey and George Walker working for him, and who once boasted that he could put 300 men on the street. His great and envious rival was Jack Spot, so called because he was always 'on the spot' when trouble occurred. His real name was Jack Comer, and he was toppled from his pretender's position when he had a gory knife fight in the street with Albert Dimes from Clerkenwell. Known as Italian Albert, he was Billy Hill's right-hand man, and eventually came off best. Jack Spot eased himself off the scene. He was last heard of working in the Wall's sausage factory in West London.

The Krays became prominent and were well known in South and North London, as well as their native East End. They helped Billy Hill out when he had trouble in some of his clubs, although there are feasible theories that the brothers engineered the trouble in the first place. When the Krays became too powerful, Billy Hill went into exile to Tangier, where he apparently lived a contented life.

Over time, the Krays made many enemies, amongst them the Richardson family, with whom Frankie Fraser was closely associated. Like most feuds, it ended in violence; shootings and murder at Mr Smith's nightclub in Catford and the Blind Beggar in Whitechapel, leading to arrests, imprisonment, and the break-up of some of the gangs.

THE GREAT POTATO RAID

JD was an old friend who I'd known since he was sixteen. He was about 5'9", quite thickset, inclined towards pudginess, with dark, heavily Brylcreemed hair, dark eyebrows, and who rarely smiled - except in the company of good friends, which made him quite intimidating to people who never knew him. In fact, even people who knew him were slightly nervous in his company. He was fastidious in his dress, always wearing beautifully tailored suits and expensive, highly polished shoes, which he kept on lasts. He'd done some boxing, like most of his close friends, some of whom, such as Jimmy Daly, Ronnie Gilbert and Jackie Bowers, were fairly successful professionals, but when he was younger, JD always seemed to get into street fights, and somehow or other, people seemed to get offended by him, and it was often a 'straight-up' outside. In fact, he was such a nuisance that I recruited him to be my fellow minder when we were running the Big Beat club upstairs at the Puddings, otherwise we would have had to bar him.

This was some time before I became the licensee and we'd been running the dancehall upstairs very successfully for about six months. Everything was going great, and we were so packed that, if the fire brigade or the council had actually checked the amount of people, the licensee would have been sacked. Being young and cocky we, of course, ignored all the rules. I remember Harry Alden, the governor of the pub before the Quills bought it, asking anxiously how many customers we had on a Friday night. 'I'm only licensed for one hundred and fifty, and you look so crowded,' he had said. I reassured him by saying, 'We are getting near the limit, Harry. There's about one hundred and forty. I won't let anymore in tonight.' I didn't dare tell him the full truth: we had almost four hundred in.

During the day, upstairs was quite a nice restaurant. There were two posh waitresses, Edith and Maisy, both of whom served big dinners, real English trencher fare, roasts, pies and puddings, all freshly cooked - no freezers or frozen chips in those days, and certainly no microwaves! There was the famous market across the road at Angel Lane, along which was an excellent butcher and fishmonger. Cooking was done by Kit, who'd been at the pub since the war. She was superb.

One Friday night, someone had left a hundredweight bag of King Edwards potatoes for Kit in the lobby, sat between the kitchen and the men's toilets. A little 'firm' from Canning Town happened to be in that night and were having a good drink. There was JD, Jimmy Clark, Billy Burns, Jimmy Daly, Terry Herring and a few others. One of them found the bag and decided it might be fun if they pelted all the boys and girls enjoying their dancing with spuds.

Whilst me, Kenny, Peter Ferdinando and Johnny Bruce were standing at the entrance, there came a sudden rush of people, packed tightly together, all screaming, shouting and pushing, with the boys just as eager to get out as the girls. The throng was so tightly packed that two old-fashioned hat and coat stands, still with hats and coats on their hooks, were carried along with the crowd. Everyone was screaming 'Get down! Get down!' and I noticed one of our regulars - a self-styled hard man who called himself 'Nutter' Murphy and who wore sovereign rings on each finger and was covered in tattoos - was shrieking in a near falsetto voice, 'Help! Help! Please don't shoot me! Let me through!' as he elbowed past, shoving his girlfriend out of the way and who stared at him in horror as she realised he wasn't the tough protector she thought he was. Bernie, our DJ, was lying on the floor behind his equipment. Kenny, Peter and myself finally forced our way against the surging tidal wave of bodies, and reached the end of the dancehall, only to find there, by the bar, JD and his little gang laughing their heads off and still pelting our customers with potatoes. Somehow we managed to stop them and, although Kenny was absolutely raving and wanted to smash into them, I knew them and their reputation, and so it all finished a bit strained but eventually good humoured enough, with customers slowly drifting back in, all talking about what had happened. Someone was convinced a gun was being fired, had screamed it out and that had caused the panic. Fortunately, no one was hurt, and it even became quite a talking point for many years and a matter of some pride if you'd been there on the night of 'the great potato raid'! The only customer that I never saw again was 'Nutter' Murphy, which was a shame as I enjoyed his lurid tales of how he terrorised Dagenham.

The upshot was that, after talking to Kenny, I asked JD to be my number two in the dance hall. He proved the perfect man. Kenny, Johnny Bruce and Peter would stay on the door, and JD and me would stand at the bar downing bottle after bottle of Guinness. We had very little trouble, and when there was any it seemed to be all over in minutes. Such trouble was normally just a bit of jealousy - one bloke talking to another's girl, that sort of thing.

Jimmy Clarke, Jimmy Daly, me, Jimmy Grant and JD in the Big Beat Club.
(photograph by Alf Shead)

THE WEDDING

Around this time, in the early '60s, Kenny and me were asked to our friend Jimmy Clark's wedding. Jimmy was a very good welterweight, and despite being an amateur, he was sparring with pros and knocking them over one by one. He was one of JD's best mates, and he worked on the door with us sometimes too. Everyone from Canning Town went to the wedding, which was quite a boisterous affair, but Kenny and I couldn't go because of an urgent previous commitment, yet I often wondered whether we could have helped stop the trouble that ensued.

At the wedding reception, JD and friends, as was customary at East End weddings, got quite drunk. Another crowd, a bit younger but also drunk, were there. Both firms had bad reputations. A fight inevitably erupted and mayhem ensued. JD and company apparently came off slightly better, but reputations were at stake and the younger mob swore vengeance.

For weeks and months over the next year, the two gangs stalked one another. Sometimes a member of one side would get cornered and beaten, and then the other side would go out looking for one of the others. They were prowling the streets in cars, carrying choppers, knives and guns. It was a tense time for us at the club. I spoke to everyone on both sides and everyone respected my ruling that they stay away from the Big Beat, as it was still called.

It was very sad because most of the people involved were pretty good people who, under different circumstances, may have become good friends, but ultimately both sides hated each other with a ferocity that, in many cases, has still never dissipated.

At one point, JD was standing outside the Greengate snooker hall when a car suddenly screeched to a halt. The doors flew open and out jumped members of the opposing faction, all armed with machetes and coshes, and simply rained blows down upon his head. He was beaten unconscious and left for dead. Of course, he never said anything, but he ended up with over 38 stitches to his head and body.

They also laid siege to the house of one of JD's closest friends, breaking down the door and rushing up the passage, but the intended victim was well prepared, lying on the floor with a shotgun at the ready, and just blasted away, shooting his attacker in the face, blinding him on one side.

There were many other confrontations, all equally nasty. A member of JD's firm held a gun to a rival's head, pulled the trigger but the gun jammed. A couple of others were shot too. Of course, it couldn't go on. I was approached - along with Stevie Hegarty, a good friend of mine from the docks, and who was respected in the area - and asked if we'd go on a meet at Bianchi's Café just to see fair play and try and broker a 'truce'. Both sides knew this war was absolute madness, but neither would back down. We duly turned up, but none of the younger crowd appeared.

Eventually, although none of the main protagonists ever went to the police and most kept their mouths shut, members of both sides were nicked for affray, assault, possession of firearms, and various charges related to this feud, receiving sentences of up to eight years in prison.

The Odd Couple

In one way, JD was lucky because he was still convalescing from wounds received in action, so to speak, he avoided getting nicked. He was, however, a chastened, changed and more dangerous man.

He'd always been known for having a fight in the street; his coat would come off and outside he'd go with whoever the grievance was with. Some he won, some he lost, but no one could say he wasn't game or fair. But after he was so badly wounded in what was a surprise attack, he swore he'd never have another 'straight-up'. 'I'll always be tooled-up from now on,' he confided.

Some months later, after the feuding had ceased and most of those involved were in prison, he came to meet me upstairs for a drink. He'd packed the 'bouncers' job in when the feud was on-going, and he told me that his brother Danny had been savagely beaten at the Hammer Club in Plaistow by members of a notorious family from Upton Park, the eldest and most notorious of whom was a tall, hawk-faced man who'd been to prison for running a protection racket. There were several brothers, and apparently it was some of the younger ones who were involved in the beating of JD's brother. Danny was a huge man, looked like JD but was six foot three, had a large physique, loved a drink, and wanted to dominate whatever crowd he was with. He seemed to never fear anyone, was very outspoken, and consequently always seemed to be rowing with someone or other. But on this particular night he was surrounded, and they gave him a thorough beating; punching, kicking and taunting him. It was a liberty because, for all his faults, Danny really was a good-hearted man, always willing to shake hands with people even after the worst of rows.

I told JD it was best to leave it. 'I dare say,' I said, 'Danny had a lot to drink and insulted them. You know what he can be like.' I knew as I was talking I was wasting my time. 'Anything I can do,' I said, 'I'll make one if you like' - which meant I'd go with him if he went after them. JD was almost my family in importance, and I was quite willing to go along with him. He never answered. He often left questions unanswered. One never knew exactly what he was thinking.

A week later, on a Monday morning, someone picked me up outside my flat in Wood Street - this all happened shortly before I lived above the Puddings - to give me a lift to work. 'Have you heard about the shooting at the Hammer Club?' he said. 'It's all in the *Mirror*.' As he was talking, I knew it could only be JD.

The *Daily Mirror* had bold, black headlines:

'MAD DOG GUNMAN ON LOOSE IN LONDON!' There followed a description of JD and another man who'd shown up at the Hammer Club, shot and wounded two men, stabbed and slashed another couple, and then disappeared into the night.

A police manhunt had been initiated.

The other man was a young, most unlikely looking villain known as 'Sykes'. He was a mild-mannered, very courteous, and personable man. He wore suits from Savile Row and Sulka Ties from Bond Street. I liked him very much. Sykes' usual partner, also very well dressed, was someone who avoided the limelight and tried to keep well in the background. He was known as 'Boater'. I liked him very much too, and really enjoyed their company - provided it was in a relaxed atmosphere and away from other villains, that is, otherwise there was too much tension because they always seemed alert and on-guard. Sykes would never let anyone get too near him; he would back away slightly and would always position himself so he could clearly see any doors so that no one could get behind him. They both worked with the Krays and used to collect any dues the twins thought they were owed by the various crooks in the area. If those two turned up looking for someone, that person knew they were in very deep trouble unless they paid up very fast.

A discrete flat was arranged for JD and Sykes by their business associates. Whilst in 'hiding' they dressed like city gents, complete with bowler hats and umbrellas. I used to speak to JD on the phone and pass on messages to his mum, telling her he was okay. The flat was in Knightsbridge, and they lived like the 'odd couple'. JD said the worst thing about being holed-up with Sykes was his strict insistence on etiquette, making sure they ate soup with the correct spoons, ensuring all cutlery was laid out in the correct positions on the starched white tablecloth, buying only the finest wines from Fortnum and Mason, drinking out of cut glass goblets from Harrods, always insisting they wore a jacket and tie for dinner. The food, by the standards of the '60s, was very exotic: tinned snails, pheasant pate, smoked salmon. JD would wearily complain down the phone that he was dying for his mum's grub.

After some months, their business associates had apparently 'straightened out' the family from Upton Park. JD gave himself up at the police station and went on an ID parade. The victims said it was definitely *not* him, and so out he walked a free man.

This made JD a well-known name throughout the East End and, although I didn't know it at the time, shortly before I was granted the licence for the Puddings, he made it his mission to seek out all the local troublemakers in the area and tell them they were barred from the pub. It had an amazing effect. I don't think there was a fight in the Puddings for nearly nine months, which was a record.

JD was fastidious in his dress and wore beautifully tailored suits and expensive, highly polished shoes. (photograph by Eddie Johnson)

THE DRIVE

A week before I was due to go to court for the Puddings' license, JD turned up at my flat in Walthamstow and asked if I could borrow Johnny Prentice's car so we could all go and pick up our mate Boater from prison and take him home. In those days, not everyone had a car. We turned up at the Puddings and asked Johnny, but he refused; full of apologies, he said he wasn't insured for any other drivers. It was probably an excuse - and I couldn't blame him as he hardly knew JD, and he was the one who was going to drive. A bit crestfallen, we went on to the local snooker hall, where I spotted Charlie Vickery, an acquaintance I didn't know too well, yet he had no hesitation in handing over the keys to his big black Humber Snipe, which was ideal for us. At this time, JD had quite a reputation in East London, and Vickery was probably a bit too nervous to refuse, but it was still nice of him.

We made our way to Jimmy Clark's house at Forest Gate to pick him up, along with Jackie Bowers. Jimmy had been quite ill with a mysterious wasting illness that the doctors at the time found quite baffling. He couldn't eat anything without being sick, and from being the most promising amateur fighter in East London - eight straight knockout victories and talk of him representing England - he'd become quite weak and ill. He always had a pocketful of salted peanuts, as he said it was the only food he could keep down.

When I was in Whipps Cross Hospital, being treated for TB, Jimmy was also there under observation in a different part of the hospital, where they would weigh him every couple of days, trying to get his bodyweight up. 'Been weighed yet, Jim?' I'd say to him.

'Yeah,' he'd answer, with a mischievous grin, 'but I put stones in my dressing gown, I'm putting an extra one in the pockets every day, so me weight's going up. I'll be out soon.'

We'd arrived at Jimmy's place and, inside, as I was kneeling down admiring some of the many books that lined his shelves, I felt something cold and hard pressed against my neck. I slowly turned around and it was JD wielding a huge revolver, 'stick 'em up or I'll blow your head off!' he said, laughing manically.

I went mad. 'Is that loaded?!' I shouted, and when he nodded I berated him, 'Don't be so fucking stupid! Never, ever point a gun at anyone unless you mean to shoot them!' Someone had died playing Russian roulette in my army regiment, and another friend of mine had been nearly killed when a Bren gun on fixed lines had slipped and mown him across the chest. I was very wary and respectful of guns. I didn't even like to possess one, and when I did I'd always made sure the bullets were in a hidden place away from the revolver.

It was still sunny and warm when we left Jimmy's flat, and we were all in high spirits after collecting Boater from the Scrubs as, being a Friday, we were looking forward to a great evening of celebration.

There were five of us in this big black car driving through the city, and if you wanted to cast the 'Wild Bunch', it would have been hard to find a better five. Jackie Bowers, with his flat nose, looked as hard as iron; JD looked like a cross between Edward G. Robinson and Neville Brand; Jimmy Clarke, although quite emaciated, looked even crazier than usual; Boater, sitting in the back, was quiet, bulky and menacing; and me, I suppose, big with a flat nose nearly as broke as Jackie's. We must have looked a tasty lot. Suddenly, we were 'belled'; no sirens in those days but the police were signalling for us to stop. They overtook us, slowing to a halt, and forced us to a standstill.

In the early-1960s, a month never went by without some daring bank robbery. The raids always took place on paydays - a Friday or Thursday. They had no barrier screens in the banks, and the tellers were vulnerable as it was quite easy for someone to jump on the counter, scream a few obscenities, wave a shotgun about, and get away with a few thousand. There was no Securicor in those days, and banks had yet to wise up on any special security measures, so the police were especially vigilant on these days.

Two coppers got out and walked slowly towards us, one holding his warrant card high for all of us to see. I looked over at JD, his face completely impassive as he instinctively, and discretely, pulled the gun from his jacket and slowly placed it under his seat, something I discovered later that anyone with a gun does automatically. I looked at the others: Jackie and Jimmy looked quite tense, but Boater seemed very relaxed, still luxuriating in his new-found freedom, no doubt - but then he never knew about the gun!

All that was going through my mind was, 'Well, that's me fucked for the pub!' The policeman asked me, as I wound my window down whilst JD just stared straight ahead, who the car belonged to. I felt a bit of an idiot as I explained it belonged to a man whose address or phone number I didn't know, but who was probably still playing snooker in Stratford. 'I haven't got the number of the snooker hall either Officer, but if you look it up I imagine he's probably still in there,' I explained whilst trying to smile nicely. The policeman just nodded. 'Well, let's look in the boot then shall we?' he said. JD got out of the car and opened the boot which, thank God, as Charlie was a bit of a thief, was completely empty.

He asked where I lived and I told him. I also explained that I was hoping to take the license of the Two Puddings the following week. He didn't seem a bad bloke; in fact, a smile hovered on his lips. He was probably thinking it was all such a ludicrous story that it must be true, and so off they walked, back to their car, and drove away.

JD whispered to me not to say anything to Boater about the gun, but we were all just so relieved the police hadn't been more concerned. If they had searched more thoroughly and found it, we would all have been nicked for 'suss' for sure, and not only wouldn't I have got the license for the pub, I may have even gone to prison.

THE SCAR

A year or so later, Boater, Sykes, Big Morrie and Lennie Alexander came into the Puddings one evening and, after a few drinks, asked me to go to the Pink Elephant with them. At the time, it was the trendiest club in the West End, and I would have loved to have gone, but I was very conscientious in those days, and said I couldn't leave the Puddings, especially on a Thursday night, which was busy, and we always tended to get a few drunks and nuisances in.

At the Pink Elephant, my friends were sitting at their table, enjoying a drink and generally having a nice time. But on an adjoining table was seated a very obnoxious type that one tends to get in certain nightclubs. In a booming voice, this man kept shouting out insults to all and sundry - real, low-life insults. Boater found this deeply offensive. It may seem odd to some people, but even though my friends were sometimes classed as gangsters, when it came to old fashion virtues, like manners and loyalty, I found them far more respectable and trustworthy than most middle-class types. But Boater did have a ferocious temper and, after being forced to endure more of this buffoon's continuous outbursts, he snapped, walked over to the neighbouring table, punched the offender from his chair, and attempted to slit his throat. He half succeeded. The obnoxious loudmouth turned out to be none other than Oliver Reed, the renowned drunk and actor, who wore the resulting facial scar for the rest of his life. I'd seen him interviewed and, of course, he told the story rather differently, making himself seem a bit of a hero, but I know who I believe, and it's certainly not Ollie.

After this fracas, they had to have it 'on their toes' and hide out for a little while until the fuss died down. No one was ever charged nor caught, despite the uproar it caused at the time. Another time, Boater was locked up in Pentonville and he'd arranged an escape attempt with two friends, which involved him having to be in the hospital so that 'Coolman' and the 'Dutchman', two of his associates, could snatch him from the ward. He'd sharpened a spoon so he could slit his own throat, just bad enough to seem like a suicide attempt whereupon, he calculated, they would rush him to hospital and his escape plan could be facilitated. The trouble was, he got completely carried away and really overdid it; the blood was pouring from his neck as if from a loosened tap, and he almost died. He lost so much blood and was so weakened that any escape was completely out of the question

Some years previously, he'd been involved with Sykes in sticking a shot gun down the trousers of a well-known East End hard man who'd been carrying on with one of their friend's wives. Boater and Sykes had swagged him outside a pub in

Stratford one night, punched him about a bit and then tried to blast off his privates, succeeding only in wounding him in the upper groin area.

When I visited Boater in Pentonville, he mentioned that their victim of that night was also locked up as he'd recently been nicked for a silver bullion robbery in Essex. I asked him if he ever said anything, but Boater laughed. 'No, but he did say that I walked like the bloke who shot him!' Anyone who saw Boater walk wouldn't forget; he was a bit flat-footed, and his walk was quite distinctive to say the least.

JD, Kenny, me, PW, Lenny Clarke and friends. (photograph by Alf Shead)

THE PUNCH

Sykes wasn't very tall, but he was compact and surprisingly strong. One night, a particularly troublesome customer - a huge, heavily muscled and tee-shirted Liverpudlian - refused to drink up, and instantly started swearing and snarling abuse when I'd asked him politely. I managed to shepherd him to the exit door, but he still carried on being abusive, glass in his hand. Sykes said, 'Take his glass, Ed.' I asked the man and tried to grab the glass, but he raised it instead as though to strike me. Sykes stepped forward and swiftly walloped the big man on the chin, swinging his right hand with such ferocity that down the man went, unconscious, before he'd even hit the floor. We left him there on the pavement and went back inside. A few minutes later Albert the potman came to see me. 'He's still out cold!' he gasped. So Albert and me dragged the huge man by his ankles a few yards and left him in the doorway of Dunn & Co. He was still there when I finally locked up the pub. We checked that he was still breathing okay and left him to sleep it off. It was such a devastating punch that I always wanted to ask Sykes if he'd used a knuckleduster.

Later on, Sykes was involved in a terrible feud with a famous boxing family from Canning Town, in which cars and even a café got blown up, and rumours abounded that he became an informer. Some members of the boxing family went to prison, as did many others, but Sykes disappeared. Someone spotted him in the Midlands many years ago, and it's rumoured he made a fortune selling plastic knives and forks to airlines. But apart from an occasional glimpse, I never saw him or spoke to him again.

THE TWINS

Wednesday was always our night off. Normally we'd go to a restaurant, sometimes a pub first to have a drink with a fellow licensee. One night Shirley and I decided to pop in to see Patsy and Cusher at the Beggars before heading off for dinner. As I pulled up outside, I saw so many blue uniforms and blue lights flashing I just drove away. We went straight to the Dick Turpin at Ilford, another favourite venue of East End publicans. The talk there was all about the shooting at Mr Smith's, a nightclub in Catford. There was quite a buzz about it, and some of the people I knew were saying, 'There's bound to be comebacks'. I didn't know till the next day that one 'comeback' had just happened. If Shirley and I had gone out half an hour earlier, we would have witnessed the shooting of George Cornell by Ronnie Kray in the saloon bar of the Blind Beggar.

I first heard of the twins when I was about seventeen. Someone mentioned that there'd been a big 'bundle' - a vogue word in the late-1940s - at the Tottenham Royal, a popular dance hall at the time, and that the Kray Twins had been involved.

Over the coming years, throughout the '50s, their names were mentioned increasingly often, usually in the context of violence; they'd bashed a policeman, they'd 'upped' some well-known street fighter, they were 'on the trot' from the army after tying up the guard's sergeant - a number of different and colourful stories, some undoubtedly true, others exaggerated, and maybe some completely invented. But they became famous, first in Bethnal Green, Bow and Mile End, and then throughout the rest of the East End - and finally, the world.

One school friend of mine, Roy Tanner, claimed to be their cousin, and when we were down the lane, hanging round Solly's record stall in Wentworth Street, they would sometimes saunter through, dressed in smart lightweight suits in summer or camel coloured Crombie overcoats in winter. They'd give Roy a distant nod - hardly the greeting a cousin could expect but maybe he was a distant cousin. I remember Roy and a couple of his mates got into a fight on Stepney Green station, and they came off worse, and he said he'd told the twins about it and they were going to sort the culprits out. But I believe Roy was just saying that to salve his pride at receiving a black eye.

Soon enough, I became a nodding acquaintance with the twins myself. We'd always exchange a nod or a brief 'How ya doing?' without ever really conversing. The more trouble they got into, the more notorious they became, though initially only in an East End context.

Then, later on, I started visiting their Double R club. It was just a big old Edwardian style house in Bow Road, converted into a drinking den by the twins. It was before I took over the Puddings, and I became very friendly with people like Harry Abrahams, Limehouse Willy, and Sykes, all of whom used to help run the club, as well as with Reggie and Ronnie themselves. Whenever they were there, they always sent over a drink, which I always tried to reciprocate. They were quite generous and bought all their customers a drink at one time or another.

They were also both very charismatic. A completely overused word today, but they definitely had this 'presence' so that the very air surrounding them seemed different. Reggie was more of a George Raft figure, an old Hollywood film star famous for his gangster roles and who they eventually got to know well. In his old age, Raft was on the door of a West End casino, the Colony Rooms, as a celebrity 'greeter' when the twins were 'minding' the place for the 'mafia'. Reggie was always beautifully turned out - shoes highly polished, silk tie, sharp suit, his dark hair heavily Brylcreemed. He would smile and greet people as he walked along the streets. Ronnie, just as expensively dressed, had a more brooding presence. As he got older, he became much heavier set than Reg and rarely smiled. If he glanced anyone's way, they would quickly avert their gaze. I'd seen people in the pub shudder, drink up and leave the premises if he looked at them. When either of them walked into a place, no matter how noisy, there was an almost imperceptible silence, and, for no longer than the beat of a heart, all eyes would look their way and a frisson of expectation would ripple through. Of what, I can only wonder; violence, maybe?

They often came in the Puddings for a drink, mostly with a big crowd, as much as twenty-handed, but they were always unfailingly polite and I liked them, especially Reggie, who was more the affable and easier to talk to of the pair. They had soft voices, actually quite gentle in tone, and although Ronnie always came with lots of henchmen, Reggie came in a few times with just Frances, his wife, and another couple, and I enjoyed his company.

When they opened the Kentucky club in Whitechapel, I'd pop in there occasionally and would find it hard to buy a drink. An old ex-boxer, Georgie Last, would be behind the bar, and he'd stick a drink in front of me, whatever I'd asked for, and say 'Tommy bought that,' nodding in the direction of someone at the bar, or Johnny 'Little Legs' or 'Two Grand Tucker' or 'Fat Pat'. Everyone in the East End seemed to have a nickname in those days for some reason or another, and the drinks would just keep on coming over. Whenever I'd get the chance, I'd just say, 'Get a drink, George, and 'ave one yourself,' and he would take care of it. That's how it worked.

It was a nice little club, dimly lit and carpeted. A small group of musicians were normally playing in the corner, and there always seemed to be plenty of celebrities in there - Joan Littlewood, Judy Garland, Billy Daniels, George Sewell, Diana Dors, Daniel Farson, Barbara Windsor and James Booth, to name a few. In fact, Joan Littlewood was so taken with the brothers - as many famous and artistic people were - that she wanted to make a film about them. James Booth, fresh from his success in *Sparrers Can't Sing*, was her choice for Reggie, and how we all fell about laughing at the time, although it was a lot less ridiculous than the Kemp brothers of Spandau Ballet, who eventually played them on screen.

Shirley shared a birthday with the twins - October 24 - although they were a few years older than her, and we'd sometimes have a drink to celebrate. However, one night at the Kentucky, Ronnie was sitting at a low table entertaining a couple of black Americans, and as she walked from the ladies room, Shirley's coat accidentally caught the glasses on their table, spilling the drinks all over Ronnie and his guests. My wife was mortified, but Ronnie Kray, the apparent 'monster mobster', couldn't have been sweeter and, despite my protestations, refused to let me replace the drinks that had soaked his trousers. Added to the drink that one of my barmen had sprayed all over Reggie's suit a few months previously, their dry cleaning bill must have been adding up!

In some cases, though, a personal invitation to the Kentucky, especially if it was a Monday night, wasn't to be welcomed. It usually meant trouble for the recipient. That was when the twins settled scores. They'd invite people who maybe owed them money from some criminal activity that they were due a cut from, and if things didn't get settled satisfactorily, the 'guest' would then be taken into a side room or out the back and 'dealt with'. One Monday night I was in there. It was winter, bitter cold, and had been snowing heavily. I was having a drink with Sykes, who told me that, just a short while earlier, the twins had taken someone out the back and beaten them senseless with a shovel that had half a hundredweight of frozen cement on it.

Another night I was in the Regency, another drinking club in which they had an interest, and the twins came over and invited me to meet them at the Cambridge Rooms in Surrey. It was a club, or a roadhouse, they'd recently 'acquired' from someone or other. When I arrived, Marion Ryan, a famous singer in those days, was there along with Ray Ellington, a top band leader, and some other well-known faces. A young South African boy was also singing, although white. He was an entertainer in the mould of Sammy Davis Junior, and I was told he was Ronnie's current boyfriend, which was probably true. As I was looking around the place, I started to notice a lot of familiar faces scattered about in the darkness. Terry Murphy and Davie Sammons, two friends who were well-known boxers, were sitting at one table; Alfie Parsons, a friend and fellow publican, and his wife Sylvie at another; Laurie O'Leary, who I'd been to school with and who was a show biz agent and close friend of Ronnie's was at the bar. Oddly, I also noticed that all the waiters had very familiar faces, but that I knew them in a different capacity. There was a couple of ex-boxers, a night club bouncer and a petty thief, all dressed up in these odd, tight-fitting waiters' outfits and all doing their best to wait on tables, but all looking very embarrassed, uncomfortable, and not being terribly efficient.

A close friend of mine, Jay, who was working as Ronnie's driver and bodyguard, whispered to me that the Kray twin wanted a private word with me at his table. I went over and we shook hands, and he asked me to sit down and have a drink.

'So, what do you think of it here, Ed?', he enquired.

'It's great, really great, Ron. I love it,' I said.

'D'yer think we'll make money?' he asked in that soft voice of his.

'I reckon so', I replied. Then I suddenly realised I'd fallen right into his trap.

Ronnie went on to ask me if I could put a thousand pounds in and become their partner, considering I loved it so much.

My heart sank. I looked over at Jay, but he seemed engrossed in the cabaret. 'I haven't got that sort of money, Ron,' I said. 'I owe so much I'm virtually working for someone else.' *Here it comes*, I thought, *the old demand, the blag, the extortion, this is where it starts*. He went on to press me further, asking me what I thought of the set-up, the waiters, the food operation; asking whether he had the right sort of cabaret, etc. Of course, I told him that everything seemed excellent, holding onto my real opinion that I didn't think much of it at all, and certainly not enough to put any money into it - even independently. He seemed to gradually lose interest. 'Okay,' he said, 'I just thought you might be interested in joining us. Go on, enjoy yourself,' and that was that. It was never mentioned again.

The only other times I was asked was when fruit machines first started to appear in pubs and Watneys was continually pestering me to have them installed, which I resisted as long as

I could as I couldn't stand them. Reggie asked me if he could supply a couple of the machines, and I just told him the brewery wouldn't allow me to. He said it was a shame as we could have done alright. Another time, which was the closest I came to being asked about protection, was when Tommy 'the Bear' Brown, an old heavyweight fighter, and Ray Moore wandered in to the Puddings one night. They came up to me and said Ronnie had sent them, and asked if they could borrow a hundred pounds, stating that, in exchange, they would always look after any trouble for me. I immediately phoned Ronnie and told him I couldn't lend them or him any money, and I would take care of any problems myself. I thought perhaps he might get threatening, but he never, ever did. Ray Moore was an ex-lighterman who I'd known slightly down the docks. He was Charlie Kray's brother-in-law and was, reputedly, a bully. He was later shot, murdered by a wronged husband called Murphy with whom I'd worked and been friendly with in the docks.

Although it's obviously become a well worn-out East End cliché to say this, but I never thought the twins were all that bad compared to a lot of the other villains of the time. They could never be said to be jolly Cockneys, of course, as they were both very violent and emotionally complex people: they committed fraud, they blagged other crooks for a share of whatever crime these others did, especially when it was on or near their 'Manor'. They also 'minded' pubs, clubs and gambling joints. Lots of people were very frightened of them. But over the years the level of violence they are supposed to have committed has gone up and up, mythologised like Dick Turpin or Robin Hood. This mythologisation will only increase as the people who knew them die off. Yet, without wishing to sound like Monty Python's

'Piranha Brothers' sketch, those who did know them remember they *were* unfailingly courteous to elderly people, wouldn't swear in front of women or children, and would make it clear to anyone else in the company that they didn't like it. They never tolerated bullies who targeted the weak outside of the criminal world. They didn't like a certain 'firm' in South London, which delighted in torturing their victims and whose behaviour was beyond the pale to Reggie and Ronnie. Clichés become clichés, I suppose, because they do represent some sort of collective truth.

Nowadays, there is so much worse going on. Killings and torture are so commonplace in the twilight world of hard drugs and people smuggling, and many crimes committed today are so much viler and shocking, yet the culprits rarely, if ever, get as long a sentence as the twins. It was an injustice they were locked up for the length of time they were. Their sentences were savage and politically motivated. Even more vindictive was the government that kept them in long after their sentences were finished, just because they wouldn't grovel to be allowed out: they were men of principle who wouldn't lie and apologise when they didn't mean it, whereas many lesser men would.

The problems really started for them after all the publicity with Lord Boothby, a well-known Tory peer and broadcaster who was photographed in his Eaton Square home with Ronnie. The twins were also found innocent in a high-profile protection racket case, so they started to believe they were inviolable. But the police they knew and who, to a degree, had protected them, were now out of the picture. There were these new so-called 'gang-busters', whose main aim was to ensnare the Krays. The twins had upset the 'establishment', the ruling elite of England - who, of course, never, ever forgive.

Reggie and Ronnie's time, although they didn't know it, was fast running out.

I'm sure if they had been released from prison like normal offenders they would never have committed another crime anyway; they would have been lapped up by the celebrity circus, and the very newspapers that most condemned them would have been queuing up to hand over vast sums of money for exclusives of their stories.

Charlie, the elder brother with whom I became friendlier, was on a different level to his brothers. Without them, he would have made a living possibly as a small businessman who operated at a shady level. He was easy going, always laughing and joking, but he received his ten years for being loyal to his family, which is considered a virtue in any other walk of life. He deserved even less for his last sentence, which meant he died in prison, and which was caused by the spiteful, illegal behaviour of an over-zealous policeman.

Today, our problems are so much worse; murder is now so commonplace, and we seem overrun with psychopathic crime barons from overseas. Guns and shootings now seem to be the norm and occur in most cities across the country with such regularity that not many murders even make the front page any more. It actually makes the Krays era seem quite genteel in comparison.

'Upstairs' with Peter, Tommy Christian, Kenny, Harvey, Ronnie Gilbert.
(photograph by Alf Shead)

The stairs to 'upstairs'. *(photograph by Johanna St Michaels)*

THE DOCKERS' HOOK

Friday seemed to be the worst night for trouble, closely followed by Thursday. I hated Thursday because it was payday for the dockers, and so you could guarantee some of them would leave the docks, go to a pub, then on to an afternoon drinking club, and finally venture in to the Puddings. I knew because I'd done it myself when I was a docker.

One Thursday night, I went down to the pub. The band was in full swing and, as usual, we were very busy. I did my usual checks - the tills, made sure ashtrays were being emptied, glasses collected, counters were clean, said my hellos and smiled at all the regulars. I then noticed two men standing at the bar; both big, both obviously dockers as they had hooks stuck in their belts. These hooks were the tools of the trade for dockers and stevedores, and lots of them carried them in their belts, even when they'd left their place of work. These men had quite a space round them; the other customers were evidently steering well clear.

A friend of mine, Johnny Jaggs, was at the bar and he called me over, nodded in their direction, and warned, 'That's the one who glassed Tommy Kemp upstairs.'

I'd never seen John Hill before, but I'd heard about him. He was known as a terrible nuisance, and he'd started a fight with four of our bouncers upstairs and, though they eventually got the better of him, one of them, Tommy Kemp, had been scarred for life by having a broken glass shoved into his face.

I walked up to them. They were both big, but John was huge. He was taller and heavier than me, and I'm 6'2" and weigh 16 stone. The other one was big, too, but more fat than muscle, so I didn't much worry too much about him.

Keeping my eyes fixed firmly on Hill, I politely asked them to leave.

Hill stared at me, then grinned. 'We ain't leaving till we've seen your brother.' And still smiling he said, 'Look, you're alright. I don't mind you.' He paused. 'But your brother's a cunt!'

I didn't even think, I just punched. It was like a lightning-fast reaction.

You always know when you land a good punch. I hit him solidly, smack on the chin, and down he went, over a table, glasses everywhere. I glared at his mate, and he just backed away, not wanting to get involved.

A normal man wouldn't have got up after that, but Hill did, so I hit him again with everything - left hooks, uppercuts, jabs - until my fists were sore. He kept going to the floor, but he just kept getting right back up again. He seemed as strong as a bull and, at one stage, Johnny Jaggs handed me a stool to hit him with, but I pushed it away. I could have kicked him as he lay there, but he seemed so game that I didn't want to.

He got to his feet for about the fourth time and started to grab the glasses off the counter and hurl them at me. Then he lunged at me with his hook, but somehow I wrested it from him. Whilst this was going on, the pub had cleared: girls had run out screaming, lots of the customers ran to the other bar and watched in safety from there. I was told after that it was better than any Wild West fight anyone had ever seen at the cinema! His mate hadn't interfered but had just watched in a daze.

Witnesses said the fight lasted a full fifteen minutes, which is a long time for a brawl. During a pause, as I was gasping for breath and he was glaring at me like a mad bull about to charge, the police walked in. I was leaning on the bar panting, my collar askew, my tie on backwards, my jacket torn (yes, we publicans all wore suits in those days, and I hadn't had time to take off my jacket!), he with two empty pint glasses in his hands, prepared to throw. One of the policemen asked me what was going on.

'Only having a friendly chat, Officer,' I gasped.

'That's right,' said Hill, putting the glasses down.

After a few words and a very sceptical look from both of them, the two officers walked out.

After they left Hill came towards me with an outstretched hand, prepared to shake on it. And so was I. Just at this point, Kenny appeared with Johnny Bruce. My heart sank as I knew Hill then wouldn't let it go.

Kenny marched up and demanded to know what was going on. As I was explaining, trying to cool the whole situation down, Hill shouted at him, 'I want you outside!' I whispered to my brother that Hill had been bashed about by me and wouldn't be able to put up much of a fight. Kenny never said much, just nodded, but as we got outside he swiftly pulled a hammer from his coat. He went to whack Hill, but the head of the hammer spun off into the air before he could.

At the same time, Johnny Bruce pulled a cosh from his pocket and started beating the other docker, who curled into a ball, screaming, 'Leave me out! Leave me out!' Kenny, by this point, had 'nutted' Hill, had him on his knees, and was dishing out a ferocious hiding. I jumped on my brother's back and pulled him off as I was terrified he would kill the big man - and I'm sure he would have done if I hadn't and if Hill hadn't been so strong.

By this point, Hill was on his hands and knees on the pavement, soaked in blood, but somehow still conscious. I couldn't help but feel sorry for him. I walked to the other one, pulled Johnny Bruce away from him, and he covered up as if I was going to hit him, but I just told him to get his mate round to the local hospital as soon as possible and don't say a word of how it happened. He picked his mate up and they both staggered away.

'Why did you have to go in so strong?' I shouted to my brother.

'He's a nuisance! He's the one who started all the trouble upstairs and cut Tommy Kemp's face up! He deserved everything he got!'

If he felt he'd been wronged Kenny was very unforgiving.

When we walked back into the pub, the music had started playing again, custom had resumed as normal, and we spoke about it for a while, hoping the police wouldn't suddenly come marching in, but we never heard anymore. I knew instinctively Hill wasn't a grass.

Some months later, I walked into the Steamship pub in Poplar, which was run by some friends of mine and was a popular venue for East Enders. Sitting in the corner of the pub with the Tibbs and Readings, both well-known boxing families, and some other Canning Town faces, was John Hill. I steeled myself for another violent confrontation, but he just nodded to me, acknowledging I was there. Later in the evening he came over, we had a chat, and shook hands. I admired him for the way he didn't take advantage of that situation.

Another reason I came to regret the fight with Hill came later on.

Kenny could be very unforgiving if he'd been wronged.
(photograph by Alf Shead)

One evening, Peter had chucked out a group of nuisances from upstairs as one of their number had been harassing a female customer, reducing her to tears. When the club closed he left the premises with a girlfriend and was walking to where his car was parked. After a few yards, the nuisance who'd made the girl cry, George Skullface, approached him and said he wanted to settle the matter with Peter, one-to-one with a 'straight-up' round the corner. Peter handed his car keys to the girl and told her to wait in the car as he'd only be a few minutes. Upon following Skullface round the corner, however, he was confronted by the entire gang of thugs he'd thrown out earlier. They quickly surrounded him, punching him from all sides, knocking him to the floor, whereupon they proceeded to viciously kick and jump on him. Out of nowhere, a huge man rushed up, laid into the crowd, and put them to flight. He didn't hang around, just helped Peter to his feet and left. Peter was in a terrible state; his face blew up the size and shape of a football.

Later that night and tooled-up, Kenny, Johnny Jaggs, and Johnny Bruce stormed into the local snooker hall where they suspected the culprits might be. They found one, Gary Frayner, and Kenny smashed him about with a baseball bat whilst Johnny Jaggs, wielding a bayonet, kept the bystanders at bay. Little did they know that Skullface, who they were mainly hunting for, was listening to this all whilst hiding beneath the counter of the pie stall there.

It was ironic that the man who rescued Peter - and who we didn't know at the time - turned out to be John Hill. It was a long time after that we found this out. He'd possibly recognised Peter as a fellow docker in distress whilst walking past.

Hill's mother also worked for us as a cleaner in later years, and she was a lovely lady.

Skullface went into hiding for a while, but eventually Peter and Jackie Bowers tracked him down, cornered him round the garages in Chant Street at the back of the snooker hall, and gave him a thoroughly deserved slap.

Hill's brother Pete became a regular. He was tall but not so heavily built as his brother. He'd come in with a crowd of boys from Canning Town, a friendly, generous lot who I liked and, though younger than me, I used to drink with them on a Thursday night. Shirley would sometimes join us, and we enjoyed their company.

One night when I went upstairs, quite late after locking up, Shirley was making me cocoa and she called out to me to come into the kitchen. 'Look out of the window,' she said. We could see from our flat down into Dunn & Co., the men's shop next door, that there were a half-dozen shadowy figures pulling down raincoats, hats, suits and sheepskins from the racks and piling them up at the front door. It was no other than my Thursday night drinking mates, Pete's tall figure prominent amongst them. Of course, we couldn't grass.

The next night, in they marched, bold as brass, all wearing brand new overcoats or sheepskins. 'Wanna buy a mac, Ed?' they asked. I told them what I'd seen. 'We'll do the gaff again in a couple of months,' they said, 'it was so easy.'

THE DRUNKEN SAILOR

One time, we had a regular band called the Foresters, who were a nice bunch and I asked them to do a version of 'What Shall We Do With The Drunken Sailor', adopting a type of rock 'n' roll sound. It sounds a bit corny now, but it proved to be very popular in the busy pub and became a regular part of their repertoire. They normally played on a Thursday as they were busy doing weddings and functions weekends, which they preferred as they not only got paid more but they normally had a more refined crowd.

This particular evening, Les, one of my barmen, by prearrangement had brought a rifle into my office and asked to leave it there. He'd picked it up from somewhere as he was a member of a shooting club and didn't have time to take it home. When I came downstairs the Foresters were dismantling their gear and taking it out instead of bringing it in and setting it up.

'What's going on?' I asked, perplexed.

The leader of the group, Peter Braithwaite looked at me. 'We can't play here anymore,' he said in a trembling voice, 'Bobby Clark has just smacked Barrie, our singer, in the mouth and warned us if we dare play 'Drunken Sailor' one more time he'll bash the lot of us up!'

This particular bloke was a bit of a nuisance who I'd chucked out before. 'Where is he?' I demanded.

I ran into the street and spotted Clark talking to someone outside Dunn & Co. I ran up to him and grabbed him. The other man tried to intervene, but I shrugged him off whilst proceeding to punch Bobby Clark on the jaw. Whilst down on the floor I screamed at him never to come near the Puddings again. The other man then shoved a warrant card into my face. He was a plainclothes policeman and he'd been questioning Clark about some incident or the other.

I walked back into the pub and persuaded the band to start playing again. They were so nervous and had been badly frightened by him. He was such a bully and had been drunk, but finally they agreed to start playing when, halfway through the song, about twenty men suddenly rushed into the pub, some of them armed - and all in plainclothes. I thought, 'Blimey, this is a bit strong! I only punched him on the jaw and they've come to arrest me!'

It transpired someone had seen Les, my barman, carrying the gun into the pub, and imagined there was going to be a shooting of some sort. The man in charge, a Detective Sergeant Diamond - who I couldn't stand as he was one of those policemen, like many in those days, who treated people, like myself, as complete criminals for no just reason - told me what had been reported, and so I lead him into the office and called Les in to explain that he was an accredited member of a rifle club and that everything was in order. They still, quite rightly, I suppose, gave the gun a good going over and demanded Les take all the documentation to Stratford nick the next day.

The Foresters were a great band, but they never played in the

Two Puddings again, no matter how hard I tried to persuade them.

Bobby Clark was barred and, despite his protestations, never got served in the pub again.

THE DEAF MOB

One particularly hectic Christmas Eve, I'd had about four fights to sort out in different parts of the pub. My hands were feeling very sore (bruised and swollen), when there was another big upheaval in the public bar. There was one seething mass of bodies all struggling, punching, screaming and swearing. 'Quick, Ed! It's off again!' someone shouted. As I ran through, thinking of my aching hands, I picked up a broom and charged into the crowd, bashing and crashing into them. Some of the barmen and some friends joined in to help out, and between us we sorted things out, chucked some people out, and went back to serving.

Jimmy Murphy was standing at the bar and was sporting a huge black eye, recently acquired, by the look of it.

'What's up, Jim? How d'yer get that? I asked.

Jimmy, who was a fine boxer from a famous fighting family, gave me that cynical, what I called *Murphy look*. 'You did it!' he said. 'Who d'yer think was helping you out, and then you turn round and nearly poke my eye out with a broom!'

Sometimes during a melee, it was hard to tell who was who, but Jimmy took it all in very good heart.

The main culprits in this particular incident were a large crowd of deaf people who used to regularly visit the pub. They were a really nice bunch who would 'listen' to the music by feeling the vibrations through the counter. Someone must have really upset them on this particular evening, though, because they went berserk and were laying into another crowd like complete madmen! I was never quite sure what had transpired because I couldn't quite make out what they were trying to tell me, so I just chucked everyone out that was involved - although I did let them all back in again after a few weeks, and they were never any trouble again.

I had so many fights and scuffles in the Puddings that, half the time, my hands and knuckles were swollen up, black and blue, and seemed to permanently throb and ache. They were broken so many times over the years that I now pay the consequence by suffering with arthritis.

THE HARD MAN

One Saturday night I was standing at the bar drinking with some customers. It was the usual madhouse. The place was packed and I'd stopped for a break from behind the bar. Kenny was on holiday, as was Peter, and JD no longer worked for me as he now held an illustrious position with the brothers from Bethnal Green. As such, in their absence, I had to keep going upstairs to check everything was okay before rushing back down again.

Norman the barman suddenly sidled up to me and whispered, 'Bloke down there won't pay for his drink.'

I looked down to the end of the saloon bar and, standing there, bouncing on the balls of his feet with about seven or eight men, all unsmiling, was a thick set man with a big face and jaw, black curly hair, and intense black, pebble-like eyes. It was 'PB.'

I felt instantly depressed.

There'd been much talk of this man. He was the new tough guy of East London. Stories of his villainy abounded; how he'd knocked out two policemen in East Ham High Street and then stuck them both upside down in dustbins; how he'd terrorised the Hammer Club in Plaistow; how he'd had a row with Willie Malone, a much-feared Stepney man, and come off best. I'd recently been told by someone in a position to know that the Krays had apparently even planned to kill him and dump his body in the lake at Victoria Park. I acknowledged that, even if half the stories told about him were true, it still made him a handful.

Undoubtedly, he was a real maverick and out of control.

I took a deep breath, got behind the bar, walked over to where the group was standing, and confronted PB. He was team-handed, and no one on my side that night was tough enough to help me if it came to violence. I knew some of them might try, but they would be ineffective. Essentially, I was surrounded. All of this was going through my mind.

He had his back to me whilst his mates were all sneering and jeering together. What their motive was I wasn't entirely sure, but they were obviously out to provoke me or frighten me into something.

'Oi! You haven't paid for the rum and black, and I want the money!' I shouted.

He slowly turned round, stared at me with emotionless eyes - dead like a shark's. 'Fuck off,' he said, 'or I'll jump right over that bar and punch you in your fat gut!'

Good old Joe Hopson, loyal as ever, who was standing beside me warned him not to try, said if he did he'd come well unstuck. Joe had more faith in me than I did myself, though, strangely, Joe's words did seem to make him pause. The refusal to pay had stemmed from the fact that he'd seen someone round the other side - a man called Neal, who'd been in prison with him - and he'd asked him to have a drink. Neal didn't particularly care for him, but had accepted a rum and black and, when PB refused to pay for it, Neal offered to pay me himself. But I couldn't accept it. It was just too much of a climb down and they'd still be there to face up to.

PB stood there a while, all the time shouting and swearing whilst I was tensing up, waiting for him to jump. At the same time, Tony Collins, a friend and barman, slid along the counter a sharply pointed butcher's boning knife. I discretely took it and held it below the bar, out of sight. From what I'd heard of this man, he was about to make his move. I knew he wasn't going to be content with just verbal abuse; he was spoiling for a proper fight. I could see his face was contorted and boiling with rage. His friends were also exacerbating the situation, shouting things like, 'Where's your fucking minders now?', so it seemed like a real 'put up' job.

In one way, although I was missing them, I was actually pleased Kenny and Peter weren't there as it would have ended up a complete bloodbath.

I don't know why, but PB never did jump over the bar. Perhaps it's because I stood my ground and didn't flinch? Maybe because I swore back just as vehemently as he swore at me? I'm certain that, if he had attacked, I would have stabbed. It would have meant the end of my license; he might have died; *I* might have died; I could have finished up in prison. But I was determined not to retreat anymore. Maybe it showed in my face as we were both hurling abuse at each other.

The jackals who were with him weren't quiet either. These men, who I'd never even noticed before, were suddenly brave and snarling along with their leader. We were still confronting each other, hackles stiff, when the bell started to ring for 'time'. So I started to shout 'Drink up', and asked them to leave along with all the other customers, many of whom had left by now anyway. Suddenly, the police walked in - and there were a lot of them. I suppose a customer must have tipped them off. They asked me if there was any trouble. 'No trouble,' I said, 'these gents' - and I emphasised the word *gents* - 'are just drinking up'.

The police looked at them and the mob just glared back, not taking too much notice of me or the constabulary. Eventually, with more glares directed at me, they drank up and slowly walked out. All the other customers had gone by now, and the police, after a brief word with me about making my customers drink up on time, also departed.

That was far from the end of the matter.

I was going to Paris the following weekend. When we were away, with Kenny and Peter looking after the pub, PB and his crowd turned up again. Johnny Bruce joined my brother and Peter, and they stood adjacent to the main man all night. They were tooled-up and in a state of excited readiness but, this particular night, nobody did anything out of order, thankfully. They just had a drink and enjoyed themselves.

The following Thursday, early evening, I was sitting upstairs, reading the newspaper with a cup of tea and waiting for my dinner before heading down for the evening session. Norman called up the stairs. 'PB wants a word with you.' I let out a long sigh. I really wasn't in the mood for all this. I was just trying to enjoy a moment's peace and a nice cup of tea whilst catching up with the latest restaurant reviews.

Shirley, who was preparing dinner, looked worried. 'Be careful, Eddie,' she said. 'Shall I call someone?'

'No, don't worry. If he's on his own I'm sure it'll be alright.'

When I went downstairs the bar was practically empty. PB was chatting to one of my regulars, who seemed to know him quite well - a huge man, a quiet, nice type of customer, apparently, who turned out to be one of his old prison mates. PB's raincoat was laid out neatly on one of the tables. I remember thinking how strangely it was folded.

We greeted each other cordially enough and ended up having quite a nice long chat. He said he was sorry if he'd been a bit of a nuisance. According to him, a lot of people had been stirring things up and, if anyone came in and started threatening me with his name, he said I wasn't to respond because they would then go running to him and tell him what I was supposed to have said. All this time, I'd assumed it must have been something like that: maybe someone I'd chucked out of the pub had gone running to him and told him some cock and bull story of what I was supposed to have said in order to mix it. I also assumed someone I knew had spoken to him and maybe warned him off.

'Face' was a very finely balanced thing in the East End.

But this man was a very unpredictable force, and no one quite knew the best way to handle him.

He started to reminisce about his time in prison, how he stabbed a fellow inmate in the throat with a sharpened spoon because the convict had been telling him, and laughing about how, when his kids were naughty, he'd force them to swallow mustard. *He can't be such a bad bloke*, I thought to myself, *at least he likes kids*.

Someone I knew, Colin Hall, then came in and, after greeting me and asking how I was, started to shout at PB and tell him off a bit, who then laughed a bit sheepishly. As he picked up his coat to go, I realised why Colin was so annoyed: it was wrapped around a shotgun!

'Good job you were friendly,' he said, laughing. We shook hands and off he went. Many of the East End's best known pubs of that era probably have similar tales to tell about him.

One day, he dropped in to see me *en route* to Kent where, along with some others, he robbed a bullion van of ninety thousand pounds - a vast amount at that time - for which he received eighteen years' imprisonment. Whilst in prison he was alleged to have killed another prisoner and was committed to Broadmoor, where he lead a famous roof-top protest. He also spent a lot of time building up his already impressive strength and boxing ability. When he eventually came out of prison he made a big name for himself as the undisputed champion of unlicensed fighters. He is, by repute, quite a wealthy chap these days, and has published a best seller about his life and made numerous TV appearances. I met him about ten years ago at a gala charity benefit night for the former champion boxer Terry Spinks. He was sitting with the Bowers family, and I enjoyed having a drink and reminiscing with him. I also, sadly, see him at funerals now and again, which I suppose is inevitable, but I wish him all the best as characters like him did add a bit of spice to the old East End.

THE SHOOTING

Friday was always the busiest night, but it was also the most troublesome. I always felt on-edge on a Friday night until I'd had about three light ales; then I'd be cheerful. Another three and I'd be positively happy and wondering why on earth I'd ever felt edgy in the first place!

Most fights we had were upstairs. Kenny and his doormen would quickly take care of it. Very often I never knew a fight had even occurred until someone told me at closing time. If we had trouble downstairs, it was normally after ten o'clock when people's brains were inflamed by alcohol. The combination of testosterone and booze makes most young males foolishly brave; they imagine they're twice as tough and strong as they are really. Near the end of a session, when everyone was charged-up by the drink and very loud rock 'n' roll, aggro usually occurred.

We were very strict on time and tried very hard to have everyone out by the required hour. The police showed absolutely

Friday night in the Puddings: George Bush, Peter, Lenny Murphy, David Hopping, Johnny Bruce, Lenny Clarke, Terry Docherty, Mickey King, Kenny, Tommy Kemp, Norman Baptiste. (photograph by Alf Shead)

no mercy to us - unlike today when they believe the softly softly approach is best. But personally, I'm not so sure.

This particular Friday had been very busy, even by our standards. The place was so crowded that the customers were all jammed together. I was trying to get around the place to collect glasses and, at the same time, trying to persuade everyone to drink up. But I noticed one group of men standing in a circle and, as they were finishing their drinks, they were chucking their glasses and bottles onto the floor in front of them. There was a growing heap of broken glass in the middle of their circle. What the point of it was I don't know - I didn't even bother to ask them but just told them, in no uncertain terms, to fuck off and that they were all barred. They didn't back off but just looked towards one man, who was sullen, heavily built, fair-haired and thuggish looking, who just stared at me. I held his stare with as much hatred in my eyes as I could see in his. He sniggered, looked at his pals, then turned on his heels and walked out, followed by the others. *Thank God,* I thought, *they were a nasty looking bunch.*

When the pub emptied I went into the office to do the tills. The bar staff, after unwinding with their customary free pint, said goodnight and went home, leaving just Albert the potman sweeping and clearing up the pub. Albert always tried to make a good job of it, took a bit more care than any of the other potmen, because he was married to Rene, my cleaner, and so I think he acknowledged that the more he did, the less she had to do in the morning.

As I was sitting in the office I heard an almighty crash. Albert rushed in. 'Eddie, they've smashed our windows!' he said.

'Bastards!' I said. 'That's the little mob I chucked out.'

We went to the front door and considered the damage. As I was inspecting the windows, two policemen on routine patrol wandered from across the road. 'What's the problem?' one asked. I started to explain what I thought had happened when one of the policemen, having a closer look whilst fingering the glass, exclaimed, 'Your windows have been shot in! These are bullet holes!'

They quickly got on to their radios, requesting urgent assistance. When they went into the pub with Albert to ask him some questions, I waited outside, picking up a few stray bottles and glasses. Suddenly, a car pulled up and out jumped two men in civilian clothes. They were detectives in an unmarked car, answering the call the uniforms had put out. As we were talking, another car screeched up, and I saw a gun poking out of the back window. 'Look out!' I shouted. I threw the bottles and glasses I had in my hand at the car, but it didn't stop them firing again. I can remember hearing about three shots and instinctively ducking as I threw the last of the bottles at them. I heard more glass shatter, and someone yelped as if they'd been stung, and the car quickly sped away. One of the coppers was holding his head moaning that he'd been shot. When I looked there wasn't much blood as it was only a small nick on the ear, lucky for him.

Then, of course, the questioning started.

It was March 1969. The previous summer, Shirley and I had decided that, after seven years' hard slog, we'd had enough of living in Stratford. Fed up of constantly being on call, having money but little time to go anywhere, fed up with the bad education our kids were receiving in an under-resourced school in a poor district, we'd been looking at houses in the countryside and had finally settled on a pretty thatched cottage in Suffolk. After lots of excitement, second thoughts, misgivings, some tears, arguments, and lots of visits to the cottage to be utterly certain that it was what we wanted to do, we finally exchanged contracts.

We arranged for Shirley's brother, Peter, and his wife Kay to manage the pub, and we were moving in March. The removal men had been hired, our farewell party was on the Sunday, and new schools had been sorted for Andrew, Matthew and Eugene. It was an exciting time.

The shooting took place on the Friday; my family and I were moving out a couple of days later on the Monday. The date had been arranged at Christmas. By another bizarre twist of fate, this was following the week the Krays received their savage sentence. All completely coincidental.

But the police never believed it, nor did the press. All night long there were newspapers banging on our door, telephoning, trying to prise the 'real' story out of me. What gang was it? Were they East Enders or a South London gang from across the water? Was it a revenge attack? Now the Krays have been removed they can no longer protect you, can they? Who's trying to muscle in on the East End? What should have been a pretty routine story assigned to the middle pages of the 'nationals' was headline news in the tabloids. I tried to explain that it was just some louts who'd been smashing glasses and I'd chucked them out of the pub. What I didn't know was that, after they'd left the pub, they'd been involved in a fracas with Kenny and JD, and a couple of them had received a well-deserved slap. I couldn't help the police with their descriptions as that wasn't our policy. My plan was to find out who they were and deal with it ourselves. I had to go not to Stratford nick but Bethnal Green police station on the

Monday - the very day I was moving - to answer questions. The detective could not, or would not, get it into his head that I'd planned this move many months before. He was convinced I'd been frightened and had managed to swiftly buy a cottage, arrange removals, take on a manager, and change the kids' schools all in the space of a single weekend. I appealed to his logic, but his logic was different from mine. He desperately wanted to believe the Krays had been getting protection money from me, and that now they were away a new 'gang' was taking over.

What made things even worse was that one journalist, Alan Shillum of the *Daily Mirror*, who I'd been friendly with at the time, asked me if I was worried over the incident. I told him of course I wasn't, that I knew it was just local louts and no big deal. 'Surely,' he said, 'you worry over your kids?'

'Well, yes, I suppose so,' I said, as anyone other than a monster or a fool would answer.

The next day, in the *Daily Mirror*, a big headline read: 'EAST END PUBLICAN EDDIE JOHNSON MOVES OUT! WORRIED OVER FAMILY'. This was so untruthful I felt extremely annoyed - not to mention humiliated. You never publicly acknowledged any fear or you would be finished; the hyenas would soon start to gather. It taught me a lesson: you can never fully trust even journalists you are friendly with as the story always comes first. I've never fully believed, without question, anything reported in the media since.

The police eventually tracked the culprits down, and it was the people I'd chucked out - the big, sullen one, who was known as 'Chopper'. They both received a couple of years' imprisonment.

THE NEW SUITS

Chopper went on to become fairly notorious in certain circles as an unlicensed fighter, crook, and all round nasty piece of work. In later years, he even co-wrote a book about his criminal and violent behaviour. When he came out of prison, unbeknownst to me, he started going upstairs at the Puddings to drink. One night there was an altercation after he threw some food over Dick, one of our waiters, and he was chucked out. A few weeks later, all 'tooled-up', he reappeared. The situation was handled and he was chucked out again. But what really disappointed everyone was that he then headed straight round to the police station to try to get my brothers nicked for assault! Bad enough being a nuisance and unnecessarily provoking all of this trouble with us in the first place, but to then go to the police about it as well? It just wasn't done in the East End. As a consequence, Kenny was arrested and locked in a police cell overnight. Eventually Chopper offered to drop all charges against him if he bought him a nice, new suit. Which Kenny duly did.

Over the years, there were quite a few nuisances sauntering around the East End with nice, new suits down to Kenny - many negotiated by our old mate Frankie, who was a good customer and friendly fellow who Kenny knew from West Ham Boxing Club, and who ran the pie and tea stall in Stratford snooker hall. I used to think of him as like a 'shop steward' for all the villains and nuisances of Stratford. One day he came to see me with a fellow called Brian, who Kenny had had a row with 'upstairs', the consequence of which was Brian's suit soaked in blood. Frankie negotiated with me, said he'd manage to talk Brian out of going to the police but that he would need a nice, new suit. I pleaded with Kenny to stop fighting as it was costing us a fortune in new suits. Brian later became one of Kenny's best customers and a great friend.

The Wiretap

Our move to Suffolk went ahead on the Monday, albeit a couple of hours later than planned. It was a relief to start living in our cottage, but there was a downside: because of all the adverse publicity, the Pudding's trade went down and was never to reach such extraordinarily high levels again. I felt particularly sorry for Peter and Kay because the downturn coincided with their move. I felt even sorrier for myself because it meant even less money just when I needed it most.

The shooting incident had other repercussions, though. A young customer who Kenny was friendly with informed him that my telephone at the cottage was being tapped. His brother-in-law was with the Cambridge and Suffolk police. I knew it must be true because he described to Kenny in exact detail our cottage and its layout, and said the men who had recently been outside, apparently repairing the phone lines were, in reality, preparing the tapping of our phone!

This customer, who Kenny introduced me to, had never met me before and had never even been to Suffolk, and so it seemed very odd that he knew so much about our domestic arrangements. The authorities obviously believed there was a direct link with the underworld they were tapping into. It was useful to receive this tip-off and I never complained as there was nothing they would ever hear over those telephone lines that could harm me.

Nowadays, the events described above all seem rather old-fashioned and would barely make the newspapers. Back then, they were quite sensational. In the meantime, the world seems to have got much worse, but I'm still living in Suffolk.

Devil's Kitchen poster. *(from the Johnson Family Archive)*

Disco Ticket. *(from the Johnson Family Archive)*

THE WORLD'S GREATEST PUB

THE STEAMSHIP

It became a fashion in the mid-1960s for successful young publicans to branch out. There were not many multiple license holders before then. Even the busiest and wealthiest publicans seemed quite content to run a single pub, but everything was starting to change.

With the Puddings, we became the first pub to advertise. We had big day-glo posters plastered all over the East End. At that time, it was unheard of for pubs to do this, and it seemed to be frowned upon - it may even have been illegal - but it didn't take long before other music pubs started doing the same. We installed ultra-violet lights in our night club, employed an artist to paint the walls and ceiling completely black and then paint large images of King Kong, Frankenstein, Wolf Man and other monsters in luminous paint, and re-christened it the Devil's Kitchen. It was such a sensation and became so busy that the brewery sent a high-powered group of executives to meet me, including the directors of St. George's Taverns, Watney's group of managed houses. I was quite flattered at being bought drinks and made a fuss over, and was happy to answer all of their questions. But soon after, they opened a heavily advertised chain of 'discos' called Bird Nests, entirely based on my original concept. It wasn't long before dark, ultra-violet lit nightclubs opened all across Britain!

My customers were always asking when I was going to join my contemporaries like Patsy Quill or Bob Wheatley, and expand. Bob was a good example. His parents had run one of the most successful music pubs in the East End's history. It was called the Rising Sun in Bethnal Green, and was famous for its singers, bands and comedians.

They even had a dwarf cowboy country singer, Big Tex, who would ride a live horse onto the stage. The compere was a limping blonde man with a walking stick called 'Welsh George'. Shirley and I often popped over there on a Wednesday before we went for a meal, and I remember Bob would be working away behind the bar and I'd always buy him a light ale and have a chat. He finished up, in partnership with his Brewers, Ind Coope, running Wheatley Taverns, a pub empire of over a hundred pubs. Patsy Quill also had extra pubs so when Doug Blake, my area manager from Watney's, asked if I'd be interested in taking another one, I agreed to have a look.

The pub they offered me was called the Steamship in Naval Row, Poplar. It was run single-handedly by a sweet little old lady called Mrs Lennon. 'Any relation to John?' I joked.

'Not as far as I know,' she replied.

She was probably asked that question every day, I realised as soon as I asked it. 'How do you manage the barrels and the deliveries?'

She smiled and replied that there was always someone in the pub or a drayman to help out, and if there wasn't she would wait till a customer came in.

The trade was pretty much on the floor, and the brewery was anxious to install a fresh tenant. When a publican's wife was widowed, they were allowed a 'widow's year', and then they had to go. The breweries didn't like the idea of a woman running a pub alone, especially in a rough part of London. That policy, which was prevalent till the '80s, seemed to make sense; in modern times, however, it doesn't - or you're not allowed to say so, at least.

I liked the look of the pub, and although it was a bit off the beaten track, there was a factory along the road from where most of the lunchtime custom came. I thought it had the potential, if some money was spent on it, to be a busy evening venue.

Doug Blake seemed to think it would be successful. He often told people, 'put Eddie Johnson on the moon with a pub and it would take money.'

Before agreeing to take on the pub, I approached my brother-in-law Peter, who was living with his wife, Kay, in a little flat in Plaistow. Peter and Kay were both keen and excited. She was a lively girl with lots of personality, very pretty, and not afraid of hard work. As for Peter, he was more like a brother than a brother-in-law, loyal; tough and lively, he was well liked by everyone he came into contact with. We had a good look at the pub, the living accommodation was quite spacious, and, as I explained the plans I had in mind for the place, they both seemed very happy.

After looking at the pub, we all went to the Park Lane Hilton to celebrate. The impression Shirley and I gave, I suppose, was that the publican's life was one of plenty, of money and socialising, and far better than struggling down the docks, living in a poky little flat.

After several visits to Watney's HQ at Whitechapel, during which time I introduced Peter and Kay to Doug Blake and Mickey Grant, who was a director not only of Watney's but of Grants Whisky, his family's business. Mickey was one of the best directors Watney's ever had and became a great friend. As well as being a brewery man, he was a Scottish international rugby star, and the Observer's rugby correspondent. After a couple of favourable interviews, it seemed as if Peter and Kay had passed with flying colours. All was all set for a grand opening.

I engaged an architect to draw up some plans, paid regular visits to the Steamship, and was introduced by Mrs Lennon to the various trades' people there. Peter accompanied me when he could, but he was still earning his living in the docks. In his spare time, he would come over to the Puddings with Kay, and they would work behind the bar and I would show him how to do the tills and clean the cellar pipes, etcetera.

One morning, as I was serving in the Puddings, a former work mate of mine and friend of Peter's came in. His face was white, and he looked very nervous. 'What's up?' I asked.

'Peter's been nicked,' he blurted out. 'Can you go down to North Woolwich police station to try and bail him out?'

He was a bit evasive when I asked him what Peter had been nicked for, and when he finally explained I exploded 'What's wrong with him?' He'd been caught selling meat to a couple of lorry drivers. An Argentinean boat was being unloaded, and he was one of the clerks off-loading the ship. It was a common enough crime; in fact Ronny Christmas, the bearer of these bad tidings, was one of the worse culprits in the docks, and if Peter had been working on the same ship as him, sure as eggs is eggs, Ronny would have persuaded him. It was out of character for Peter whilst par for the course for Christmas, who was notorious in such an arena. He'd bought shops and big cars and seemed to live a millionaire's lifestyle - and all down to the goods he'd fiddled as an OST Clerk. As far as I know, he'd never been caught, and he even retired early from the docks at an early age to run a 'swag' shop.

Ultimately, there wasn't much I could do. We engaged a good solicitor, pleaded his previous good character, but all to no avail as the evidence against him was too overwhelming.

He lost the case, lost his docker's 'brief', as we called the registered dockworkers ticket, and so he also lost his job. And add to the mix that we both lost the Steamship, which was a huge disappointment. Peter had to go and work with his dad, helping him paint, decorate, and do odd building jobs. I managed to find a friend to take on the pub and, although I was no longer directly involved, the people I helped put in there made it, for a time, a very busy and fashionable pub.

A few years later, Peter and Kay managed the Puddings for me and, subsequently, became tenants of their own pubs in the East End including the Blind Beggar. They ran that pub for many years, and were its most successful landlords since its heyday before the shooting in the '60s.

Keeping it in the family. Kay and Peter, who ran the Puddings for us in the 1970s before taking over the Blind Beggar. (photograph by Alf Shead)

THE MITRE

I was still keen on having another pub, so when Kenny asked if I wanted a share in the Mitre in Tunnel Avenue, Greenwich, I jumped at the chance. It was a Courage pub, so I had to keep secret my involvement as neither Brewers, Watney's or Courage, would have approved.

This proved to be successful for a couple of years. The lunchtimes were very busy, full of Irish navvies working on the new tunnel and motorways that spread out from the area. They were heavy-drinking, big-spending customers, most of them large, genial men, even when they'd had a drink. The volume of beer we sold was huge, but we kept the prices low as our overheads were small. Consequently, our percentage wasn't very high but Kenny booked music and bands for the evenings and put the prices up for those sessions.

It was a bit of a rough area, so we did receive a few threats from South Londoners who despised people from our side of the river encroaching on what they saw as *their* patch. There were a few fights initially, but we stood our ground and, in the end, things ran fairly smoothly.

One incident, however, stands out. We'd received a tip-off that local nuisances were coming over to start trouble one evening, so Kenny, Big Lenny Clarke, Johnny Bruce and Rocky Bob were standing by. Sure enough, trouble flared up in the shape of three nasty looking characters who turned up and provoked a fight, but Kenny and the others laid into them and chucked them into the street without too much effort. As they were standing at the bar celebrating the evening's excitement, Billy Newell, our manager, said, 'Hold up, there's cozzers everywhere!' They looked through the frosted glass windows and saw blue lights flashing outside, and lots of silhouettes running towards the doors. Lenny and Johnny ran through to the gents' toilet and both managed to squeeze through a window that opened to the yard outside, but Kenny and Rocky ran upstairs to the pub kitchen. Unfortunately for them, the police were looking for four men they had an accurate description of, and insisted on searching the entire premises. Kenny and 'Rocky' were hiding behind the door, but could hear footsteps getting closer and closer. In the kitchen were two large catering tables with all the pots, pans and various equipment laid out, all covered up with white dust sheets. 'Quick,' Rocky whispered, 'under the sheets!' He and Kenny quietly but quickly pushed the cooking gear to one side, laid flat on the tables, covered themselves with the sheets, and lay motionless as corpses. They heard the door creak open as the police came in, and listened to them slowly walking around the kitchen, opening cupboard doors, checking everywhere until one of them, leaning against the very table Kenny was lying on, said, 'Well, that's a mystery. I was certain they'd be up here.' Kenny and Rocky waited till the sound of the policemen's footsteps receded back down the corridor before getting out from under the sheets.

Kenny said that, when he'd heard the copper's voice, he was so terrified he'd burst into a giggling fit that he bit his lip until it bled.

When the navvies moved on, there was no passing trade to take their place, and the Mitre became quieter and quieter. The cars just whizzed straight by along the brand new roads our old customers had built. Eventually, after we moved out, it became the Tunnel Club, a notorious venue for comedians made famous by the late Malcolm Hardee.

I did have some other pubs later on, but that was when I'd stopped physically living above the Puddings and was able to have a more 'hands on' involvement. Most publicans who had several pubs always admitted to me that they were just as well off running one really busy pub than several because breweries were very crafty and they'd only let you have another pub if no one else could run it successfully. So the consequence was that the busy pub a multi-operator owned subsidised the ones that lost money.

A 'hands-on' tenant who was always in his pub ran the best pub. It was a hard life and hard work, and it paid financially if not health-wise. I used to say that customers 'wanted your blood', and it was true. For your regulars, you had to be there all the hours you were open.

THE WORLD'S GREATEST PUB

One of Kenny's favourite sayings was 'Don't spoil the ship for a ha'porth of tar,' which I wholeheartedly agreed with. The trouble was, a lot of our disagreements were because he did just that! We used to advertise, tongue-in-cheek, as 'The Two Puddings - The World's Greatest Pub,' and once I asked Kenny to get some car stickers made. He duly delivered about a thousand, nicely designed, colourful, correct size and shape, but then I noticed there was no adhesive on the back. 'They're not sticky, how are people going to stick 'em on?' I queried. 'Oh, to have them self-sticking was a lot dearer, so I thought people could buy their own glue,' Kenny answered. I don't think a single person bothered to stick one on.

At one point I decided we should have a very large banner made with bold writing stating the same sentiment as the stickers. We would string it up across the front of the pub. Kenny arranged to have it done, and duly delivered a wonderful looking poster but which was, I noticed, made of extremely thin paper. 'I managed to get it done really cheap,' he said proudly. Of course, it barely even lasted a day. It rained slightly, was a bit windy, and so it quickly tore off and floated off high above the rooftops of Stratford, looking as forlorn as our boasts about the pub.

Roger (foreground) and Jackie Bowers, keep the customers at bay on a Friday night. (photograph by Alf Shead)

THE UPSTAIRS

We'd been discussing for some time the possibility of 'doing up' the upstairs. The Devil's Kitchen, as it was then called, had been very successful for us but had been copied by so many other people that we wanted to keep ahead of the pack, so we started thinking of various new themes. I was semi-retired at this point, around 1971, and Peter and Kay were running the Puddings enthusiastically and efficiently, and I'd only visit weekends and Monday lunchtime.

One day, whilst out shopping in Cambridge with Shirley, she said, 'Why don't you do it like this?' We were in a very fashionable new boutique called Snobs, and it was decorated a bright pillar-box red with black and lots of chrome, and looked quite spectacular for its time. I was really taken with the idea and discussed it with Kenny at our next Monday meeting, and he was also very enthusiastic. 'We'll even call it Snobs,' he said, all cock-a-hoop. I urged him to go to Cambridge to have a look for himself before any work was done. 'No, no, no, I've got the idea. I know *exactly* what to do.'

Kenny, as well as his various other business interests, had also bought a lot of property over the years that he let out as bed-sits and flats, so he thought it made economic sense to employ a full-time builder and decorator to maintain them. This builder's name was Tom, whose assistant was his wife, Rose. He was a friendly, talented man who seemed able to handle anything in the building and decorating line. Rose, who would labour for him was, like Tom, quite petite, and though always wearing heavy lipstick, she would also dress in one of his old suits. She would mix cement, wheel a barrow, and clean his paintbrushes. The main reason she accompanied him, though, was because of her insane jealousy. She was also an alcoholic. Tom, a mild-mannered, moustached cockney, who resembled Private Walker, the spiv from Dad's Army, would quite often turn up with a black eye or fat lip, always given to him by Rose. He was once innocently watching Miss World on television when she leapt upon the coffee table and screamed at him, 'What 'ave they got that I 'aven't?!' and then proceeded to perform a striptease whilst beating him about the head with her shoe. It was such a shame as he never even looked at another woman. Kenny called her a 'husband basher.' So, it was this pair who was going to redecorate the upstairs.

I asked Kenny once again to go and take a look at the Cambridge boutique, but he said he never had the time and he knew exactly what I wanted anyway. 'Stop worrying, it'll look terrific.' Of course, it was my fault, I should have kept a closer eye on things, but living in the countryside and enjoying life, I just left it to Kenny.

On my next visit to the Puddings I was so disappointed I felt like crying. Everything about it seemed bodged, and it looked absolutely nothing like the original idea I'd so painstakingly explained. Even the colour was wrong; instead of pillar-box red it was a bright industrial orange! Kenny had managed to get hold of a job lot of so-called 'red' paint much cheaper than the paint I'd recommended, and so another row erupted between us with more expletives, but eventually we just let it lie and duly reopened as Snobs, though I have to say it was really disappointing to me, and never looked right. But Kenny seemed very happy with it.

We had several 'makeovers', to use a modern term, the final one occurring in the '90s. I employed a young designer called

Kerry, who worked for my son, Matthew. A pretty girl, she had quite a reputation and some brilliant ideas; she even traced some of the original tiles from the '20s used on the London Underground and incorporated them into the design. But Kenny didn't seem to like her for some reason. At first I was completely puzzled, but my younger brother Michael - who, by this time, was running the pub - said it was Tom's fault, that he had kept telling Kenny that she wasn't up to it, didn't know her job, and he couldn't work with her. The root of the trouble, Michael deduced, was, in fact, Rose: she was so consumed with jealousy as a result of Tom working with a young woman that she never left his side for a moment, instead resorting to swearing at him, warning him not to dare talk to her. 'Stop chatting her up!' She'd whisper aggressively in his ear whenever he'd ask Kerry even the most mundane question, such as where she wanted a certain picture hung. His life was made utter hell as he was being abused mentally and as well as physically. I told Kenny this and, inconvenient though it was, we arranged that Kerry only make an appearance when the other two were absent.

Kerry herself, who was a charming and bubbly person, was totally bemused by Rose's behaviour, and felt sorry for both her and Tom. The work was eventually finished and looked great.

THE CON MAN

In the mid-1970s, Kenny opened a restaurant in Woodford, Essex, and called it Bunters. It had a large illuminated clock made in the likeness and shape of Billy Bunter, which was fixed above the entrance to the restaurant. It was striking and was a big talking point in the area. The publishers of Billy Bunter, D. C. Thomson of Dundee, however, took a completely different view, and actually threatened to sue him if he didn't remove it immediately. I was all for leaving it up as I thought the publicity he'd get would offset any damages, but his solicitor thought otherwise and strongly advised him to take it down. Despite all this, the restaurant was successful, so when Dunn & Co., the men's outfitters next door to the Puddings, became vacant, we had little hesitation in buying the lease.

We converted the premises to a bar and restaurant and called it Keneddy's, an amalgam of our two names. We had it fitted out by a young designer and architect, Terry Hines, and it looked wonderful. It was the best designed restaurant of its sort the East End had ever seen, and it cost us a lot of money. The Who's manager, Bill Curbishley, an old friend and guest on our opening night, said it reminded him more of New York, where he was then spending a lot of time, than London. 'This would go down so well in Manhattan,' he said, 'but Stratford?' He laughed as he said it, but it sounded a bit ominous to me.

The problem was that our experience of not eating but presenting high-class cuisine was so limited. One day, the bank manager called me into his office, sat me down, looked me in the eye, and asked if I had any idea of all the pitfalls of running a restaurant. 'Of course,' I lied robustly adopting a confidence that was starting to drain. I'd read somewhere that sixty percent of new restaurants close within a year, but we were still both sure of ourselves for some reason. We spent all the budget on the look of the restaurant, but very little in the kitchen; we stupidly bought domestic equipment, a household cooker, little microwave, small fridge, and thought when the cash rolled in we could then buy better and bigger. In essence, we really neglected the 'engine room'.

I contacted a friend, Mick Harper, who'd been the chef at Quaglino's for many years, and asked if he'd manage the place for us. He'd be happy to, he said, but only as a partner. He even offered to stick some money in. I was delighted with his response as I thought he'd make the perfect partner. With his expertise, Kenny's energy, and my promotional talents, what a combination we've have, but Kenny wasn't very keen: all he could see were arguments on the horizon when the money started to roll in. Basically, he didn't want to share.

It's easy to be wise in retrospect, but that's where our trouble lay: we lacked experience and knowledge, and between the pair of us, we couldn't even poach an egg.

We never did make any money. In fact, we ended up losing a small fortune. The first chef we employed was called Kevin, a fat, rather miserable gay Irishman with dark curly hair. He had all the right credentials, of course: he'd been working at the Flask in Hampstead, a renowned bar and restaurant. He cooked sublimely but untidily, and the kitchen, under his direction, was a chaotic mess that failed to ever look clean, despite the help of three kitchen staff. The place was a lock-up, and when we closed in the afternoon, I'd leave Kevin there to rest and relax as it was too far for him to go all the way home to North London and get back in time to open.

One afternoon when we closed, after a week of fairly satisfactory trade, I'd left Kevin in the restaurant, as usual, and headed off. Two hours later, I realised I'd forgotten some important papers so needed to pop back. When I entered the place, all was deathly quiet, and there was no sign of him anywhere. As I walked across the restaurant to retrieve the papers, I almost tripped over something on the floor. To my horror, it was Kevin! Not asleep but just lying there, semi-conscious and mute, spittle drooling from his mouth, one eye open, staring up at me and following me around the room. He was completely paralytic having downed an entire bottle of vodka. No wonder he wasn't still at the Flask - he was a raving alcoholic! Of course, he had to go, and I chucked him out after a session that saw him hardly able to stand. I'd forced him to drink cup after cup of black coffee and, miraculously, we had no complaints about the food he cooked that night, but we were turning into Fawlty Towers.

The first night without Kevin was a Monday, a quiet night. In the kitchen was Nora, the washing-up lady, and Brian, our new chef. He was a middle-aged man who looked like a labourer that had just wandered in from a building site. He spoke in a twisted accent; a mixture of Cockney, Geordie and Irish. I could never quite make out what he was saying. Nora, a Canning Town girl, always looked extremely puzzled whenever he spoke to her, too. He explained he'd also been a kitchen porter in all the best hotels in the West End. I had no reason not to believe him as it wasn't much to boast about and, for some reason, it gave me confidence. If we had any customers, surely Brian would have enough knowledge to help us get by. He said he would - at least, I think he said that.

We had four early customers - two couples, middle-aged, smartly dressed, the women attractive with lots of nice jewellery, just the sort of custom I was aiming for. I made a big fuss of them in the best Basil Fawlty fashion, and led them to our best table. I explained that it was quiet, as Monday's normally are, and that we'd only been opened two weeks, early days yet, etc. They were all very nice and quite chatty. They normally went to

Bloom's in Whitechapel on a Monday, they said, but this looked so nice and it would be much more convenient. I poured their wine and said it was on the house. 'Well, we've never had that at Bloom's!' one of them said to the others.

They all ordered the same: four egg mayonnaise and four T-bone steaks that I'd highlighted on the menu as *Specials*. I wanted to get rid of them as Kevin had ordered too many.

I took the order to the kitchen. Brian and Nora looked apprehensively at each other and then at me. Brian muttered something to me that I couldn't quite understand, whilst Nora looked at him and back at me, completely puzzled. I went out and conversed with the customers for about twenty minutes until the waitress, a young Greek girl, beckoned me urgently to the kitchen. On the table were the remains of about 12 eggs, none of them hard-boiled, some soft, some semi-soft. Brian and Norah both looked desperate, mouths wide open, with real fear in their eyes. They obviously didn't have a clue, which I suppose was what Brian was trying to tell me earlier, albeit in his own mangled way. I phoned Shirley in a panic, who told me to calm down, explained that we would need to boil the eggs for ten minutes, slice some tomatoes, and serve with Hellman's.

After the longest ninety minutes of my life, the customers finally got their steaks. They had become extremely quiet by now, just a whispered mutter now and again, and they were all frowning and looking at their watches. They'd finished the bottle of wine and hadn't ordered any more, and I agonised over whether or not to give them another bottle for free, but I felt too embarrassed at having any further conversation with them so I'd retreated behind the bar and was doing my best to look busy, polishing glasses in between forays into the kitchen. I let the young waitress deal as best she could with them. They paid their bill in silence. I wasn't going to charge them, but I thought the damage had already been done, reasoning that they were never going to come back anyway so I'd take their money. They left quietly, stony faced, so different from the eager, laughing foursome two hours before. They never left a tip.

I was managing the place Monday to Thursday, and my aim was still to attract what I regarded as 'nice' people as customers. I refused anyone that just wanted a drink, and never let anyone who had already had too much to drink past the door. I wanted a place that attracted families and couples in their thirties and older.

Kenny ran it Friday, Saturday and Sunday. His style was rather different: he let all the bouncers from next door come and drink at the bar, and lots of his mates, too. Bobby Fourway and company were the nicest people on earth, and I was very fond of them, but their language was often a bit over the top, and they were far from being quiet. I tried to explain delicately to Kenny how I thought the family trade I was trying to encourage might be unsettled and put off by lots of large, intimidating men drinking noisily at the bar.

Ultimately, both of us found it too much: it was a full-time job and we did our best, but being involved with other things, there was no way our full attention could be on the restaurant. However much our styles differed, either one of us could have been successful with enough time devoted to the project.

I advertised for and eventually found a manager. His name was Phillip, and he was in his early forties. A suave, well-spoken and unctuous man with dark gingery, well-oiled wavy hair and grey pallid skin, he produced numerous references with enough letters of personal commendation to have landed him the job of Captain on the QE2. He said reassuringly, 'I'll take all the troubles off your shoulders. I'll pack this place out.' I was sceptical to say the least but, like all good salesmen, he was telling me what I was desperate to hear.

He certainly packed the place out, yet we never seemed to earn any money. We were taking a small fortune, some weeks eclipsing the Puddings takings, yet it all seemed to evaporate before Kenny or I saw any of it. The wage bill was higher, there was equipment to be paid for, all plausibly explained by Phillip with a smile and a confident reiteration that, 'We're getting there.' *When?* I used to wonder miserably.

We held a large family party at the restaurant for my son Andrew's twenty-first birthday. It was a wonderful evening and, at the end, I asked Phillip to arrange a taxi to take us home. I remarked to the driver of the brand new Mercedes what a lovely car he was driving. 'He wanted us to supply a Rolls Royce for you, but we couldn't get one in time,' he replied. He continued, 'That Phillip, he's doin' so well in that place, taking an absolute fortune, he tells me. Mind you, my boss is getting a bit worried about him as he books nice cars for all his customers. He already owes us well over a thousand pounds!'

Sitting in the back of this expensive saloon, my heart sank. I was shocked. I can't say I liked Phillip and, in retrospect, I trusted him only out of sheer desperation. Many years later, when I first heard Tony Blair make his apologies over the 'Bernie Ecclestone affair', he reminded me so much of the plausible way Phillip had explained things that I never, ever trusted the prime minister.

I rang Kenny immediately, and we arranged to meet Phillip

in the restaurant the next day.

Of course, he never showed up; he must have sensed the game was up from our voices. We found out he'd been up to so many dodges. He really took us to the cleaners. All the money paid out for new equipment, he'd given us false receipts - we still owed for all of it. There was phantom staff, food that was never delivered. What utter folly it all was. It took a while for us to recover from this setback.

We never saw Phillip again. He left his wife and children to fend for themselves, and ran away. Eventually, someone did track him down for us, and found him living and working in Blackpool. He was asked for the money back, which he swore he never had, and so we sold the debt on.

Keneddy's became Frederick's Wine Bar when Freddie, our sister Doreen's partner, managed it for us. He was a quiet and reassuring presence, a steady hand on the tiller, and a man we could trust and who wouldn't be easily fooled. Freddie was very well liked with lots of friends, and under his guidance it got packed again and we started to get some of our money back. He ran it for a year or so before we sold it.

But Kenny is still my best friend, in business or out. He's the first one I turn to whenever I've got a problem, personal or otherwise, and he has always responded so positively. There have been times in my life when I just don't know how I would have carried on without a brother like him.

Kenny, for his part, carried on at his Lotus nightclub for a while after we left the Puddings and, but for the landlords wanting it for redevelopment, he would still be there now.

The oldest Rocker in town.

THE NEIGHBOURS

Our neighbours in Stratford were, a hundred yards to the right, the Swan, a beautiful Georgian building four stories high, and a hundred yards to the left, the Black Bull, another handsome building. Both pubs, like ours, were owned by Watney Manns. They were good pubs owned by various 'governors' during my tenure as the longest serving licensee in London. The most memorable of the Swan's proprietors was David Edwards and his brother John.

The Edwards brothers were both very young to be publicans, but had lots of style and flair. David, still a good friend to this day, is very flamboyant, a free-spender who loves the high life. He had lots of friends from the Soho set, who thought it quite thrilling to venture into the 'jungle' of East London on a Saturday night. One of the crowd was Francis Bacon, the famous painter. He kept promising David that he would visit the Swan on a Saturday night, and as he was noted for only drinking the finest champagne, David would tell his brother to stock up with plenty of Dom Perignon. Francis consistently failed to show up. When he eventually did, John, not knowing and not particularly caring what a famous person he was, really told him off. 'All that champagne stuck in my cellar, it's about time you started to drink it, don't mess me about!'

Bacon, quite bemused that someone should tell him off like this, was quite struck by John's appearance: he was a good looking, well-built and charismatic young man with a shock of dark curly hair, quite Italianate in appearance and always smiling, with real warmth in his smile. Francis and John Edwards took a real liking to each other, and John became his model and confidante, their relationship becoming like father and son.

When the most famous living painter in the world, as he became, eventually died, he shook the art establishment by leaving his entire estate to John.

The Black Bull on the left was, for a time, under the auspices of Bobby Moore. I never knew Bobby very well but, as he was partnered in his pub ventures by my old friends the Quills, I met him a few times and was always struck by his natural modesty and unforced friendliness. At one party he came to he stood talking to my younger brother Michael and his mate Johnny Edwards for hours, mainly about football. It was true what they said about him, he was a lovely man. He and the Quills changed the name of the Black Bull to Mooro's, and it had a grand opening attended by lots of celebrities, Georgie Best and his current girlfriend, the dancers from Top of the Pops, Ronald Fraser, Harry Fowler, most of the West Ham squad. The event was hosted by Eamon Andrews and televised live. What a wonderful boost that was for the pub! They employed lots of famous DJs. and the Broadway was thronged most nights. All the local pubs, including the Swan but mostly the Puddings, benefited from the publicity.

The week before its opening, however, Mooro's was almost burned to the ground by an arson attack. I went into the ash and cindered pub, its beams like charcoal, to give my condolences to Patsy Quill, who told me they had no insurance but were still determined to open on time, and miraculously they did. Over time though, the pub became quite a trouble spot and despite a refit and a name change to Moonlights it eventually reverted back to its old name: the Black Bull.

THE PUBLICANS

As the '60s wore on, we became good friends with lots of other publicans who started to make their pubs busier by following the model we'd set down. We used to give a lot of advice to people who wanted to get pubs of their own.

Eddie Roberts, a well-known West Ham boxer who I was already quite friendly with, and his wife, Pat, decided to become publicans and took the tenancy of a pre-fabricated Whitbread pub in Forest Gate - the Golden Lion.

Shirley had actually met Pat when they were collecting the children from the school in Salway Road. She'd recognised her from the dances they had both frequented at Poplar Town Hall, and as her son, Edward, was in the same class as Andrew, they got chatting. She also had a daughter, Tracey, a year or so older, and they would all walk back from the school together and became good friends.

Their one night off, like ours, was on a Wednesday, and so we often went out in a foursome to the theatre or a nice restaurant, and they became life-long friends. Sadly, Eddie died at quite a young age, but Pat and her family have remained great friends of our family to this day.

Philly Jacobs took the Plough and Harrow in Leytonstone, which wasn't a very trendy area, but by putting on top-class groups it became a great rival, and we started to lose a few customers; but of course, competition makes you try harder, so we hired better and better groups, at one time even having a sixteen-piece show-band on stage.

The Bird brothers had the Greengate in Bethnal Green, and their compere and pianist was Lenny Peters, who became famous with his partner as Peters & Lee. My old mate from the docks, Alfie Parsons, took the Ship in Stepney from Philly Jacobs, and later moved to the Dover Castle in Old Bethnal Green road, where he stayed almost forever. Alfie remains a great pal. Barney Slattery made waves at the Deuragon Arms in Hackney, where he featured go-go girls suspended in golden cages whilst dancing to the bands.

Some publicans, such as Georgie Walker at the Black Swan in Bow, didn't have live music, but just a superb collection of LPs, a good sound system, and a strong personality. George used to sing himself, sometimes doing impressions of Dean Martin, Perry Como or Tony Bennett, and his customers loved it. He got nicked once for receiving and, thinking he was going to lose his license, sold me his record collection. I put all the sleeves round the walls of the Puddings. In the end, he was found not guilty of receiving. I was on the jury.

Tommy Kemp and his wife Carol took a pub down Vallance Road, opposite Jack's the old Beigel shop, which, like its successor in Brick Lane, was open all night. Tommy would let his customers stay a while, and they would tumble out two or three in the morning for their smoked salmon beigels.

Terry Murphy took over the Bridge House in Canning Town and turned it into East London's most famous music house of the '70s and early '80s. He went one step further than us, and even launched a record label from the pub. My son, Matthew, played an early concert there with his band The The, although Terry didn't know he was my son at the time.

The Rose & Punchbowl in Stepney was run by Harry Gerrish and his wife Maureen for the Quills, and we'd often see them with Patsy and Cusher at the Dick Turpin. Harry Later took over the running of the Blind Beggar for Patsy before finally taking a pub of his own - the Globe in Stepney Green.

Alan Wheeler, who had the Bakers Arms in Stratford, became very popular when he started cooking eggs, bacon and chips for Bobby Moore and the other West Ham players when they came in for a drink after the game on a Saturday night. He became very successful and, at one time, had a few thriving pubs.

There were dozens of other publicans with whom we got very friendly in those days. There was such a sense of community amongst East End pub owners, which doesn't seem to exist so much these days, especially as so many of the pubs today are managed houses without a proper governor.

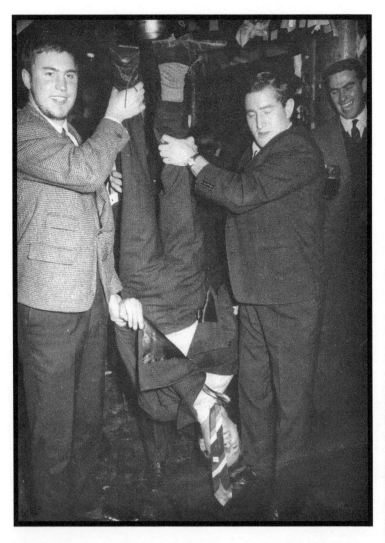

We managed to deal with the nuisances a lot better than the police could. Kenny and Peter in action! (photograph by Alf Shead)

THE VINDICTIVE COPPER

We used to get so crowded on certain nights of the week that, if I left the bar to go out amongst the throng to try and get some fresh air outside or to maybe have a word with Kenny or the boys upstairs, it would take me nearly twenty minutes to get to the door. Sometimes fights would erupt, but it never seemed to take long to get to the centre of it as I suppose everyone must have been shoved to one side with little ceremony. In fact, the more crowded the pub was, the harder it was for the nuisances to cause damage to each other, and I - normally with the help of Sid, Jackie or Don - would manage to chuck them out with a few swear words, and they would disappear into the night, sometimes helped on their way by a swift boot up the backside.

In the mid-1960s, Stratford nick had a particularly nasty inspector. His name was Nellaway. He'd often march in *exactly* on closing time to make sure I was getting everyone out on time, which could be very difficult, especially on a Friday night, but I knew that if I was even a few minutes over, his little book would swiftly come out. Although I must have offended many of my customers without meaning to, I always did manage to get them out on time, to the extent of taking their glasses out of their hands if they wouldn't drink up fast enough. This is not something to be recommended and can cause all sorts of trouble, but our laws then - or the way that policemen like Nellaway interpreted them - meant we *had* to or we faced being dragged to court by the police.

One very busy Saturday, Nellaway barged into the pub with a squad of policemen, ordered me over, and shouted at me that I was overcrowded. He was a tall man with a white, podgy face, and his eyes bulged as he spoke. He was staring at me as if he'd finally caught up with Ronnie Biggs. He said they were going to wait there until closing time and count every single person that left the pub. I think we were licensed for about 500 customers downstairs; if we didn't have live groups it wouldn't have mattered as there were no numbers restrictions without a music license. Another example of a silly law.

As it neared closing time, Kenny and me went round to as many customers as possible asking them to exit via the back doors and through our yard where we'd rigged up a ladder so they could climb over our wall and into the yard of Stratford Town Hall next door. Most of them were only too eager to co-operate - girls as well as boys - as the police were not loved in this part of London, and besides, everyone thought it was a great lark.

We managed to get well over a hundred out that way without the police twigging, but Nellaway was patiently waiting outside by the front doors, flanked by his officers, all stony faced. I went up to him. 'Everything okay, Chief?' I asked.

'You!' he screamed, his face now a deep shade of crimson and his eyes almost bulging out of their sockets as he pushed me against a wall, 'I want you round the station, we've counted over 800 people tonight! You're only licensed for 450! I want to see you round the nick!' As the police were counting, they were also checking on the ages of our customers, and I thanked my lucky stars that we didn't seem to have any kids in, although I had a strict policy of not giving an inch on the age question: one never knew, especially with girls, if you got their age right.

The inspector's face was contorted in fury. It was probably wrong to let so many people in, but some pubs that had a DJ were packed to the rafters with no restrictions on numbers at all, which seemed quite unfair. I was at a loss to understand the extreme hostility shown in general by the police to a publican like myself who, in the seven years I lived there, never once called them in, even when we had a serious incident, as we managed to control the nuisances a lot better than the police could. In addition, we always closed on time and never, ever had 'afters', never served kids, didn't buy stolen goods, never watered the beer down, and kept the pub nice and clean.

I was never sure if the real reason certain policemen loathed me and Kenny with such intensity was because we happened to know so many notorious East End characters, or that we weren't Freemasons or that I wouldn't give them a 'drink'. Apart from Christmas, when I'd send the local police the same as every other publican in London - a bottle of scotch and a couple of crates of beer - that was all they ever had out of me. I never bunged them or let them drink late on the rare occasions they did come into the pub socially, whereas most publicans were 'on the square' and would 'treat' the police if they got a 'visit'.

'I can't understand this harassment. I think he must be after a drink,' I said to Kenny.

'Looks like it,' he said. 'Perhaps you should arrange it.'

'No,' I said, 'once we start that it'll never end. And in any case, I don't like the bastard.'

I made the appointment to see Nellaway the following week. I also telephoned the Brewery and arranged to see my area manager, explaining what had happened and telling him I feared I might be blackmailed into giving this inspector a little 'pension', so he agreed to come with me. In those days, lots of the area managers were people of what used to be referred to as the 'Beerage' - men of some substance. This particular man,

Clive Gurton, was an ex-Guardsman, old Etonian, and his father was the Managing Director, in Britain, of Coca Cola, and he could really turn on the gravitas.

Clive was dressed in a sharp Savile Row suit, his assistant, also ex-public school, was dressed the same, and we marched into the police station with the air of the Lord of the Manor and his entourage visiting the serfs. Nellaway marched out eagerly enough, obviously expecting to see me alone, all ready to usher me into his office, give me a thorough dressing down, and perhaps come to some 'arrangement'. When he saw Clive, his demeanour changed instantly. A sickly subservient smile appeared on his face and, as soon as he heard their rich, plummy, old school tie voices, his own voice instantly went up an octave, became shriller and more suburban, and his manner utterly fawning and obsequious.

We then arrived at a civilised solution. I would station someone outside the pub, count the customers and, when it reached a certain amount, we would stop them coming in.

I'm convinced that, if I'd gone on my own, he'd have lambasted me and tried in his cunning way to squeeze something out of me or threaten to keep raiding us until we had no customers.

We put a man on the door and used to make people queue but, after a few weeks, this had a very negative effect and we gradually dropped the idea. I don't think that particular policeman ever visited the pub again. He seemed a spiteful, jealous sort of man, and shortly afterwards, to my relief, was moved on.

THE PLAYBOY

One morning the telephone rang at 4am. It was Anne, Kenny's wife. She told me that he and our younger brother Michael were both locked up in West End Central police station, and asked if I could do anything. Of course, I went straight up there. They let me see my brothers and Kenny, who was stripped to the waist, was battered and bruised about his body; beaten expertly so there was no blood.

It transpired Kenny, Anne, Michael, and some gambling friends, Teddy Lemon, 'Little Legs' Edwards, 'Jump Up' Roy Smith, 'Plump' Patsy, and a couple of others had arrived at the Playboy Club in Park Lane late the previous night, and somewhat the worse for wear. It was a place Kenny was very fond of as he loved gambling with cards. As they stumbled into the club, it seems one of their group brushed against a woman that a party of Arab gamblers were with. The accused was shoved hard in the back and, when he turned round to protest, one of the Arabs in this other group cleared his throat and spat straight into Kenny's friend's face. Of course, it was off.

All of them were experienced pub brawlers, it was their game, and they were a hard crowd to handle. Mayhem ensued. Michael ended up horizontal with his head being crushed by the repeated opening and closing of the elevator door, whilst Kenny had picked up one of the Arab gamblers and thrown him straight through a closed window. Thankfully for all concerned, the fellow landed on a hedge below. More screaming, shouting, punching had ensued, and The Playboy bouncers, headed by an ex-pro boxer, Denis Booty, did their best but couldn't cope, and so the police were called in. About forty officers charged in and arrested them - that is, just Kenny and his crowd; no one else was taken in. The custom of the Arabs and the money they were bringing in was just too valuable, and so they were virtually untouchable.

In the back of the van, a policeman attacked Michael, who then head-butted the officer in retaliation. Kenny then grabbed the other one, who had also started attacking Michael, and my brothers then held the two officers firmly to the floor, imploring them to calm down. The van reached the station and screeched to a halt, the doors flew open, and in piled six policemen, all wielding truncheons.

The pavement outside the station was also teeming with agitated boys in blue, all waiting to grab, kick and manhandle them as they were dragged into the police station. Five of them, all tooled up with truncheons, followed Kenny into his cell and dished out a thorough beating.

Kenny was due to appear in court the next morning so I got in touch with Sykes and Boater to find him a decent brief. Sykes contacted a solicitor called Abrams, who did a lot of work for the Twins, and Boater made himself frantically busy contacting 'Red Face' Tommy, a famous bent cop who had a network all over the country of other like-minded policemen.

The message came back: 'Nobody wants to know.' The oldest taboo in the country amongst criminals was hurting a policeman. Although Kenny was far from a criminal, the police now regarded him as one because of his various dance hall activities, his connections, and, more importantly, because he had bashed up a couple of policemen. Regardless of their revenge on him in his cell, they still wanted to see him banged up.

The George Best of East End nightclub owners, Kenny, en-route to the Playboy Club in the '70s. (photographer unknown)

I sent back a message that I'd be willing to pay a thousand pounds, which was a huge sum in those days. It was a week's takings, you could buy a new car with that amount, but I knew it was vital for the future - not only of the Puddings but the Lotus nightclub and Kenny's other interests, which included his show biz agency at 100 Charing Cross Road, that he be kept out of the jug.

In the event, after tortuous negotiations by others, the offer was finally accepted. They never let him off completely - he and Michael were both charged with ABH - but they did water down what they were going to present as evidence and passed a few quid on to the injured. In the end, they got a heavy fine and I had to hand over the grand.

The Playboy Club instantly barred Kenny after this fracas, which seemed to upset him more than the arrest and the fine, but its days were numbered anyway: it was very much part of the '60s scene, and didn't last much beyond that. Denis Booty, the Playboy's bouncer, was a good man who did his best to help us as a witness. Later he became a publican himself in Bethnal Green, and eventually took over Daniel Farson's old house in Narrow Street, Wapping, converting it into Booty's, a riverside wine bar which is still there today. Eventually, Denis also managed to persuade the Playboy to reinstate Kenny's membership, which of course cheered him up no end.

THE MURDEROUS MILE

Michael, my younger brother, got pinched a couple of times years later when he was running the Two Puddings, both times for chucking nuisances out a bit too enthusiastically. As he was licensee at the time, it was essential he didn't get a conviction and, by this time, the '80s, 'Red Face' Tommy and his ilk had long since gone, swept away by the anti-corruption squads that were a feature of that time, and so we employed the best barrister our money could buy and also managed to get all hostile witnesses out of the way. Both times his case was 'chucked'.

I got quite friendly with the barrister, and he would give me a quizzical look when the witnesses could never be found. He used to imply in conversation that he thought they'd been done away with or threatened so much that they were too frightened to make an appearance, whereas in reality they'd been given a nice few quid to take a holiday.

Liaisons between the police and publicans gradually improved and took a huge turn for the better when Stratford got a new Chief Inspector, Albert Patrick. He was a huge man who had won a Commonwealth games medal for wrestling. He had a nice, open face, seemed very intelligent and magnanimous, as is often the way with big men. He spoke with a soft Edinburgh burr, and I warmed to him immediately. He had a relaxed view about misdemeanours and petty offences - unlike Nellaway, who would become almost hysterical about even the most minor incident and therefore perpetuate the resentment the police engendered in working class areas. Things had moved on in the pub game when Patrick was in charge in the '80s, but one of the main worries was drugs, and with drugs came even more violence. Drugs were seen as the key to the increase in gang violence, with such huge sums of money involved and drug crooks were arming themselves as never before.

Stratford was going through a real bad patch. There had been a vicious murder of a local gangster in which guns, knives and an axe were involved. This was at a pub in West Ham Lane, round the corner from the Broadway. There had also been a huge fight in our neighbouring pub, the Swan, which needed scores of police to control and lots of people had been badly hurt. There was yet another murder in Moonlights, also on the Broadway and formerly known as Mooro's - Bobby Moore's old pub - in which another well-known gangster had been stabbed and left to bleed to death.

And so it seemed the death knell was struck for the trade in our area. Although we, as a pub, had been relatively trouble-free during this period, because all the trouble was centred on and around Stratford Broadway, our trade was suffering terribly: understandably, fathers wouldn't let their daughters near the area. The local press were having a field day, too, and 'Murder Mile' was just one of the epithets used.

In an attempt to try and deal with this problem head-on, I decided to form an association of pubs in the area where we would look out for each other. When I suggested this to Watney's, they embraced the idea and were full of enthusiasm. They even briefed one of their area managers, Terry Godfrey, to become my aide in setting it up. Chief Inspector Patrick threw his considerable weight behind the scheme, and was one of its most ardent advocates. All the Watney pubs in the area were roped in. The Brewery paid a PR firm to help attract the attention of the local press and radio, and we held a launch day at which the Brewery, the police and various dignitaries attended.

Terry Godfrey said a few words of introduction, and I gave a speech, which was very well received and applauded. I also gave lots of press and radio interviews. I called it the Broadway Association of Pubs for Crime Watch. The *Daily Telegraph* did an especially large spread, their Chief Crime Reporter, Barry O'Brien, wrote a good piece and gave special prominence to a part of my speech in which I mentioned that the streets were a lot safer in the '60s despite the presence of the Krays. Of course, this was highlighted, and even now people repeat and embroider this as meaning that the lesser violence on the streets resulted *because* rather than *despite* the brothers' presence. This version has been mentioned countless times since I first said it - completely misconstrued.

Because of the favourable publicity, trade started picking up considerably and, because of the help we gave each other, telephoning ahead when a nasty crowd was about, letting each other know when 'dud' money was being circulated, reporting any sort of 'con' trick or 'dodgy' bar staff, co-operating fully with the police, who, by this time, had set up a special liaison officer who understood our problems, the whole Pub Watch scheme started. It is now an integral part of the pub scene all over Britain, and I don't think there is a pub in the country that doesn't take part.

Thankfully, nowadays, the police are far more understanding and treat decent publicans as allies in the fight against crime, rather than enemies to be leaned upon.

Because of all the adverse publicity the Puddings trade would never reach such high levels again. (photograph by John Claridge)

THE GETAWAY

I suppose life was always going to be a bit dull after the frantic pace of the Puddings, especially moving to a quiet village, deep in the Suffolk countryside, but that's what we were longing for; some peace and respite from the constant noise and fighting, a school that wasn't overcrowded and understaffed, and where the pupils were a bit more genteel.

Our cottage was a townie's dream. It was thatched with a huge inglenook fireplace that you could sit in. It had low, dark heavy beams (that I constantly bashed my head on), the garden was nicely laid with lots of trees, including a beautiful willow tree and a large copper beech, whose leaves in summer were dark red and burnished, half an acre of mainly lawn surrounded by a tall hedge, but not so twee that the kids couldn't play football on it. Shirley, who hadn't been as keen to move as me, seemed to become a country girl overnight, and the transformation delighted me as I really worried she'd miss the intensity of city life and find it hard to settle but she ended up enjoying it more than me.

She loved the rustic features of our new home, and the small village with its church and pub were like a scene from Radio 4's Afternoon Play land. The vicar popped in for tea and asked Shirley to help arrange the flowers in the church. The landlord of the Red Lion, Stan, lean and saturnine, and his wife, Rene, plump and rosy cheeked with a smiling bespectacled face, were welcoming characters who, as well as serving pints, would make massive meals for anyone who was hungry whilst, at the same time, retailing all the latest gossip about the other residents of the village.

In London, living on a very busy main road, our kids never went out alone, but here we felt they'd be safe amongst the haystacks and fields that stretched endlessly under the big Suffolk sky.

Andrew, along with his new friend, Mark, played football for a local boys' team. He scored some goals and won many medals whilst I jumped up and down on the touchline and, to my shame, hurled abuse at the referee when he made what I thought was a bad decision.

Matthew, to be different, became friends with a boy who Stan, the publican, warned me was a 'ne'er do well from a broken home'. Matthew and this boy, Gordon, were reportedly spotted driving around a cornfield in a tractor at high speed, and later that day the field was set ablaze and the fire brigade were called. No one was brought to book for this crime, but everyone blamed Gordon and, by implication, Matthew. 'Of course,' said Stan, 'your boy was led astray by that Gordon.' This seemed to be what all the locals thought. I questioned Matthew at the time but he denied everything, despite his blackened face. I told him that he mustn't mix with Gordon in future, but he ignored me and continued to play with him regardless. The boy seemed nice enough to me compared to some of my children's schoolmates from Stratford, and so I let him carry on. Some years later I found out that Matthew and Gordon would regularly creep around to the bottle shed behind the Red Lion, grab armfuls of empty bottles, bring them into the pub's off-license where Stan, having no idea of their little fraud, would pay them the deposits and feel quite pleased with himself as they then spent all this money buying crisps, drinks and sweets from him.

At first country life was idyllic but not dull. We toured the surrounding countryside and villages, Cavendish, Kersey, Clare, Fressingfield, Walsham Le Willows, all delightful places of real character and beauty. We shopped in Cambridge and would walk alongside the river, by the famous 'backs', before having afternoon tea in Auntie's. We'd go to Bury St. Edmunds and walk round the Cathedral close on a warm summer's evening, before having dinner in the ivy-covered Georgian Angel hotel in the town square. And racing at Newmarket became a frequent treat. We'd invite relatives, such as Uncle John and his wife Aunt Flo, down for a weekend racing, as I knew they loved to gamble. All sorts of people would turn up; having someone to visit in the 'country' was quite rare for Londoners of my background, and our cottage became a favourite place to visit.

Everyone was made welcome, we were delighted to show our friends and relatives around the village and take them on our favourite walks; our lifestyle was now so different. Antique auctions and sales got to know our faces, I joined a golf club, Shirley took up pottery, we became part of the saloon bar crowd in the Red Lion, and each Saturday, when the pub was closed, we'd go to a neighbour's house for supper and carry on drinking whilst listening to James Last on the 'stereogram'.

In the summer we attended the village fetes, including our own local one, which were held all through the summer at surrounding villages. Spaced so that they didn't clash with each other, if the weather was fine they'd be thronged with masses of good-natured people. One time I even won a pig, and it was a debate in the family whether or not we should keep it as a pet, but we accepted a fiver in lieu. By the mid-1970s, the organisers of these fetes started to get a little greedy and introduced beer tents and, naturally, the events tended to become a little rowdier than before, and we always tried to avoid any place that had such outlets.

Our lifestyle became more and more rural. I bought an Irish thorn-proof tweed suit and a leather trilby with a feather in it, and started to take an interest in shotguns. I bought a fishing rod for Andrew, and we spent hours on the river bank with no particular luck, catching only sticklebacks, odd bits of wood, and frog spawn. Shirley's dress started to become tweedy with cashmere roll neck jumpers and fashionable long leather boots. We both took Timmy, our wire-haired fox terrier, for long walks over the fields. Our holidays were taken in places like Scotland and the remoter parts of Wales or Ireland as we preferred mountains, lakes and rugged walks to sun-drenched beaches.

But still, every Friday and occasional Saturdays, I went to the Puddings to keep my hand in, and every Monday I did the books in the office and met Kenny for discussions on the business, but the rest of my time was free. This routine went on for three years until I said to Shirley one day, 'Do you realise we're in the Red Lion nearly every night spending? We could do that in our own pub and earn money.' Although I was reading lots of great books, going out to lovely restaurants and taking nice holidays, I was getting bored. And our money was running out. So we started to look for another pub.

In the years that followed, we lived in three more pubs, which we ran concurrently with the Puddings. Plus I also had an interest in and helped run a couple of restaurants, but none of these ventures were ever as successful as the Two Puddings in its heyday. That dear old pub that I loved and hated at the same time.

THE LOST WORLD

When I became a publican in 1962, it was seen as a desirable way to earn a living. I was young for a publican - barely thirty; publicans were very often retired policemen or sportsmen who thought that pulling pints would be one long holiday.

The breweries were strict, though. A prospective buyer would have to attend the head office with his wife at least four times. He had to show his marriage 'lines', his birth certificate, and have two reputable businessmen as character references. Any misdemeanours could rule him out. It was normally a cash payment for the pub -not a huge amount; just the stock, fixtures and fittings, plus an amount for what the previous licensee had spent on the pub. This amount was defrayed by 'dilapidations'; in theory, the amount that had to be spent to bring the pub up to decorative 'scratch'. In the contract, a promise was made that you obeyed all the laws, that you never bought outside the 'tie', and that the pub was kept in a reasonable state of repair, inside and outside, some of which was responsibility also befalling the brewery. Any 'goodwill' money was paid 'on the side'. Ostensibly, the broker knew nothing of this but, in many cases, it was he that actually arranged it.

When I entered the trade, the large breweries were, by then, fully committed to keg beer. This was seen as the future, and the road they were all heading down together. Red Barrel was the brand leader, and Watney's was determined to keep it that way. It wasn't exactly new; it had been developed in the 1930s to allow ships, mainly liners and troop carriers, to serve draught beer on a long voyage. It was a godsend to rugby clubs and the like, the bars of which were only used at weekends, but it came into its own with the advent of commercial television in the mid-1950s. Red Barrel was one of the most prominent adverts on ITV's opening night. It was played in between rounds in the fight at Shoreditch Town Hall between Lew Lazar and my old friend, Terry Murphy, for the Southern Area middleweight title. It was very successful and, after the fight, it seemed that almost everyone headed to the nearest pub to ask for a pint of Red Barrel.

A huge amount of our trade was bottled beer, though, mainly light ale, brown ale, Rustic, Guinness or Cream Label, a sweet stout. Most young men drank by the half-pint as drinking pints wasn't very fashionable in those days. It was considered something only old boys did. I'd order 500 cases (12,000 bottles) of beer each week. Pubs don't serve that amount anymore. Some of our customers would order beer by the case to drink at

Watney's Red Barrel was one of the most prominent adverts on ITV's opening night. it seemed that almost everyone immediately headed to the nearest pub to order a pint. (photograph by Alf Shead)

their table, and so we'd just take the tops off the bottles and pass the entire wooden crate over the bar. It was all recycled, too. Even the lemonade and fruit juice bottles were put back in their crates and collected by the suppliers. The girls drank either Babycham, Snowball or Wicked Lady out of fake champagne glasses, always with a cherry on a stick, or maybe gin and lime or gin and bitter lemon, and the occasional port and lemon were also popular, but in the early '60s we had no bowls of ice or slices of lemon to garnish the glasses with - that was left for the more sophisticated bars in posh hotels.

The ordinary bitter and mild of the day took a lot of looking after compared to keg beer. A knowledgeable cellar man would keep his beer in bright and sparkling condition. At the end of the night, all the slops, including the leftovers in any bottles, all went, filtered through finings and a clarifier into the mild. Light ale, brown ale, Guinness and even lemonade, in it went.

Most older people would judge a pub on the quality of its mild. A good mild in past times was treasured because, early on in the week, most pub customers would be scraping for pennies, and mild was far and away cheaper than any other drink. Before the war sixty percent of beer sold was mild, but by 1962 the pattern had changed to approximately thirty-three percent mild, twenty-five percent bitter and thirty-six percent bottled. By the mid-1960s, mild started to disappear altogether as everybody switched to keg. The trouble was, even though you could buy mild in five-gallon wooden pins, if your trade was the younger set and you didn't sell enough of it, by the third or fourth day it would taste sour and have to be thrown away. No businessman is going to keep stocking something for one or two old boys in the corner if he ends up throwing most of the product away.

Bitter still sold well enough if it was properly cared for, but very hot weather could cause very big problems for the publican. Although the cellars were cool we had no refrigeration, and the beer could easily start to turn, at which point the customers would complain quickly enough if it tasted even slightly off. Some bright spark once advised me to spread wet sacks over the beer barrels in hot weather, despite the ale in the wood being susceptible to outside smells and the beer subsequently tasting of damp Hessian sack - which is awful!

Keg beer, on the other hand, came in metal containers, and was gassed with carbon dioxide, which ensured it never went off. We had flash coolers, and it tasted consistent everywhere you went. I suppose it was bland and characterless in comparison to well-kept cask ale, but to a population that often missed work on a Monday morning with a bad stomach due to sour beer, it was a novelty, and so it started to dominate.

THE CAMPAIGN

In 1971, CAMRA, the Campaign for Real Ale, began. They did have a point, but I found some of their members got a bit carried away. In 1972 I had a very quiet pub in Ongar, Essex. I was lucky to get *any* customers on a Monday or Tuesday and only bothered opening because the brewery were adamant their tenants should open all available hours. One Tuesday evening, Gary, a young lad working for me, called up the stairs asking for my help. I was delighted when I got downstairs to see there were twenty customers, men and women, all waiting to be served.

'They want twenty pints of our least gassy bitter,' a delighted Gary exclaimed.

After we'd served each of them, they made a pretence of

taking a sip and then, as if rehearsed, all put their pints back on the bar together as one of their number said, 'We're not drinking this! *And* we're not paying for it! It's gassy *and* it's tasteless! We asked for a *real* ale!' Meanwhile, his protégés were going around the pub, laying out CAMRA leaflets on all the empty tables. I was quite shocked. I went from elation to depression in seconds. The spokesman was triumphant in what he seemed to regard as his victory over the big powerful brewery, ultimately represented by me and this little pub I was trying to run. I said it was quite obvious that he knew this was a Watney's pub, and that he also must have known that Watney's never sold cask-conditioned beer. He also knew that it was no fault of mine that I was not allowed to sell it. He still, unreasonably, insisted that no one was going to pay. I appealed to his better nature - didn't he realise that I'd have to pay for it myself? That this was a small, quiet pub that couldn't afford this sort of loss? - but all to no avail.

They weren't going to pay for it, and that was that.

I went round from behind the bar, pushed my way through the crowd that, initially, I'd been so pleased to see, and stood in front of him. I never touched him, just stood very near and stared him in the eyes.

'I'm only going to ask you once, no more, just once,' I said, emphasising the word *once*, speaking in my gruffest and roughest voice. 'Are you going to pay for these drinks?'

He crumbled like a brittle meringue and paid up amidst the clamour of his companions that we pour their drinks down the sink which, as I'd been paid, I was only too happy to do.

My area manager was an ex-army major called Giles. I'd been in the pub about nine months, and I'd never seen him once, nor even had the courtesy of a phone call, so I was quite surprised to hear from him the day after this incident. He wanted to come down and see me that very day. Apparently, the man who'd refused to pay had been in touch with the brewery and complained that he'd never been so near to being assaulted in his life. This was a lie: I never laid hands on him, nor would I have done, but I was more annoyed with Major Giles, who hardly listened to my side of the story, preferring instead to believe the sworn enemies of Watney's. I wrote to our trade paper, *The Morning Advertiser*, detailing the story and its aftermath and, in particular, Giles' behaviour of non-support for one of his tenants. This didn't go down at all well with the brewery Top Brass, and I was told that my area manager was quietly but very firmly told off. I went to a function on a Thames river cruiser shortly after this, at which Giles was present. He wouldn't acknowledge me or even look in my direction. He was never promoted, and it was said this was because of my letter to our trade newspaper.

I also wrote a long letter to *The Sunday Times* criticising CAMRA for their behaviour, and they became quite vindictive towards me and bombarded the newspaper with spiteful replies to my arguments. I considered this quite small-minded behaviour, particularly as the founder members of the organisation were all media people with lots of access to radio, TV, and newspapers. I must have touched a raw nerve.

The truth is, I'm actually a big fan of cask-conditioned ale, and like nothing better than sitting outside a quiet village or country pub on a warm summer's evening, sipping a half-pint of Adnams or Nethergates's ale. If there is a heaven, that's how I want it to be. Watney's had to eventually reintroduce it, as did all the breweries, but, thank goodness, there are still small breweries surviving, as well as some new 'designer' ones using the old fashioned, more traditional methods to revive long-forgotten brands.

THE CHAINS

Nowadays, there seems to be just one or two giant conglomerates dominating the entire industry, although it's a puzzle who actually owns what anymore. All pub-letting is now done by the greedy pub companies, which have sprung up in the wake of the infamous 'beer orders' that ultimately ruined the trade in the '80s. These were brought in by the government to give customers more choice by stopping the 'tie', but it actually had the opposite effect: the 'tie' had been the custom for over a hundred years in which the tenant agreed only to buy a particular brewers' products at the full price in exchange for a below market rent. This worked fine, everyone seemed reasonably content, and then the Thatcher government, in its Free Market insanity, decided to deregulate everything. It has been, sadly, to the detriment of the pubs, the landlords and the customers. There is *far* less choice now, with pubs the length and breadth of the country going out of business on a daily basis.

I find the majority of pubs nowadays quite depressing. The Wetherspoon chain, for instance, sells cheap drink and food, but is soulless: no one knows the manager or even if they've got one; the staff are like robots, not unpleasant but devoid of personality or conversation; you'll be quickly served but quickly forgotten. They trumpet as a virtue the fact they don't play music, but there are blaring fruit machines all over the place, which is just as bad. They are the Tesco of the pub trade. The trouble is, just like Tesco have killed off many of the small retail outlets surrounding them, Wetherspoon are similarly killing off many of the small pubs.

Many of these remaining small pubs are now forced to rely on big-screen sports, filling the places up with lager-swilling loutish types, swearing, shouting, burping, and getting drunk as quickly as possible. They also sell a huge volume of luminous-coloured alcopops and cheap, strong wine to young people who just cannot handle such excessive alcohol abuse. New figures seem to be released every few months from the various medical associations, all detailing the terrible rise in alcohol-related liver disorders amongst younger and younger people.

Then there are the pubs that decide to sell food, of course, but more often than not it's the microwaved-straight-from-the-freezer slop with special prices for OAPs Monday to Thursday lunchtimes, Sunday roasts for under a fiver, the same supposedly, hand-written chalk board with items like 'Giant Cod and Chips' written on it, or perhaps they'll advertise 'Thai' or maybe 'Mexican', which seem exotic until you actually taste it and realise it's the same pre-packaged mush supplied by the same firm that supplies the lasagne, chilli, and 'home baked' meat pie. They'll even do Shepherd's pie - that great pub standby - with the same chemical format.

Unfortunately, most of the great British public will forgo quality any time in favour of quantity and cheapness.

Lager has the highest sale and also the highest profit. In my early days, we didn't even sell draught lager; it was unknown in most pubs. But they have solved many of the problems with efficient refrigeration in the cellars, serving very cold without so much fobbing. With the old flash coolers, this was a big problem: the beer in the pipe was always warm, so when it collided with the cold coming through the cooler, it would foam up, causing tremendous waste that the publican had to pay for, which was one of the main reasons for the price of lager being so high. They have cut the extent of this problem to some degree, but it's still a comparatively expensive drink. Very little bottled beer is sold nowadays unless it's the 'beers of the world' type glamour bottles from all over the planet. Mexico, Japan, Canada, Belgium, Czech Republic have all had their day in the sun, all deemed by youth to be better than the old humble English pale ale or brown ale - for years one of the staples of the drinking classes.

There are some good pubs making a comeback, though, well-run places with dedicated owners where the food is good, not too overpriced, and made by good cooks on the premises, the beer well looked after, the red wine a reasonable quality, and the white wine well-chilled and served in a nice, decent-sized glass, the staff courteous and friendly. These are normally 'free houses', which means the governor does not have to worry about the huge rents that the pub companies impose. These pubs do well, but they are oasis in a desert, and one must be dedicated to seeking them out - and, when one is found, you must tell all the pub lovers you know; they must be encouraged, the English pub must be nurtured back to health and quality.

THE HOURS

The campaign to liberalise our licensing laws was started by a group of restaurateurs and hoteliers. The group was led by a dynamic American who came to London in the '70s and started the famous Chicago Pizza Pie Factory. He helped revolutionise the eating out trade with other venues such as Chicago Rib Shack and Peyton Plaice. His name was Bob Peyton, and he made a tremendous impact in London. He thought it absurd that a restaurant could serve food all day but customers couldn't have a drink between 3pm and 5pm or after midnight. He had a point, and he, alongside such food luminaries as Robert Carrier, spearheaded the group that was ultimately successful in their aims. The brewers, distillers and wineries seized the opportunity to jump on the bandwagon Peyton had started

I personally was against all-day opening. Over the years, I wrote many letters to various prime ministers, including Mrs Thatcher, different MPs, Tony Banks and John Biggs Davidson, amongst them. I was interviewed by journalists, and seemed to have a lot of support from other licensees. Sir Bernard Braine, who was the Father of the House of Parliament, gave me his utmost support and quoted me at length in the House of Commons, which was, as always, reprinted in *Hansard*. But, of course, the law was eventually passed by New Labour. I still believe I was right and that the law was agitated for by a powerful lobby - not for the good of the public, but rather for pure greed and gain. In many places, drinking is no even longer remotely civilised. We always had drunkenness, of course, but now it's a national epidemic. It's hard to believe the complacency of government and ruling bodies as they watch this country drown in alcohol abuse.

If I was thirty today I would not even *consider* becoming a publican. The hours are much longer, and there is a plethora of new legislation, all apparently intended to simplify licensing; in reality, however, it makes everything far more complicated. The small businessman's life is becoming hellish, and he has to employ a solicitor as well as an accountant to unravel the complex rules hedging him in like a barbed wire fence. Making a 'living' takes second place to keeping within the framework of legality.

Although some may argue that it was people like me who paved the way for the modern pub, one of the reasons I'm so critical, I suppose, is because I saw over the years how damaging alcohol is - not only to the body but to the brain. I have watched, up-close, as the personalities of many lovely people became deformed out of all recognition. Essentially, drinking heavily shortens lives, and the bedlam that binge drinking causes creates so much misery and sometimes fear for everyone else. The world has changed so much in the last fifty years; it has become much more violent, advertising is more untruthful and misleading, and due to the power and pervasiveness of the lobbying industry, the government seems to allow pretty much anything if it makes money.

If I *was* one of the instigators of the modern pub in Britain, I can only apologise and say that I did really care for my customers, looked after them to the best of my ability, and although I loved money as much as most people, I was more interested in running a place I could be proud of. In most parts of Britain, the image of the cosy inn, with its pretty garden in summer and roaring log fire in winter, has receded into a distant past... A paradise lost.

Incidentally, Bob Peyton's life was cut tragically short when his Range Rover went out of control and crashed, killing him outright.

THE LAST ORDERS

After a long period of low and difficult trading, during which time our rent went through the roof, Watney's ceased to exist, having been absorbed into Courage, which remained the main beer supplier, and Nomura, a Japanese investment firm became owners of the property.

Tenants were always wary of these takeovers because, inevitably, rents would go up, more ties would be imposed, and more pubs taken from the Tenanted Estate and put under management. This is what did happen to hundreds of established hard-working tenants who, in some cases, had been in their pubs for more than twenty years. They were told their leases would not be renewed and were then forced to leave their pubs with very little or no compensation. For the remaining tenants, a new agreement was foisted upon them, known as a 'turnover lease'. The rent was based on takings or annual turnover, which meant quite a significant increase in revenue for the brewery. Not everyone had these turnover leases. The Two Puddings remained on a three-year lease, albeit at a much higher rent, but the Crown pub I had at Loughton was a ten-year turnover lease.

This situation resulted in many publicans standing together, hiring solicitors, and trying to make the case that the brewers were acting illegally, which they were. Many publicans withheld their rent in the belief that they had a cast-iron case and would be paid compensation, which would outweigh the large debts they were running up. The various agreements had, instead of releasing the publican from any tie, bound him or her ever closer to the designated supplier whilst subjecting them to outrageous and punitive rent.

The publicans' case against Inntrepreneur started in 1996 and lasted over 12 years. We won our case in the courts, they appealed, we appealed to Europe, and their response was in our favour, too. Inntrepreneur appealed again, we won once again at the appeal courts, and Inntrepreneur appealed yet again. Finally, it went all the way to the House of Lords and, in circumstances that many publicans are still bitterly unhappy about, the Lords voted in Inntrepreneur's favour by three to two.

Then, Inntrepreneur sought their revenge. Hounding everyone for the money owed to them, many ex-publicans lost their homes, were made bankrupt, became blacklisted, and were ultimately driven into the ground. Yet another example of how the British government works on behalf of big business against the common man.

Michael, me and Kenny during the case against Inntrepreneur. It started in 1996 and lasted over 12 years! (photographer unknown)

"Time Gentleman Please!" In 2000 the writing was on the wall for the Johnson Boys. (photograph by Johanna St Michaels)

The 'office' was piled high with all the paraphernalia that comes with running a pub. (photograph by Johanna St Michaels)

Goodbye to all that. JD looks out of the Puddings' backyard to a fast disappearing sixties Stratford. (photograph by Eddie Johnson)

THE FUNERALS

Sadly, many of the characters told about in this book have now passed away. Every other month seems to bring a dreaded invitation to yet another funeral. Just a few months ago I attended the funeral of Jackie Bowers, a friend and one of the best barmen the Puddings ever had. Jackie always did have a mordant sense of humour and, in keeping with his strict instructions, as his coffin slowly rolled towards the furnace, 'Fire' by the Crazy World of Arthur Brown began blaring from the crematorium speakers.

A few years previous to this, I attended the funeral of JD, one of my oldest and best friends. He wasn't particularly old by the standards of today - he was seventy - but he'd been ill and bedridden for some months, and though not in great pain, he slept most of the day and seemed to gradually waste away and descend into everlasting sleep.

JD was a very popular man, very well-known in the East End, and there were five or six hundred people at the crematorium to see him off. The reception was at a hotel where his family had seen to it that there was lots of good food and plenty to drink.

My mind wandered back to when he came in the pub one night and introduced me and Shirley to his new girlfriend. Her name was Sylvie, and she was a beautiful, dark-haired, blue-eyed girl from Poplar. Quite serious, but with a good sense of humour, she introduced a certain levity into his life. Shirley and I were both impressed by her, and liked her very much. JD had never been much for the girls, and it was if he'd been waiting for Sylvie all his life. She was a good influence on him and he on her. He changed his ways after meeting her, and they complemented each other perfectly, and after they were married he became a model father to her son Mark, and later they had another son, Danny, and were a tight-knit loving family. Later on, before they took the Essex Arms in Canning Town, they came and did a few sessions in one of my pubs to learn the ropes. We remained very close friends and had lots of good times together.

Funerals vary so much. It's odd, really. Grief, one would suppose, is a universal feeling. Of course, it depends on the age, the circumstances, the closeness of the deceased. If they are very young or struck down in their prime, their parents and siblings, wives and children are overwhelmed with unutterable sadness and a feeling of such desolation and misery that one's very limbs will not function properly. The grievers' gait is slow, and they are bent as if in very old age.

There are cultural differences, too. The traditional Irish, who have the recently departed stood upright in their coffin, and celebrate their life with song, dance and drink. West Indians also treat death less reverentially as a celebration of past life; deeply held religious beliefs where death is believed to be a bridge to another world helps mourners stay relatively cheerful.

Forty-seven years ago, I went to the first funeral of my life when I was thirty-three years old. I haven't stopped going to them since.

The early events I went to were sombre, often heart-breaking events where the chief mourners were dumb with misery and tears.

As I've become older, so many of my friends have died, as have my mum, my dad, my wife, one of my sons, and all my uncles and aunts. When a friend dies, if one hasn't seen them for some time, there is a feeling of detachment. After the usual expressions of regret to the family and children, there is acquaintance and friendship to be renewed with fellow mourners who haven't seen each other for years.

JD's funeral all seemed so unreal to me. I was surrounded by friends and family, and we were all laughing, joking, eating and drinking, and telling each other what a wonderful send-off it was and how JD would have loved it. I guess he would have. Aside from tears from some grandchildren and a few muffled sobs in the chapel, there seemed no evidence of overwhelming grief.

I felt a loss within me; a sadness that I'd lost a great friend. But it's as if a stoic acceptance comes with age, that it's a natural and normal process, as if only in the last stages of life this awareness becomes fact. All through youth and middle age, one regards death as unlikely, and so it's not really contemplated and is so deeply shocking when it comes to those around you. But in the elderly it is embraced, not eagerly but with equanimity and a sense of the inevitable.

I decided when I got home from JD's funeral that I wanted a small one; a muted affair for immediate family and close friends. In many ways, my life has been a sad one in recent years, particularly with the loss of Shirley, my wife, and our son Eugene and other illnesses and tragedies in our family, and I don't want jokes and celebration around my grave. I would like some tears to fall upon the freshly opened earth.

The Puddings Gang in 2012.
From left: Eddie, Michael, Kenny and Peter.
(photograph by Matt Johnson)

Would the last one to leave the Two Puddings, please turn out the lights! (photograph by Andrew Johnson)

Milton Keynes UK
Ingram Content Group UK Ltd.
UKHW011547080324
439166UK00003B/138